Story as Vehicle:
Teaching English to Young Children

Multilingual Matters

**Please contact us for the latest book information:
Multilingual Matters, Bank House, 8a Hill Road,
Clevedon, Avon BS21 7HH, England.**

Story as Vehicle: Teaching English to Young Children

Edie Garvie

MULTILINGUAL MATTERS LTD
Clevedon · Philadelphia

Library of Congress Cataloging-in-Publication Data

Garvie, Edie, 1928–
  Story as vehicle : teaching English to young children /
Edie Garvie.
  Bibliography: p.
  Includes index.
  1. English language—Study and teaching (Primary)—Foreign
speakers. 2. Children's stories—Study and teaching (Primary).
3. Language arts (Primary). 4. Storytelling.
I. Title.
PE1128.A2G29   1989 / 88-27020
372.6'5'21—dc19

British Library Cataloguing in Publication Data

Garvie, Edie, *1928–*
  Story as vehicle: teaching English to young children
  1. Great Britain. Primary schools.
  Curriculum subjects: English language. Teaching
  I. Title   PE 1128
  372.6'044'0941   A2 G29
                                                               1990
  ISBN 1-85359-050-9
  ISBN 1-85359-049-5 Pbk

Multilingual Matters Ltd

Bank House, 8a Hill Road   &   1900 Frost Road, Suite 101
Clevedon, Avon BS21 7HH   Bristol, PA 19007
England   U.S.A.

Copyright © 1990 E. Garvie

Reprinted October 1990

Index compiled by Meg Davies (Society of Indexers)
Typeset by Wayside Books, Clevedon, Avon
Printed and bound in Great Britain by WBC Print

Contents

Acknowledgements

'Nobody writes a book entirely on his own. The words that appear on the page have a long history of past discussions, of the unconscious adoption (and adaptation) of other ideas, of the influence of other minds.' So writes Henry Widdowson in the introduction to his book, *Learning Purpose and Language Use*. I am very much aware of this 'deep well of unconscious cerebration' as Widdowson goes on to call it, and of the many colleagues and fellow-authors to whom I am indebted. My special thanks go to the staffs of the Literacy Centre at Brighton Polytechnic and the Education Department of Loughborough University, to Richard Collet of the Kent Education Authority, to Marcel Leclerc, formerly of the Bradford Education Authority, and to my brother Alex for the time spent in reading and commenting on the manuscript.

I would also like to thank the following people for permissions and help in various ways: Elaine Abrahams of Harmony Publishing Ltd, for permission to reprint one of the illustrations from the book *Topiwalo the Hatmaker*, and for writing to explain her rationale, which seems to incorporate so much of what is presented in this book; Geoffrey Broughton and Longman Ltd for permission to use *The Hat Song* from his course for infants entitled *Go*; Eve Burch of Cecil Road Infant School, Gravesend, Kent for her ideas on how to develop a story across the curriculum from the book *Daniel and the Coconut Cakes*; Henrietta Dombey, Principal Lecturer in Education at Brighton Polytechnic, for permission to reprint a quotation from her letter to *The Times Educational Supplement* of 15th May 1988; Eric Hawkins and Cambridge University Press for permission to reprint a quotation from his book *Awareness of Language;* Keith Johnson and Thomas Nelson & Sons Ltd for permission to reprint a section from his book *Now for English*; Jenny Du Plessis of Kathorus Teacher Training College in South Africa for permission to use the story, *The Mischief Maker*, a useful source for classroom narratives and her ideas for carrying it across the curriculum; Joan Reed and Susan Kelly, students from Avery Hill College, for their ideas on Shared Story Writing; Harold Rosen and the National Association for the Teaching of English for permission to reprint material from his book *Stories and Meanings*; Louisa Shippey for the Italian version of *The Hatmaker and the Monkeys*; Mike Simpson of the Educational Support Service, Birmingham, for the illustrations of the story *The Old Woman in the Bottle*; Bradford and Ilkley Community College for permission to reprint a section from their information sheet on *The Storybox Project*; and the State Department of Education, Adelaide, South Australia for permission to use 'What the Graded Objective Approach Is' from *Tongues*.

Finally, I would like to thank my publishers for all their encouragement, and to Rachel Evans who put me in touch with them in the first place.

Edie Garvie, February 1989

Prologue

The ideas for this book have arisen from recent work in the United Kingdom and other places, particularly Malaysia and southern Africa. Primary teachers of English in various workshops of differing lengths have produced story kits which now act as useful prototypes for other teachers and contribute to the multiplier effect in situations where those with some training act themselves as trainers of others. In Britain, teachers working abroad have come together with those working at home, focusing on story at Loughborough Summer School courses. In Kent a group of teachers, concerned with the needs of the bilingual child in particular, have organised a story working-party. Tutors in teachers' colleges in Malaysia and Africa have encouraged trainee teachers to make more use of the story vehicle and to design teaching materials accordingly, while serving teachers in many parts of the world have shared on *their* courses the wonders and potential of story. All of us have come to see the importance of this vehicle for language work, not only in the story product itself but also, in terms of teacher awareness, in the process where so many ideas about language and its relation to thought and experience have been engendered and fostered.

By way of a forerunner it may be helpful to consider two kinds of context in which the book is set. First there is the theoretical state-of-the-art kind of background, which it is necessary to bear in mind in all discussions of a practical nature; and second there is the more immediate, professional context which provided the impetus for the topic of the book. The opening chapter deals with the first context, looking briefly and somewhat simplistically at certain trends which appear to be affecting language issues in one way or another and which must at least inform our thinking as we proceed into the rest of the book. The next chapter offers statements of aims, readership and general strategy, and endeavours to place the work within the wider picture of Chapter 1.

So, the first part of the book attempts to answer the question of — why story? The second part highlights the issues to be carried by the vehicle, issues of language, learning, and teaching, and these are matched in Part 3 by options of story theme, classroom activities and materials, and techniques within the methodology. Part 3 is really the core of the book where we consider story at work with children in classrooms. Then, leading away from it, come the implications that this kind of methodology suggests for teacher training, curriculum and policy. That is the business of the two chapters in Part 4. Finally, in Part 5 I have offered one or two samples of materials which augment the text but which have been kept separate to prevent distraction in the discussion. These appear in Appendix 1. There are no footnotes as such. Most notes have been included in brackets in the text itself except for a few longer ones which appear at the end of the relevant chapters. The bibliography has been divided into those works which appear in the text and are listed at the end under 'References' and those which are suggested for further reading and are grouped under topic headings in Appendix 2.

The book is dedicated to all those children and their teachers with whom it has been my privilege to work over the years in so many places and circumstances. It is also dedicated to those who train and support teachers in one way or another, many of whom have become close colleagues and friends especially in the last five years. To you all — this is *your* book. My thanks to everyone who has contributed and provided the stimulus which has prompted me to put it down in writing. The better parts of the book are the things I have learnt from you. The rest is *my* responsibility.

Edie Garvie
Peterborough
June, 1988

Part 1
Why Story?

1 Theoretical Context

The Communicative Approach

Over recent years the tendency to conceive language in terms of communication rather than as a set of structures has become all-pervading. There is now a vast literature on the topic — almost a cult — and certainly a whole new glossary of terms and jargon. For those who would pursue the subject, suggestions for reading are given (see Appendix 2). Meanwhile let me try to outline the parameters to some extent.

There has been a gradual switch of emphasis in language matters towards greater interest in the functions and appropriacy as distinct from the form of language. For a long time the learning of language was seen as the mastery of a set of structures. The then current theories of learning linked well with this notion and the learning of language became that of linguistic habits. This had given way in the late 1960s to a concern with rule-learning and what, following Chomsky (1965), became known as transformational grammar. The learner gained language competence by manipulating the rules of syntax. A purely linguistic concept of language had become psycholinguistic. But still there was the notion of language as a set of some-things to be learnt and that once you *had* this collection you were there. It is important to remember too that the rules were those of form or grammar. There was no concern as yet with the purposes to which people put language and the diverse patterns of performance or use.

Then in the 1970s began the move towards language as communication. People became interested in the individual utterance. What were the things which made each one a unique event? How was the performance of language affected by the personal needs of the user and by his role in the social situation? Now the *social* psychology dimension had entered the language scene and sociolinguistics had become important. The term 'communicative competence' began to be used, seen as a kind of opposition to grammatical or linguistic competence, a knowledge of the conventions of use as against that of structure. This was reckoned to be a considerable advance and very soon became the accepted orthodoxy in most areas of language study and teaching. Discussions on the nature of language, its acquisition, development, pedagogy and testing have all been affected, with influence on syllabuses, methodology and techniques. It might be useful now to highlight just a few of the more salient notions of the approach which are particularly relevant to the language teacher.

Salient notions of the communicative approach[1]

1. *Focus on Message rather than Medium.* This suggests that the teacher should be more concerned about meaning and understanding than about *how* the learner expresses himself. (In this book the learner will be referred to as 'he' and the teacher as 'she'. I apologise if this offends some readers but I find the s/he attempts at unisex tedious!) The *accuracy* of the utterance is less important than the *fluency* and the communication engendered. It also carries implications for the manner in which the teacher deals with error. The communicative approach sees error as a useful indicator of a stage of learning or interlanguage and it must be allowed. In the days of concentration on form and system, error was seen as deviation from that system and must be eliminated as soon as possible. Exercises were set to prevent it and the learner was drilled in the correct patterns. There was concern to offset the interference from the first language. With its emphasis on fluency as opposed to accuracy the communicative approach suggests a more flexible classroom regime.

2. *The Information Gap.* Briefly this means that in the teaching of language the student is likely to learn more quickly if he is asked to use his learning for real purposes. The authentic text is essential, either spoken or written. The teacher should set up classroom situations where students and teacher interact, student to student and student to teacher, exchanging information that is really needed, say, for the completion of a real task which they are working on together. Questions are asked because people want to know something. This is in reaction to the kind of technique where the teacher held up a pencil for instance and asked the class, 'What's this?'. Everyone knew what it was. There was virtually no information to be given and therefore no communication, other than the message perhaps that language is boring!

In a sense this idea of *language learning through tasks* could stand as another issue here in its own right. Many who embrace the communicative approach use this kind of methodology.[2] It assumes that language is what language does, as Halliday (1969) described the developing language of the young child. To provide tasks dependent on language so that the learner has to bear the responsibility for his own mistakes seems to be both stimulating and conducive to language learning.

3. *Focus on Process rather than Product.* There is a link here with the task issue. What appears to be meant is that the outcome of the task may be less important than the talk which goes on to facilitate it. Most of us have experienced meetings where the decisions or materials produced seem to have been less important than the ongoing communication and interchange of ideas. In terms of language teaching the teacher must sometimes be prepared to devalue the end product in the interests of the learning in transit, as it were.

4. *Emphasis on Negotiation rather than Pre-determination.* This suggests that the learners should be able to participate in their own learning process. The teacher must not be afraid to throw away the lesson plan occasionally and to enter in to real (this word is constantly to the fore) conversation with her pupils, using the moment, the things the learners offer, while at the same time, presumably, linking all this with the overall aims and the general direction of the curriculum. This means a role for the teacher which is facilitative and catalytic rather than strictly instructive. The classroom becomes a market-place of negotiation instead of a place where all the time pre-determined and rigid lessons are offered to passive students sitting in serried ranks with the instructress out front. The atmosphere is relaxed or, to use Krashen's term (1982: 33), there is a *low affective filter* and students are not pressurised. This could mean at times that no language *production* is expected before sufficient time has been given for listening, imbibing and processing (which is very different from passive acceptance). But the degree to which input becomes intake depends to a great extent on how comprehensible the former is.

5. *Use of the Learner's Own Resources.* This notion seems to link with much of what has been said above. Take the last point made, for instance, about the importance of *comprehensible input.* Teachers are notoriously bad at recognising one of the best teaching resources of all, the human beings in the classroom. What each group/community brings is likewise a source of enrichment and learning and the shared experience both within the school and beyond it is something that teachers must exploit in the participatory atmosphere of the communicative classroom. The teacher must know her students so that she can guide the learning procedures from the known to the unknown.

There is obviously a great deal more that could be said about all of these, and no doubt other notions which might have been focused upon, but perhaps enough has been said to give a flavour of current thinking. These notions will be appearing again in one guise or another in later sections of the book as we consider this orthodoxy in terms of the young child. Before going on, however, there is one other issue I should like to consider in particular and that is the significance or otherwise of the acquisition/learning dichotomy, a notion which seems to spread across the others and which will feature strongly in the methodology sections of the book.

Acquisition/Learning

Ellis (1982) describes two kinds of communicative approach. There is that which is informal, designed to engage the learner in the *process* of communication in the classroom. This emphasises the *use* of language as a means to some behavioural end. The teacher here abandons her traditional role of instructress and becomes more of a participant and facilitator. The other kind of communicative approach is formal, based on a syllabus of language items to be learnt, selected and graded into units for teaching in the traditional manner except, Ellis says, that the syllabus should be based on functions rather than on linguistic items and should suit the needs of the learner if it is to be truly communicative. The formal communicative approach is concerned with the *product* of communication.

Following Krashen, Ellis links the first of these with *acquisition* of language and the second with its *learning*. Stevick (1980) has described this distinction as 'potentially the most fruitful concept for language teachers that has come out of the linguistic sciences in my lifetime'. There has been a great deal of discussion and argument about it in the literature, about the validity of the concept in the first place and about the classroom implications in the second. What is the relationship between the two? Does the learner use his learnt knowledge to sort out or monitor his knowledge acquired in the informal and natural situation? Does he in fact *need* formal learning if he can acquire on his own, and if not, where does this put the teacher?

Ellis in his article comes down in favour of both and supports the idea that learnt knowledge *does* transfer to acquisition, provided that the classroom offers communicative opportunities. It is these which activate the switch and allow the knowledge learnt in the formal situation to be *used* for authentic purposes. If he is right then there are very significant implications here for teaching methodology. Just how can appropriate communicative opportunities be created in the classroom?

It is hoped that this book will go some way to answering this question, particularly concerning the young child. It must be noted that what has been discussed so far is very much the thinking of those involved with older learners of language. The applied linguists and their colleagues in higher education are not really catering for the school teacher, but perhaps the latter should be listening and reading nevertheless. I believe that there *are* things here which are relevant to the teaching of English language to young children and will try to make this plain as we go on. It is interesting, for instance, to look at communicative matters from another angle, one which *does* bring us nearer to the young child.

Language proficiency and education

There has been a renewed interest in recent years in the relationship between language and thought and in the place of language in education. What I should like to highlight now is something of what has come to be known as the 'Cummins Debate'. Jim Cummins is a psycholinguist involved particularly with bilingualism. His contribution also to the field of special education has been considerable. Concern with the education of minority group children and also with the outcomes of different kinds of teaching programmes, such as the immersion language strategies in Canada, led Cummins to believe that an adequate theory of language proficiency and its relation to school achievement did not exist. Much of the debate amongst Cummins and his colleagues has centred on a certain dichotomy relating to *kinds* of language, an attempt by Cummins to state what *he* meant by language proficiency. He spoke of (a) basic interpersonal communicative skills (BICS) and (b) cognitive, academic language proficiency (CALP). The first he saw as the everyday surface kind of language, the face-to-face oral communication very much concerned with a shared and obvious context. The second had to do with study skills and literacy, with not so obvious contexts and with more demand cognitively.

Cummins believed that all normal children acquire BICS in their mother tongue (L1) fairly quickly as they become socialised within their family and community. CALP comes rather later and has to do with the formal education process. It was an interesting new way of looking at old truths and it opened up many avenues for discussion. It also begged many questions. For example, could the two sorts of language be quite so easily polarised? Were the matters of context and cognitive demand so simply divided? And was BICS strictly to do with oracy and CALP with literacy (shades of other debates in which communicative skills have been linked very closely with oracy)? Could not a face-to-face conversation on nuclear physics, say, be highly demanding cognitively even with shared context and could not a piece of writing to an intimate friend in a context they have not shared be relaxed and entirely non-demanding?

The acronyms, some said, were confusing and raised too many questions. Others felt strongly that Cummins had ignored the sociolinguistic component. He has since dropped the acronyms and concerned himself more with the notions of context and cognitive demand, bearing the criticisms in mind. However, the concepts underlying the original thinking seem to me to be important to remember. For convenience I intend to refer to BICS/CALP whilst noting the reservations. There may well be things here which educationists should be considering, from the policy-makers concerned with learning medium to the teacher in the classroom opting for activities and materials to meet specific needs. It is necessary perhaps that teachers should not so much align themselves with one theory or another but simply be aware of the differing viewpoints and as far as possible cover all the options as a kind of educational insurance policy. So the teacher should be concerned with ordinary everyday conversation and the child's skills in code-switching in different situations. She must also be concerned with the child's growth of concepts and his study skills relating to language.

An interesting question which this whole debate in the context of bilingualism has raised is the degree to which proficiency in the first language assists the learning of the second, and if it does, where the threshold would be? What level of proficiency is required and how can it be measured? Is there an underlying capacity which services both the first language and any subsequent language or does each language learnt have its own separate growth-points? There are adherents of both common underlying proficiency (CUP) and the separate development idea.

A belief in the first would suggest an educational regime where BICS in the first language (L1) had become CALP before a second language (L2) was attempted. Allegiance to the second would plunge the child into L2 as soon as possible. Again, these are matters for policy-makers. The classroom teacher usually has to accept the policy in which she finds herself. What she *can* do, to be on the safe side, is to try and find out as much as possible about what the child brings to her class, linguistically speaking, in order to cash in on the assets. It may be that the child has a fair proficiency in both L1 BICS and CALP. What, if anything, can be transferred? Should the teacher, especially of an older child, attempt to move straight into L2 CALP? How does L2 BICS relate to L2 CALP in the formal school situation? Is L2 BICS a necessary step? My own feeling is that the teacher of a second language, even of older learners, should not ignore the stages of development of the first, in so far as she understands them, and that to some extent the L2 learner should be provided for in such a way that he can go through them. This may be particularly important for children having to do other studies in the second language, as distinct from those learning another language as a subject only. On the other hand the latter may also benefit from BICS-like provision in their foreign language as, in achieving communicative fluency in it, they are likely to be meeting with a wide range of social and all kinds of other meanings which may be a vital pre-reading experience. Once more it is better to be safe than sorry. How important it is for policy-makers and teachers both to have a depth of language awareness.

Graded Objective approach

Another angle on the communicative approach is represented by the Graded Objective Movement in the field of modern languages. It is an attempt to define a series of short-term goals, gradually drawing the learner forward in knowledge and skill and obviously altering, many think for the better, the whole face of language testing. What is particularly interesting for this discussion is that while they are about it the movement more or less incorporates the entire communicative approach. Here, for instance, are the points made under the title 'What the Graded Objective Approach is' (from *Tongues:* Education Department of South Australia, 1982):

An approach which features a shift in emphasis, defining language in behavioural terms rather than structural terms (getting what you want rather than the conditional tense).

An approach which stresses communication, the ability to convey and receive information in the target language. This, rather than the formal study of structures, forms the focus of learning.

An approach which recognises the unpredictability of communicative situations and therefore calls for the ability to generate original sentences and not simply the ability to repeat rehearsed phrases. *This will necessitate the understanding of an underlying language system and a study of grammar* [emphasis mine, the point important to this book].

An approach which sets clearly defined objectives. The goals are achievable and make realistic demands on the students, but there is a corresponding insistence on high standards of performance.

An approach which calls for testing to be 'criterion' referenced rather than 'norm' referenced, which means that students are judged on their ability to perform the outline tasks, and not on their position in relation to others in the class.

An approach which gives the learner recognition for his efforts in the form of some sort of certification at short and regular intervals.

An approach which is motivating, because the students can see what the language is for, and how they can use it.

An approach which stresses fluency, appropriacy and intelligibility rather than formal accuracy. While accuracy is not considered unimportant, and strategies for achieving it must be constantly sought, it is not the main criterion for judging performance.

An approach which stresses learner responsibility, teaching students how to learn, as well as helping them to do so.

An approach which calls for language to be constantly placed in a context. While there is a place for language practice in classroom methodology, it must be constantly related to language for real communication, which is language that fills an 'information gap' in a situation meaningful to the student.

I have quoted this in full, not only because it acts as a useful summary of things mentioned already, but because it does bring in the language testing element which otherwise is not focused upon in this book; and in addition it points the way to an understanding of the communicative approach which suggests an eclecticism and not an opposition to grammar, which is the line to be followed in the present book. It seemed a good way to conclude this discussion. And now, as we hear on the broadcasting media, for the rest of the news!

Language Awareness

The expression was used a little while ago in a general way. In a more special sense it has been given to us as a trend by the field of modern languages, but like all the trends being discussed here it has spilt over into other areas. It was felt that children would learn another language more easily if they knew more about the patterns and strategies of language *per se*. These relate to both structure and behaviour and to the ways in which language relates to concepts. Hawkins (1984), who is a key figure in this movement, describes the aims thus:

1. It (language awareness) seeks to bridge the difficult transition from primary to secondary school language work, and especially to the start of foreign language studies and the explosion of concepts and language introduced by the specialist secondary school subjects.

2. It also bridges the 'space between', the different aspects of language education which at present are pursued in isolation, with no meeting-place for the different teachers, no common vocabulary for discussing language.

This last point is an interesting one which will be taken up again. For now let us stay with the children and the importance to them, as Hawkins sees it, of what he calls 'insight into pattern'. This has been shown to be a key element in aptitude for foreign language acquisition. Hawkins feels that it is vital to show children how language works to convey meaning.

All kinds of interesting ways have been found for doing this besides straight information-giving. The curiosity of the children is aroused by offering topics which they have probably not thought about before, things like language origins, change, dialects, borrowings, how the baby acquires his own language, etc., and this calls for a classroom method relying chiefly on pupils' activities.

It is important to see this trend as linking with another strong movement and that is the dimension of multiculturalism and anti-racism in education, something which Britain shares with Australia, Canada and very many other places of immigration. Awareness of language is seen as helping to 'challenge linguistic prejudice and parochialism'. Research work, particularly in London (for example, see the 'Linguistic Diversity' references in Appendix 2) had revealed the large numbers of languages/dialects being used in the schools there and in other parts of the United Kingdom. Diversity became something to celebrate in a new and exciting way as the language publications in the early 1980s demonstrate (see Appendix 2). The children from the ethnic minorities had brought much of this diversity and now began to acquire a new status. They were no longer the outsiders learning English as a Second Language (usually in a separate class or unit, at least to start with) but bilinguals with all the assets that could bring, assets which could be shared with the 'deprived' monolinguals.

So this sharing brought about, in the schools where it was done well, a new language awareness for teachers and pupils alike. There was more rapprochement amongst teachers with differing language interests, more enthusiasm for collaborative learning methods. The issues of the famous Bullock Report (1975) were studied afresh, particularly its three salient messages discussed in Chapter 12: that language crosses the curriculum, that every teacher is therefore a language teacher, and that every school should have a language policy. Then in 1985 came the Swann Report, *Education for All,* a controversial document which stressed the importance of the multicultural/multilingual dimension permeating the total curriculum for all children. For some it went too far: for others it did not go far enough, some of these for instance seeking a recommendation that more provision for the community languages of the ethnic minorities be made in the schools. The report is concerned with the most appropriate ways of ensuring that all children will achieve well in a multicultural society. The chapter on language stresses the importance of giving children a good grounding in the English language, the standard of the country, and suggests that this can best be done within a total school policy. It seems to imply that whilst the tasks of the curriculum act as a challenge for new learning, they offer at the same time contexts for language teaching, providing authentic text and comprehensible input. The hidden curriculum and the close working with child colleagues would support the development of the natural, everyday language of BICS.

Though much of the aim here concerned social and political factors, it seems to me that the debates and movements around bilingualism, diversity, awareness of language and language policy in the United Kingdom interestingly reflect and highlight many of the things being discussed in other areas of the world and in other disciplines in relation to both adult and child learners. In particular they appear to demonstrate the all-pervasiveness at the present time of things communicative, with Hawkins's insistence on the place of pattern in language offering a timely *aide-memoire*.

Language for Specific Purposes

One aspect of language awareness in the general sense which has been focused upon lately is that of language for particular needs and purposes. Beginning in adult education, where language programmes became carefully tailored to the needs of the learners (see Sayers *et al.*, 1979), the movement has reached school learners also where teachers considering language across the curriculum have used the 'language for specific purposes' strategies in their analysis of school subject needs.

Questions of the validity of this industry and of how far language can be special in this sense have touched off yet another interesting debate. Widdowson (1983) describes the growth of university departments in the field somewhat cynically when he says 'the field is a busy one, full of prospectors staking claims, working seams, with the usual crowds of attendant camp followers parasitic on their success . . .'. He does, however, acknowledge the work of language for specific purposes as having contributed to our theories of language generally and having helped us 'reappraise the principles of language teaching'.

There are many useful questions for teachers to consider here. When we examine the needs of our pupils in this way in their subject fields are we looking only at vocabulary, for instance? Or is there a different kind of structuring too in various kinds of writing? Does the learner have to be aware of different styles as, for example, the way in which the matter-of-fact reporting of science would differ from the more expressive essay in history or literary criticism? How narrow should this focusing be? Is it chemistry as distinct from physics, or science as distinct from the humanities; or is it even language for academic purposes, CALP, as distinct from BICS?

The whole business of the narrow/broad concept is interestingly dealt with by Widdowson, not concerning these particular questions but perhaps offering a manner of looking at them. It may be that there is a place for both the narrow and the wide and that both have to be catered for in education. It is worth pausing to look briefly at what Widdowson is saying. He follows the narrow/wide notion through a number of dichotomies, objectives/aims, training/education, instructors/teachers, skills/abilities, competence/capacity. Objectives he sees as the ends of classroom programmes, as distinct from aims which have to do with the ends of all this learning for the students, what *they* will eventually do with it. All the others relate to this in an interesting way. For instance, an *instructor* can *train* someone to master *skills* and become *competent,* thereby fulfilling the *objectives* of a programme. On the other hand a *teacher,* concerned with the wider *education* of her pupils and the *aims* of these pupils for the years to come, will provide a learning environment in which basic skills become long-term and integrated *abilities* and where a mere competence becomes a *capacity* for creative use of learning. An example of the first might be giving the learner the language appropriate for ordering the groceries; an example of the second, knowledge of the civilisation of the people whose language you are teaching.

The competence/capacity dichotomy might merit a special mention. I have already used the word 'competence' with the attribute of communicative or grammatical/linguistic. In ordinary, lay terms the word 'competent' suggests 'skilful'. A skill is acquired and possessed, allowing the possessor to perform — usually well. In linguistics 'competence' is used differently. It is still the something behind/below the performance but the latter can be at any level. There is no degree of skill attached to the term. A person performs in language well or badly according to the kind of competence he has. The important thing to pick up here with the introduction of the term 'capacity' is, I think, that the notion of performing well comes back in, in the sense that the language user is really able to go beyond the conventional knowledge and wisdom of his learning, to be creative, to make the language truly his own. With all the claims of the communicative approach in its concept of fluency and greater flexibility, there still lingers a feeling of a closed set of items to be learnt and then used, unless one accepts the implications of the monitor theory (see Krashen, 1982, around p. 30) and the kind of regime where acquisition can flourish. The T. S. Eliots of this world must have something more than mere competence, something worth considering for its educational implications, even if very few of our L2 learners may aspire to such heights.

Widdowson has been accused of being too simplistic in his use of such dichotomies, but I agree with him when he says that they are a useful means of raising questions for discussion and act as points of departure. For instance, following his idea of equating the narrower learning of competence with the narrower procedures of instructing, training, use of objectives (graded or otherwise), and the wider acquisition of capacity with the broader notions of education, teaching, aims of the students, how *do* we help the learner first of all to gain — be a possessor of — the rules of the game, and then to move on to making this knowledge and skill into an ability which he can use for his own specially creative purposes? Surely this is what the development of language is all about. However right Widdowson may be in his dichotomies, the idea of 'narrow' and 'wide' may be helpful for teachers to bear in mind. There may be times when one is called for and times when the other would be more appropriate; a place for the pedestrian instruction required for a rule of spelling and a place for the stimulus of story. So much depends on the needs of the learner at one point in time. There is a sense in which the language for specific versus general purposes debate *has* widened the pedagogical thinking as Widdowson says. There is certainly more concern now for the particular needs and interests of the learner. Learner-centred approaches, learner-friendly materials and perhaps other new terms to support, have become a further current trend and will be the next one discussed here.

Learner-centred Education

Widdowson's 'capacity' implies the kind of education which has both objectives and aims, concerned with the gaining of concepts and skills along with the gaining of strategies for how to use them and to go beyond. If the language being acquired and learnt (would that we could find a new word to cover both) is really to become the learner's own, then the experience offered must touch his own, must be capable of accommodation in the Piagetian sense (1953, 1955). Here we can see the importance of the teacher doing a needs analysis of the learner. What does he bring to the situation? How far has he got in the development of concepts and skills? What are his particular interests? Only an understanding of these things will allow the teacher to provide the kind of environment which ensures that the learner moves from what is known to what is unknown.

It would appear that many of the issues discussed above come nicely together now, matters such as comprehensible input, a low affective filter, time and provision for the learner to acquire, patience for the teacher to facilitate while at the same time being conscious of the learner's needs within the framework of the curriculum. The programme offered is as narrow or as wide as required. And lest the language teaching industry thinks it has just discovered all this, it might pay them to have a look at what has been going on in some primary school classrooms for a very long time. Through various vicissitudes of the swinging pendulum, primary education, at least in some countries, seems to have found its optimum in terms of such matters as provision for both acquisition and learning, teaching of rules and the giving of opportunity for their use, development of both BICS and CALP. That is to say, the good primary classroom offers the kind of ethos which is friendly to the learner and in which true communication can take place. If anything a balance sometimes needs to be redressed towards a little more structure and formality. But on the whole the right ingredients are there for the kind of education which offers a wide range of experience.

A good example of this is the current approach to the teaching of reading (see Appendix 2). The important thing is the message, the meaning of what is being read, and much use is made of the child's own experience and news so that he is asked to read what he understands. A vital part of the message is the notion that reading can be for pleasure and the child is encouraged to *want* this key to wonders untold. At the same time the decoding skills are acquired and focused upon so the pathway to literacy has two lanes. (See Chapter 8 for a development of this idea.) Would that this kind of balance could be the nursery of the young child everywhere coping with the acquisition and learning of a new language, but more of this later in the book.

Return of Grammar

The idea of balance brings us back full circle. The final trend to be discussed is the recent resurgence of an interest in grammar. I began this chapter by registering the swing in the 1970s from a structural, grammar-orientated approach in language teaching to one where *use* of language took precedence. Everything which has been described above has reflected this communicative emphasis. Now, in the late 1980s, we are experiencing some swing in the other direction again. It is reflected in much of the current literature along with comment and questions as to the exact nature of what is being revisited. The *EFL Gazette* of July 1987 devotes its central spread to this issue. In an article which appears there by Roger Bowers some specula-

tion as to what now may be meant by grammar is expressed. After summaris-
ing the various stages he believes language teaching to have gone through,
Bowers (1987) says:

> . . . as one bandwagon slows down but the next one has not yet
> lurched into sight, we are peering back along the road and realising
> that we left behind some rather important baggage . . .

He goes on to specify what this might be, things like *wanting* the right language in the right context, and *wanting* to do things *with* language as well
as with people *through* language. But he sees the new grammar as something which can live very happily with its communicative bedfellow. As he
says, 'accuracy is not at odds with fluency; language awareness and language skills can be developed concurrently; modern interacting students
might actually like drills'. Bowers also suggests that among the many
things we can communicate about is the English language itself — its
usage as well as its use. He reckons that grammar is perhaps something we
can teach explicitly, within, as he says, 'classrooms immensely enriched
by all that has happened in EFL over the past twenty years or more'. So
the fears of some that this trend may be a reneging on all the progress
made over these years of emphasis on language communication, need not
be realised.

The same fears are interestingly reflected in the aftermath of the
publication of the Kingman Report (1988), the most recent inquiry in
Britain into the teaching of English. The report offers a model of English
which Kingman hopes will be a basis on which the new national curriculum
can be built. What is pertinent to this discussion in particular is the argument
in the second chapter for children to have a knowledge *about* language as
well as a skill in its use. The committee asserts that knowing *about* language
improves the mastery of it. It is this assertion around which there has already
been much controversy. Henrietta Dombey, at the time of writing Chair of
the National Association for the Teaching of English, expressed her reservations in *The Times Educational Supplement* ('Talkback', 13.5.88). She says:

> despite the bold words declaring that the committee was persuaded by
> the evidence demonstrating the ineffectiveness of grammar lessons as
> a means of developing children's competence as grammar users, the
> seductively commonsense view that if you can define it, you can con-
> trol it, dies hard.[3]

She goes on to say that what is lacking in the report is guidance on how children will *develop* this competence:

The linguistic foundations are sound enough, but what is lacking is any similarly substantial expertise on how children acquire and develop their competence as language users. That surely ought to be the base of the argument. It is as if we had a document on surgery based solely on the expertise of anatomists.

It seems to me that much depends on what is understood by grammar. If the concept is restricted to arid classroom exercises on parsing and analysis, then a return of it must surely be a retrograde step. If on the other hand one's idea of grammar is more like Hawkins's 'insight into pattern', coupled with his ideas of how to handle this in the classroom, then perhaps what Kingman is suggesting makes more sense and is less to be feared. In other words, the knowing about language which the report recommends must, in my view, be seen as the language awareness discussed above, an awareness which *should* inform performance.

Another writer who deals with new thinking about grammar is Rutherford (1987). He sees grammar as a facilitator of language learning, something which raises the consciousness of what is already subconsciously familiar so that the learner can move more smoothly into the specific aspects of the language he is learning. Grammar in this sense is more of a process than a product. But Rutherford also believes that there is still a place for knowing about as well as being able to do. As he says here:

> . . . learners who live in what Krashen (1982) has referred to as 'acquisition-rich' environments and take advantage of such settings to use their communicative skills in the L2, also need opportunities to focus on the structural properties of the language and attend to form.

It is interesting to contemplate on what the *ancient* grammarians would make of all this. The Greek *grammatikos* meaning 'pertaining to letters or learning' was a pervasive concept in the Middle Ages. It gave us the term 'grammar school', suggesting a place which embodied all the prevailing knowledge. This was a new enlightenment in its day. It is also interesting to remember that the word 'learning' can be seen as both noun and verb and also that the grammar school taught more than parsing and analysis! Somewhere along the line the early meaning of grammar became lost until for many of us, in the older generation at least, it came to stand only for those arid lessons mentioned above, and to be only something which people do exercises on. Could the new edifice be about to change things for the better, its concept as both process and product not only giving grammar back its proper status, but at the same time supplying language teaching as a whole with a welcome eclecticism? If so, then this book subscribes to it.

Conclusion

In this chapter I have ranged fairly widely and theoretically over a number of current trends in language study and teaching and in education generally, which in some way or other are almost bound to have an effect on the teaching of English to young children. I have noted the all-pervasiveness of the communicative approach which was the main story. The rest of the news consisted of Language Awareness, Language for Specific Purposes, Learner-centred Education, and Return of Grammar. Throughout the rest of the book we will be meeting these again as threads being carried forward and as issues for the story vehicle to carry. The practical implications for the teacher are varied and interesting. I believe that this book is just catching the pendulum as it swings back from the extreme of things communicative. Perhaps there is little new under the sun, only currently appropriate ways of looking at things. But let us turn now from philosophy to the more practical matters of the context which offered the points of departure for the work.

Notes to Chapter 1

1. For these ideas I am much indebted to the writings of Rod Ellis and Keith Johnson and to Graham Walker of the Human Sciences Research Council in South Africa whose work led me to theirs.
2. For example, the well-known Bangalore project. See N. S. Prabhu (1980), 'Theoretical background to the Bangalore Project': *Bulletin 4/1,* Regional Institute of English, Bangalore, pp. 19–26.
3. The Association's response to the Kingman Report is available from the National Association for the Teaching of English, Birley School Annexe, Fox Lane, Frecheville, Sheffield, S12 4WY.

2 Professional Framework

Central Concern of the Book

In English language teaching (ELT) courses for primary teachers, initial or in-service, story usually features as one technique or strategy amongst many others. Few teachers of young children need to be convinced of its usefulness. There is also a fair bit about it in the literature, often linked with other strategies such as use of music, puppets and drama, and creative writing. All teachers should be as knowledgeable as possible about these things and should be prepared to use them appropriately in their own particular circumstances. What is being advocated in this book as a result of the workshops and discussions referred to in the prologue, is that story can also be used as a methodology for pulling everything else together. Instead of being just one technique amongst others it is taken out of the list and made to carry all the important things we want our pupils to learn about and do with English.

There are some who will plead for story to be simply enjoyed and *not* exploited for language teaching. This is recognised and accepted for much of the time especially if a story is presented in a child's L1. There is a strong case for allowing the comprehensible input of the appropriate story to serve as it stands, a resource for acquisition in the Krashen sense. But having said this I wish to state also my belief that exploitation or teaching, particularly in a second or foreign language situation, can be justified. It seems to accord with the intuitions of the teacher, perhaps because it so easily cashes in on the assets which the child brings with him, and it would be a pity *not* to use this wonderful opportunity for furthering the child's awareness of language.

In a fascinating booklet, *Stories and Meanings* (1985), Harold Rosen reflects on the important role of story in our lives, especially in the lives of children. He quotes James Moffet: 'They [children] utter themselves almost entirely through stories — real or invented — and they apprehend what others say through story'. Rosen goes further than Moffet and suggests that adults too make more use of story than might be supposed, and that

'. . . given proper status and respect, [story] may prove to be good for more than has been generally thought'. There are stories in current events and the everyday gossip of home and High Street. There are stories in mankind's successes and failures. There are stories in fantasy. There are even stories in mathematics and science, in other curriculum subjects and in other factual contexts. The categories are numerous and interesting if we think of story in the widest possible sense.

It is interesting also, returning to the philosophy of the first chapter for a moment, to apply the concept of grammar as it was defined there and to talk about the grammar of *story*, meaning not only its structure and form but also its process as facilitator of meaning. It is thought by some that grammar is part of the human mind and that it is activated in the young child by exposure to language. Might this idea be extended also to story grammar, innate and waiting to be quickened by experience, as though a child were programmed for it? If this is so then we have a strong justification for not only giving the child a rich diet of stories but also for using them as vehicles. However this may be, the central concern of the book is the potential that story has for carrying in particular things conducive to language development.

Expected Readership and Aims

So much for what the book is about. To whom is it addressed? This is always difficult to define exactly as there are as many learning/teaching situations as there are schools and classes within them, but broadly speaking two categories are seen as the target groups: those who teach English as a Foreign Language (EFL) and those who teach it as a Second Language (ESL). There are people who prefer not to use these terms today, considering them no longer helpful or definitive. I decided to retain them here as they *are* familiar acronyms and the alternatives might be clumsy paraphrases. In this book EFL means a situation where the pupils are learning in the language of the country (community language), with English as a subject on the curriculum. An ESL situation means that the pupils have to learn English in order to learn everything else, as it is the medium of instruction in the wider curriculum. Methodologically speaking, the main difference usually is that the EFL teacher has to follow a syllabus of English language items to be covered while the teacher of ESL has to be concerned with the implications of English as a tool of learning. She may or may not also have a syllabus for the actual English lessons. While stressing the strategies which can be shared by both kinds of teacher the book will also recognise the main difference, and endeavour to demonstrate how links can be made through story with, on the one hand, the language demands of a syllabus and, on the other, the language needs of the curriculum in general.

These two broad categories can of course cover several variations. Within EFL, for instance, there is a difference between a Malaysian or southern African situation where the children are learning English in a country using the language fairly widely within the community, and one perhaps in some parts of Europe where young children may be encouraged to learn English at that stage simply as an enrichment activity. They are not hearing it around them. Then within ESL there is the Zambian type of situation where the policy is to use English as the medium of all schooling because of the large number of community languages in the country and the difficulty of selecting one to be the language of learning. Here, everyone in the school is likely to be an ESL learner. This differs from situations in English-speaking countries of immigration such as the United Kingdom, Canada and Australia. Here there are likely to be some schools at least where the ESL learners are in a minority, immersed within a school population of English native speakers, although there will also be schools which are very multicultural in clientele and others where the situation will be close to that found in Zambia.

There is another variation which straddles the two. Sometimes the system is that children begin their schooling using the language of the community, with English introduced as a subject. At a certain point the medium for all learning becomes English. In other words, by the way these things have been defined here, EFL *becomes* ESL, which brings particular problems of approach and methodology as we shall see. Finally there is the situation of the international school, to be found in many parts of the world. The pupils come from a variety of linguistic backgrounds. They are likely all to be learning English, but whether as a foreign or second language it would perhaps be difficult to define, as two or three languages may well be used equally importantly as media for learning in the school. The term 'bilingual', or even 'multilingual', might be appropriate for the language learning situation in this case. Indeed, 'bilingual' is the preferred term today in the United Kingdom where 'ESL' is now seen by some as having an apartness and therefore racist connotation. In this book 'ESL' and 'bilingual' will be used interchangeably, meaning a child who uses more than one language, without indicating degree of competence.

The specifics of the political, educational and linguistic ecology will naturally determine and make for differences in the wider policy and provision. At the level of classroom methodology and technique it is felt that there is much in common across all the situations and it is hoped that the ideas expressed here may be generally useful, even perhaps rubbing off to some extent where English is developing as a first language. In the early years one has to be concerned with the development of language *per se* and there may be important connections between the L1, L2 and further languages learnt. One aim of the work might be expressed in fact as an attempt to bridge the ELT information gap. The bridging would be between EFL and ESL, between both of these and English as L1 and perhaps even between ELT with older learners and that with younger. We surely all have much to learn from one another.

For example, the EFL teacher could well gain from the experience of ESL where the learning of English has to be made meaningful in order to serve the needs of the other subjects. On the other hand an ESL teacher, especially one working in an English-speaking country where there may be no English language syllabus as such, might learn, by studying the task of the EFL teacher, something of the structure and conventions of her own language! The untrained (in ELT) native speaker of the language is notoriously vague about this and may find a syllabus used in EFL as usefully didactic for herself. In other words she may gain a better language awareness which could inform her teaching of both ESL and English L1 pupils.

Another example of helpful sharing might be for those who teach English to the very young to consider seriously, as has been suggested already, the issues being debated in ELT generally as they could just have some relevance to their own work. For far too long the mystique of teaching little children and that of teaching English to older learners have been closed to each other, which seems a great pity. The teacher in the lower primary school might, for instance, have great expertise in techniques of the communicative approach without giving them any fancy names! There is difficulty sometimes in looking beyond the specific to the general. It seems to me that the more teachers of language can share their experience and expertise, can cover the space between, the better it will be for the total lingualism of the learners and for the discipline of language teaching in general.

The book then attempts to cater for a fairly wide range of situations, not forgetting of course that of teacher training. It is hoped that the ideas advocated here will be useful to both teachers in training initially and to those on in-service courses. For those who train them the first chapter in Part 4 may offer some helpful suggestions, particularly regarding the organising of workshops and courses and the use of prototype materials connected with story for the indigenisation of concepts, activities and materials.

Before proceeding to elaborate a little on the varied circumstances and their special needs and to see how the story vehicle might best serve, it is necessary to deal with two further matters important to the aims of the work. One concerns what is meant in this context by the young child. There are so many interpretations depending on one's point of view. For the purposes of this book a young child means one in the age-range of six to ten years. This covers the primary classes in most countries. To go below would be to enter the world of the pre-school child and to go above would be to involve the special needs of children facing the challenge of the secondary curriculum, both areas which the present book must bear in mind but which cannot be dealt with here without extending the scope of the work considerably.[1]

The age-range of the children we are concerned with will be one factor in our discussion which the varied EFL and ESL situations share. The other matter to be focused on now is the general approach towards language teaching which is supported in the book. It has in fact been mentioned several times already in one way or another, so this is just a reminder. I refer to the eclectic nature of the work. It was while working in Malaysia and other places that I first became convinced of the value of eclecticism. The curriculum planners, recognising the swing from a structural to a communicative approach in language teaching, were anxious to bring their primary syllabuses into line with it and to train the teachers to handle the change. I was asked to help. In the course of the work I began to question at least *some* of the communicative orthodoxy. It seemed to me that like many new things in education the best of the old was often thrown out in the frenetic enthusiasm for the new. Perhaps not all work concerned with structure was arid and pointless. Perhaps not all work concerned with communicative appropriacy was exciting, meaningful and real. And perhaps if the former were sacrificed entirely to the latter there would be a loss to the student, as Rutherford (1987: 79) suggests when he says 'the purchase of thematic options . . . carries a grammatical price-tag . . .'.

My work in ESL situations also gave me pause for thought. Many of them seemed to be offering the conditions conducive to Krashen's acquisition notion but perhaps his learning and monitoring ideas were not being catered for sufficiently. My conviction grew that the good teacher of language has to be concerned with *both* structure and communicative function, with both the usage of grammar and its use in appropriate ways. She also has to recognise when it is right for her to instruct from the front and when it would be more useful to set up a pair or a group situation where the pupils would be collaborating and communicating. I began to realise that while we had all learnt much from the years of communicative emphasis, the result very likely of a need to redress a balance, it was possibly more sensible to follow an eclectic line which accepts the best of both worlds and pursues its methodology accordingly. I was particularly interested therefore to watch the development of the swing back to grammar as discussed in the first chapter. My hope is that the swing will not go too far and that a balanced eclecticism will result. It is the stance taken in this book.

A Variety of Needs and How Story Can Help

Bearing in mind these two issues of age-range and approach which apply to all our situations, let me try now to pinpoint some of the differences in the circumstances, the needs of which may imply differential handling within the general framework of the methodology.

Considering first the broad EFL/ESL distinction it will be remembered that one of the main differences is that the first is almost certain to involve an English-teaching syllabus of some kind (see Chapter 10 for a discussion of syllabus/curriculum) whilst many ESL situations will have none. The EFL teacher feels the need to get through the syllabus. Indeed in some parts of the world this becomes a kind of obsession and the teacher is often extremely wary and resistant when new things are introduced which in her view would interfere with this process. Rightly or wrongly the teacher feels pressed and can be worried about visits from inspectors who might question the new methodology and ask what it has to do with the syllabus. In these areas too there are often other constraints such as very large classes, over-full time-tables for the teachers and a dearth of teaching materials, not to mention, in some cases, a low level of education and/or training of the teachers themselves, with poor English competence resulting in lack of confidence. In such circumstances the syllabus can be a kind of life-line.

It was in situations where all or some of these constraints were operating that the idea was launched of using story as a vehicle for carrying the syllabus. In other words story could be used to *help* both learners and teachers do better what they *had* to do at the demand of the syllabus. It was not being advocated as yet another pressure on the timetable, but was a way of bringing some variety to a programme of English teaching which followed the syllabus (either structure or function based: see Chapter 10) unit by unit, with a kind of dull regularity of sequence, killing all motivation and interest. Even the statutory song which was part of the new communicative methodology could be sung to the same tune all the time! When it could be shown that stories could incorporate the language of the syllabus as well as of the story theme and that the follow-up games, songs and other activities could be made to practise and extend the same language, with the use of materials simply and inexpensively produced, then many teachers became willing to try this story methodology and usually ended by being convinced and accepting also further bonuses that story could bring.

The lack of motivation in the learning of English can be a very real problem in some countries. The constraints described above are certainly contributory to this, but there is also another factor which has to be considered. It could be that the government in its remoteness has decreed that the children learn English and that certain teachers teach it. The officials may see very clearly why this should be so. It may be that English is one of the main languages and is used both as lingua franca within the country itself (internationally) and as a means of communication with other countries (internationally), or both could be in operation. In the cities and larger conurbations the language would be used fairly widely and most children would be exposed to it to some extent, but in the more rural areas it would never be heard at all and the children learning English, and their teachers also, might not be at all clear about the purpose of the exercise. Someone has called this type of situation 'TENOR', Teaching English for No Obvious Reason! It certainly exists and is perhaps more widespread than we would like to think. Inevitably it brings a lack of willingness to learn. What better means than the good story for offering some *extrinsic* motivation? Perhaps we need at times to 'create purposes out of nothing by pedagogic invention', as Widdowson (1983) describes it. All the world loves a story and wants to know how it ends. Before they know where they are they have learnt a lot of other things besides.

Another variety of EFL was referred to above. This was the kind of situation, as in some countries of Europe, where young children learn English because their *parents* require it. There may be a number of reasons. For instance it may be desired that the children should be able to communicate with English-speaking relatives or with people in English-speaking countries in which the family may have to travel. There could be any number of instrumental reasons such as a desire on behalf of the parents that their children should be able to enjoy English literature. Again, it could be a question of educational enrichment in general, a belief that it is good for children to learn another language and especially one which is such a worldwide medium, a belief also perhaps that the earlier the children start, the better. Whatever the reason, in this kind of situation the constraints described above do not normally operate. The classes, usually in private language schools, are generally small, the teachers competent bilinguals, the materials at least adequate and the motivation with parent backing very high. One thing they might share with the rural schools in the previous situation is the lack of English in the wider community for the children to be exposed to. So, here too, story could be useful as substitute for authentic text. But also it could bring variety and cohesion to the work of the prescribed syllabus/course.

Much of what has just been said is true also for the situation of the international school. Some of these schools are in English-speaking environments but many are not. For some of their pupils English is a foreign language which they may not be very motivated to learn but which the school itself uses fairly widely. In some schools English is the medium for all the teaching. This brings us into ESL and I shall be considering that below. Suffice it to say that in the international school too the use of story as vehicle could be helpful for a number of purposes. A technique which might be particularly useful here is the bilingual handling of story. More will be said about this in Part 3. The technique in fact may have a generally useful application.

In sum, then, I see story as being helpful in all varieties of the EFL situation. It helps to contextualise the items of the syllabus/course, offering a field of learning which is meaningful, interesting and motivating, while at the same time it covers the English work that has to be done. It can also give cohesion to the work. Above all it brings a more informal, lively and communicative component to what at times can be a highly structured and often tedious programme. The structure would still be there but so would the other side of the language equation, giving the balance of the eclectic approach.

If we turn now to ESL and begin with the kind of situation where there are a few bilingual children in a school community of mainly native English speakers, we note that the balance may have to be redressed in the other direction. In these circumstances there is likely to be no English syllabus as such. The only syllabus in a sense is the curriculum in total, as its demands suggest the immediate needs (at least) of the bilingual pupils in the school setting. This means of course that the teachers must be very aware of the English needed for the specific purposes of the other subject areas and be able to focus for the children on the facilitating language. The bilingual children are having to pick up their tool of learning as they go along, amidst those who already have it (in a manner of speaking).

The problem here, as we have seen, is that the teacher may be a monolingual native English speaker herself with no training in teaching English as a second language. Whilst the learning environment could well be lively and highly communicative, with the ESL pupils benefiting enormously from the informal and participatory activities and the flow of BICS-type language around them, there might be little, if any, focus given to the particular difficulties of many children, especially perhaps to the things which make for accuracy and help to ensure CALP. It is all too easy for the teachers in this situation to assume amid the fluency an accuracy which does not in fact exist, the gaps showing up only later when the child has to cope with more advanced written work.

Withdrawal for special help, in the United Kingdom at least, is no longer fashionable and is considered racist. In my view it is equally racist to deny the ESL children the kind of language focus which the withdrawal system offered. If this now has to be done by the class teacher then she must be equipped to do it as part of her general provision for individual difference. So she needs some training, and this will be considered further in Part 4. For now it can be suggested that the teacher somehow finds herself a checklist of items to be covered. These should be of both structures and functions, the kind of lists to be found for example in a language course for EFL. (See Appendix 1.) Another source might be the items to be assessed in an accredited language test such as those of Trinity College (1988). If these are the things the testers consider EFL candidates need to know, they could be just as useful as a check for covering in an ESL situation.

Armed with this kind of guideline the ESL teacher can then adapt and devise materials which will incorporate and focus on the items in it. In addition, of course, she should be using checklists of another kind, those which list the special language of the subjects (see Appendix 1), arrived at (in the ideal situation) by a school team concerned with a total school language policy. More will be said about this in Part 4. It is suggested here that the story methodology is ideal for the teacher having to cope with a wide range of needs. The aware teacher has materials in her story kit and ideas in her repertoire for all comers (see Part 3). The story is the centre of interest in which *all* take part. Monolinguals and bilinguals learn together, a little more flexibility here, a little more structure there; a little more opportunity for stretching and creating here, a little more priming the pump there, and so on. And with it all BICS and CALP are both catered for. The story kit should provide activities and materials aimed at both fluency and accuracy. It should also offer opportunities for class, group and individual work where the learner is challenged to solve problems within the context of the tale which has interested and motivated him, so that he knows the background and the vocabulary being used and can move more smoothly and easily from the known to the unknown. What is being suggested then in this particular kind of ESL situation is that the excellent communicative opportunities be exploited to bring in something of the conditions which will enable the learner at the same time to develop a knowledge of English structure a little more quickly and easily than he would if left to his own devices, and that the story methodology can help.

In a situation where most or all of the pupils are ESL, much of what has just been suggested also holds good. There is the same need for the teacher to analyse the subject needs and to help the children to cope in English. There is the same need for a certain amount of focus on structure and language functions and to feed these into the general work. In the same way also it is recommended that a story methodology will offer a vehicle for doing this. There may, however, be certain components here, two in particular, which highlight other issues. The lack of native English speakers to help with BICS is one. This kind of support, as we have seen, may not be possible in some countries, even when English is one of the official languages.

We are brought once again to the interesting question touched on in the last chapter. If English is to be the language of study and perhaps not much else in the pupil's life, does he need BICS in that language? Does he need to be able to communicate fluently at a basic interpersonal level? As I have already indicated, my own view (and I have to stress that this is personal and intuitive) is that even if the aim of learning the language is mainly study, this will be better achieved if there is a fluent foundation of BICS. So much of what is subtly present in the literature is a written and stored expression of things shared and spoken by the English-speaking community. If children are to read well they must predict and if they are to predict they must have a command of BICS. I feel sure that the educational insurance policy I spoke of before must be taken out. It may even be important in EFL. That being said, how *does* one cope with BICS in a school situation where there is little or no help from native speakers? Here is where story could be especially useful, linked to drama and perhaps the use of native speaker dialogues on tape.

The other factor worth pausing on, and this again would be in a non-English-speaking country, is that there is likely to be an English language syllabus for use in the English lesson. In a sense this is one up on the other ESL situations where the teacher has to find her own checklists. Here is one ready made. The problem is that there is usually little relationship between what goes on in the English lesson and the English work needed in the subject fields, even when the same teacher is concerned with both. The English language syllabus is not made to serve the medium as it should. In an ideal world where it was, one can see how story yet again could help. It will be remembered that it can be conceived in a great many ways. The story of history or of environmental science or mathematics should be told by the teacher of English as much as by the teachers dealing with those subjects, and the teacher of history etc. should recognise her important role as a teacher of English. This, it seems to me, is crucial in every ESL situation. It can also be useful in EFL where the concepts understood in the subject fields are being used for the teaching of the new language. Although presented constraints may make the ideal world seem very far away, I envisage the story theme as a vehicle for helping to bring these things about.

The point about the English lesson serving the medium has an interesting significance in a situation such as that in Black education in South Africa. It will be remembered that we have here EFL *becoming* ESL, so many things from both are applicable, including the constraints, and will not be repeated. There is, however, one issue in particular to highlight and that is the matter of the traumatic change of circumstances, for everyone but especially for the pupils. Suddenly the pupil finds himself having to try to understand the context and to produce his own responses, in the language he has experienced up to then only as an academic exercise. Language-like behaviour has to become language. Exciting and motivating stories could be made to bridge the abyss. Story used bilingually, it has been suggested, might be a helpful technique in a number of situations, and here is one. It could be a major strategy for helping children, perhaps at different rates, to move in their learning medium from one language to the other. Not only the story itself but the activities and materials based on it could be made to carry over meaning and to relate to the concepts being presented in the second language. This might be worth exploring.

Story, therefore, as a vehicle for language development, appears to have much potential across a wide range of situations. It can be a wonderful antidote to the syllabus tunnel-vision syndrome of some EFL classes; it can be equally useful in situations where teachers, absorbed by curriculum needs generally, are in danger of forgetting to focus on the learning tool. The situations described here have been selected from recent experience. Many of the issues raised could apply to others and it is hoped that there will be something here which touches on the experience of most readers.

But if the story methodology is to be effective there is a big task to be done by both teacher trainers and curriculum planners. In situations where the syllabus dominates, for instance, teachers must be shown how to use it as a guide and not a straitjacket. They must also be reassured and convinced that the sky will not fall if the inspector discovers work not covered, that both syllabus and inspector are there to guide and that the ideas offered are there to stimulate and not to press. So long as the main topics/items are dealt with, the teachers can adapt, devise, augment and enrich as much as they like. In other words, many different ways should be found of approaching the content of the syllabus and teachers need to be guided along these lines. They should be shown how to record and store their own creations, perhaps interleaving notes in the syllabus itself for future use and sharing with others. Very often the good ideas of the individual teacher can be taken up by the official curriculum developers and used on a wide scale. We will be looking later at the idea of selected story kits being dealt with in this way and discussing further the importance of a network of communication and teachers working together.

In situations where the *curriculum* dominates, teachers need to be helped along two lines in particular, with the language needs of the subject areas and with the general English structures and functions, the one feeding into the other. The teachers need guidance in focusing and in what to focus on. They also need to be shown how to devise activities and materials incorporating the focus at different levels of difficulty, which of course applies also to the EFL teacher. If there are native English speakers in the class, then this differentiation of levels would be particularly important.

How easily the story methodology fits into all this. Part 3, where it is worked out in some detail, elaborates on many of the points raised here. Then in Part 4 more is said about training and curriculum planning and also something about policy generally. We have seen that the educational constraints in many places are a major factor in the quality of English teaching. Some of these constraints are hard to deal with given the political and economic climate, but perhaps there are a *few* things that could be suggested in the short term. Papert (1981), in his book concerned with computers and educational innovation, says: 'What is happening now is empirical, what *can* happen technical, what *will* happen political and this is the base-line of change'. While I accept this in principle I also believe that change can be helped along from the bottom up, and that indication of good classroom practice can suggest the conditions which would make it even better. Let us stay meantime with this practice.

Further Consideration of the Nature of the Vehicle

Language, thought and experience are inextricably linked. All the pundits tell us so. It must therefore be important for the development of language in the young child that teachers should be able to offer the kind of experience within the school situation which will stimulate thought and feeling as well as train the skills of listening, speaking, reading and writing. Story can be that kind of experience. In this last section something will be said briefly about the nature of theme.

Story can be seen as a version of the thematic approach to education. The theme, project, centre of interest or whatever one chooses to call it, has long been advocated, particularly in primary education, as a vehicle for learning. The stimulus of an appropriate theme arouses interest and engenders motivation. At worst it sugars the learning pill; at best it offers growth-points for further learning and creative activity.

The advantage of story as a stimulus over topics introduced through chart, poster, picture, model, etc. or simply discussion, is that it is structured. It is going somewhere and the learner wants to reach the end of the journey. In addition, the staging-posts on the journey offer the kind of growth-points just mentioned, potential development sources for learning and teaching (see Part 3). So far I have indicated the importance of story as a vehicle for the development of the language skills, and this is the central concern of the book, but we must not forget the cognitive and the affective, intensely human aspects of story. It is a universal experience offering gains which are personal and emotional as well as educational. In the Rosen (1985) booklet referred to earlier, T. Eagleton is quoted as saying, 'Narrative is a disposition of the mind, a valid and perhaps ineradicable mode of human experience'.

Another whole dimension is suggested by this. If story is universal as a mode of human experience it is important nevertheless to recognise that the various societies and cultures in the world will have their own specifics, including their story grammars. There is therefore a great variety of story in the world, both fact and 'fiction [which] encompasses and extends the possibilities of human experience' (Rosen, 1985). Schools, wherever they are set, must encompass the cultures of the communities of which they are a part. If the community is multicultural and multilingual, so much the better. The story resources are enriched. But even if it is not, teachers should be able to tap the resources of the 'global village' which is today's world. It is essential that all children be helped to understand life-styles and views which differ from those of their own cultures and to see that with all these interesting differences there is still much that is common and shared. How better to bring this about than a rich experience of story?

If there *is* a close link between language, thought and experience then exciting things are possible. Given an appropriate story experience the child would be encouraged to develop the language which meets the needs of the thoughts stimulated. Is it too much to hope that a careful choice of stories would lead not only to a richness of language and development of language skills but also to the kind of lingualism which is suitable for living in an interdependent world? It behoves us all to think about this and to become aware of our responsibilities in this direction. Story as vehicle, then, has more than one purpose and teachers must try at some stage to cater for all of them.

There is an interesting dichotomy which might be a useful thought with which to end this chapter on the concerns and aims of the book. It is this. Children need experience to acquire and develop language: children need language to cope with new experience. The skill of the teacher lies in helping to keep the balance, not too much new language without meaningful experience and not too much experience without adequate language. The teacher should also be able to select the appropriate kind of experience capable of carrying issues of language and including the broad areas highlighted so far. Story seems an admirable vehicle for this purpose.

Note to Chapter 2

1. Though in practice one finds in many countries that a wide age-range is permitted at most stages for various reasons. It may be that the child is a late starter or that the system insists on the passing of exams before a child can move on. It is not unknown, for instance, for adults of 20 years or more to be in some secondary classes.

Part 2
Vehicle for What? Issues of Language, Learning and Teaching

3   A Strategy and an Analogy

Issues and Options

In Part 1 I tried to answer the question — why story? In doing so I have looked at past and current trends in the language teaching field. These issues will continue to weave their way forward across the broad front of the total fabric. Here in Part 2 we move on to a more detailed consideration of what story may be made to carry, further issues concerned with the nature of language, its acquisition/learning and, particularly in the school setting of the young EFL/ESL learner, the appropriacy of the conditions for its development. The idea is that these issues should suggest certain teaching strategies, perhaps a variety from which teachers can select the most suitable.

The notion of issues and options is, I think, a helpful one. It raises awareness and stimulates action and it has been found particularly useful in the training of teachers. In this book we are starting with the issues and moving to the options. We might just as easily have worked the other way round. By focusing first on activities and materials for language teaching it is possible to arrive at the underlying issues, and more is said about this in Part 4 when we look at strategies for training. Whichever way of focusing is used, the idea of action based on knowledge or awareness has been borne in mind as has the further idea of choice of action depending on the issues concerned.

There is an interesting parallel in the work of Stevick (1986) who explores the implications of research into the formation and use of mental images, and shows in his book how an understanding of imagery can help teachers to identify and evaluate many of the options that are available for their use in the classroom. Whilst not written in particular for the teachers of young children, the book is worth looking at for the light it throws on thought and learning patterns and for its well-designed and practical option system. It is a book for any teacher, not only the language specialist.

The Architect Analogy

In order to arrive at one or two headings of issues which can then be sub-divided, it might be helpful to use the analogy of an architect. The human being, in his creation of language, can in some respects be compared with the architect of buildings. Both need a knowledge *about* and a knowledge *how* and both need the ability to do. Let us consider the architect first of all. In order to do his work efficiently he must have an understanding of the basic components, the raw materials or things in the builders' yard, and going along with this he must know how they are handled physically. Next, he must have a knowledge of their possible patterns when combined and re-combined. In other words he must know the system and rules for the usage of the components. He must also know how his building should be put together so that it does not fall apart, how to handle the scaffolding and the other components within it; and how to construct it in such a way that the users of the building will know how to find their way about.

The mention of users suggests another kind of knowledge which our architect needs. He requires to know what exactly his building is to be used for. This involves an understanding of many different functions and also a knowledge of the cultural norms. What kind of people is he building for? What is their particular life-view and what makes them tick? The building of a new mosque, for instance, is likely to differ in a number of ways from that of a church. In this connection then the architect has to be knowledgeable about the general or universal things concerned with building and also about things particular or specific to certain situations. He cannot of course know *all* the specifics, but he should know that such things exist and be prepared to deal with them. It surely goes without saying that the more the architect understands about life and the world about him the more competent he will be. He will become confident when he couples this kind of knowledge with that of his components and building expertise, confident enough to present his *own* messages through his building.

But there is also a receptive aspect to the architect's knowledge. He must know how to interpret and appreciate the buildings of other architects. They give messages to *him* and these can affect in a number of ways how he will perform the next time round. Creativity is a two-way process. The architect must know how to analyse as well as to build. Finally he must know how to plan, to see the finished product in his mind's eye, and have a know-ledge of things which make for balance and cohesion. Along with this he must know how to repair and cope with emergencies when the balance is upset or some other catastrophe occurs. He may have made some mistakes in the building which render some part or all of it useless to the person for whom it was built. He must learn about strategies for putting these things right quickly.

So, without claiming in any way to be comprehensive, I have looked at some at least of the kinds of knowledge the architect needs. I also said he requires the ability to do. It is hard to separate the acting or performing from the knowledge about it. This is probably true of any human endeavour. There are some who would say that creativity is what creativity does. I believe that there *is* a knowledge about and even a knowledge how which are not always activated, and that the ability to put this awareness into practice *is* something else. I can know about gears and how to change them without being able to drive a car or about colours and their mixing without being able to paint a picture.

What then does the architect have to do? Speaking generally he has to put into practice what he knows about building, and the components of it — all the things we have just been discussing. He has to comprehend and express, which means he uses his knowledge of the components and the ways they can be combined. He must also use his knowledge of different building functions in order to make judicious choice of the components in the first place and of their structuring and styles of combination. Components, comprehension/composition and style could be key entities in all of this.

Up to now I have been speaking of the mature architect, and if the reader can bear with me just a little longer perhaps we can consider briefly something of his learning process. As a child, of course, he would have been exposed to the buildings of his own culture, narrowly or widely depending on his home circumstances. He may or may not have travelled far from home. But at least he would be aware of the architecture around him. Without realising it he would have acquired or imbibed its forms, uses, styles, etc. He may even have had the chance to build things himself with play bricks. By unconscious imitation and acquisition of the building conventions and rules he might even be able not only to repeat the styles he sees but to create some ideas of his own. He would always be making new discoveries. All the time his notions or concepts of what building is about and how it can be accomplished would be growing, as he deduced from the finished article and induced from the bits and pieces in his brick box. In the early stages those bits in the box which were already built to some extent, prefabricated, would be a great help. He would continue to use them later but not so much after he had learnt more about using the rules of building for himself.

Eventually our architect-to-be goes to college and has formal classes. His early acquisition of the building business will stand him in good stead. In fact he will continue to acquire and to make discoveries for himself while his teachers take him through the course of learning he has opted for. Many of the concepts and skills he has already made his own may be confirmed or otherwise by his teaching. New ones will be accommodated if the teachers understand what he already knows. All his early playing about has served as a useful preparatory period for the real thing.

As he progresses, the trainee architect learns to make much of his learning mechanical. This is a great asset as it leaves him time and energy to be more creative. He can really begin to concentrate on the messages of his buildings rather than their basic construction. He may also begin to add some embellishments of his own, things which he could develop into a special individualistic style, and if he really has the capacity, he may eventually become famous for this. It must be stressed that it is not so much a part of the building process itself which is mechanical but the possession of it to the learner. Another important thing to stress is that the competent architect, which our trainee has now become, is all the more imaginative and fluent in his work if at the same time he is careful and accurate in pedestrian matters.

So the architect is now qualified and at ease in his building. Then there comes the day when for some reason he has to operate in an alien culture, an Englishman building a mosque in Iran for instance. He feels inhibited, afraid of putting a foot wrong. Although he is a trained and qualified architect with a good knowledge of the universal aspects of building and even a knowledge that things *can* be different, he is somewhat dismayed at first by the particular ways of this new community. They may use his familiar building components in strange ways or not use some of them at all. They may even have a few of their own which our architect has not seen. There may also be some different devices for shoring up the building and holding it together. The important thing to realise is that our once so competent architect has now to start learning again, not in quite the same way as before, but learning nevertheless. He has to go through the same steps but in a different cultural climate. Of course he will do it more quickly because he is mature and because he has acquired this universal knowledge of the building business. He could also be helped enormously if he employed a tutor again, for some of the time at least, someone who could just help him over the bewildering hurdles, preferably of course a tutor who has an understanding of building in both cultures and who can anticipate to some extent where the difficulties for the architect may lie. It must be remembered that as with the matter of mechanics, foreignness does not lie in the learning itself but in the learner. Things are mechanical or foreign to the person experiencing them. It should also be pointed out that unless our architect is a fairly exceptional person and/or has some fairly exceptional teaching he is unlikely to reach the heights of creativity when building in the foreign culture that he arrived at in his own, which is not to say that he may not want to go on trying.

One last point about the learning process is worth making. This architect *may* want to specialise in one particular area, for instance places of worship. He would then naturally concentrate his efforts in learning everything he could about every kind of building in this genre. He would study the real thing, study books about them, learn from his tutors etc. But so he would do in the first place about buildings in general. The specialist, I believe, has first of all to be a generalist if time and reasons of expediency allow. But enough of the analogy. Let me try now to relate the issues which it has highlighted to those of language and *its* development, the baggage which the story vehicle can carry.

4 Language

First a brief summary of the general ideas about language offered so far. It is closely related to experience, thought and feeling. It is structured and systematised and this part is called the grammar which is both product (it has components) and process (it facilitates meaning). To be a competent language user, which means performing well with the skills of listening, speaking, reading and writing, a linguist[1] must know about language, must have an awareness, not only of the grammar but of the parameters which link with it. We shall now take a closer look at this awareness, bearing in mind the notion of components and their systems and the factors of thought, feeling and experience. The thought of system also suggests not only a knowing *about* but a knowing *how*. Again, there is no claim to be comprehensive. The aim of what follows is simply to offer a few thoughts for reflection which may inform our teaching.

Kinds of Language Awareness

If language with its kernel of grammar is and does what has been suggested here then it seems to me that the linguist's awareness of it must be of several kinds. I begin with those which perhaps relate most closely to the grammar.

Linguistic Awareness: This I take to be a knowledge of the inventories of sounds/letters, words and other pieces of structure in the linguist's building-yard, which are manoeuvrable for a number of purposes. These are the basic components for the building of language. It refers also to the knowledge that there *are* such manoeuvres at all. Linguistic awareness may be said to cover also the metalanguage, the language about language, such as words like 'sound', 'sentence' and 'punctuation', a knowledge which can be helpful in particular to the learner of language. It makes a useful shorthand between him and his teacher.

Psycholinguistic Awareness: The able linguist not only knows the raw materials, he also knows the rules of the game, the accepted conventions for manipulating the components. Deep in the heart of things language is very systematised. There is the sound system or phonology, including intonation and stress; there is the system which sets the rules for the modification of words to indicate things like past tense or plural; there is the syntax or word order system; and there is the lexis or way in which words are made to fit the right slot in the sentence. I call this kind of awareness psycholinguistic as it has to do with an understanding of rules and concepts/categories.

Discourse Awareness: This is concerned with both components and rules but in a wider context, at a level higher than the sentence. This brings in another kind of knowledge. It will be remembered that the qualified architect was able to envisage the whole edifice before he began to build. In his plan he made sure that his building would have balance and cohesion. The linguist needs to be able to do the same with his *language* construction, be it oral or written, and he requires the components and rules for doing it, components like connective words such as 'but', 'so', and 'however' and devices for pointing to relationships backwards and forwards amongst the sentences as when you say, 'The man . . .' etc. and then 'he'. There are some differences between oral and written discourse which will be discussed below, but what they have in common is the need for organisation and cohesion so that communication is made easier.

Communicative Awareness: This leads nicely to the other side of the language equation bringing in yet another kind of knowledge. This is an awareness of the ways in which words, structures, total discourse, can change, depending on such things as topic, purpose, situation. It is concerned with the function of an utterance, and appropriateness of language style. The linguist has to know the kinds of changes possible in the *usage* of the linguistic items which can meet the needs of communicative *use.* Furthermore, he must know about the skill of code-switching (see below), how to recognise quickly the rightness or wrongness of saying what to whom and how to change tactics as the circumstances change.

Sociolinguistic Awareness: This links very closely with the last but has more to do with the knowing about — about the factors in situations such as status and role which affect, for instance, degree of formality in communication, and about the factors which determine code-switching. The linguist needs to know why/when the standard dialect would be appropriate or another variety or, if he is in a bilingual situation, why/when another language should be used. The greater the individual's understanding of social norms, the better awareness he will have of how to use his linguistic and psycholinguistic knowledge. Here we really see the intertwining of language, thought and experience.

Strategic Awareness: I reserve this term for a knowledge of personal strategies. The linguist, like the architect, has to have techniques for extricating himself from trouble and for repair of the edifice. He needs to know how to try other methods of building if the first attempts do not seem to work. So the person to whom the linguist speaks misunderstands. Can he reword? Another aspect of this is when he cannot think of the right word. Has he a strategy for using some other means of communication? Can he use gesture or sign language, perhaps, or is he forced not to give his message at all? I am reminded of one very good strategist I met some years ago in Bradford, a little second language learner of six. When I pointed to the picture of a mouse and asked her what it was, her eyes sparkled with understanding but the word was not known. After some hesitation she made her fingers scurry along the table and said something which sounded like, 'He do like dees'. This is what I mean by strategic awareness, a kind of competence which seems to me to be important and is often overlooked in teaching programmes.

Cognitive and Semantic Awareness: We come finally to the enveloping context. We noted how vital it was for the architect to have as wide an understanding of the world about him as possible if he was to be aware of the universals which will be a kind of backcloth to the particular work he does at any point in time or place. In a sense the more experience he gains of different kinds of particular situations, the wider his knowledge of the universals. The linguist also needs this kind of experience, a wide and deep understanding of life. He should have a large repertoire of concepts and a vocabulary to go with it. The concepts are physical and social and there is also his concept of self which has grown amongst the rest. The notions or ideas the linguist has about the world and his own world within it and the semantic field of his vocabulary are highly influential to his performance as a linguist and highly indicative of his ability.

Some general points

First a reminder that these kinds of awareness are not exhaustive. There may well be other kinds. For instance, the language of feeling may suggest a certain dimension of its own. In my scheme it lies meantime somewhere on the communicative side amongst the functions and situations, and of course links with the cognitive and semantic. Second, none of the kinds of awareness are in sealed and separate boxes. They all inter-relate. Third, there has been no attempt at a hierarchy. It would be very difficult to say which was more important than another. What might be assumed, and I think it has come through almost surreptitiously in the discussion, is that there are two main sides to language, the linguistic and the communicative, and that all the other kinds of awareness somehow filter through, especially perhaps the psycholinguistic. This would certainly be in keeping with the broader issues highlighted in Part 1. It is also in keeping with the eclectic approach taken in the book as a whole.

In this connection and fourthly, the two sides, it will be remembered, were referred to in Part 1 as 'grammatical competence' and 'communicative competence'. I have preferred 'linguistic' to 'grammatical' because I feel there may be confusion with traditional connotations of 'grammar', one of which was a restriction of it to syntax and morphology (word modification). I have also preferred 'awareness' to 'competence' though I do use the two fairly synonymously. The word 'competence' for some carries theoretical nuances from the 1970s (following Chomsky, 1965) and I would now be looking more to the ideas behind the language awareness of the 1980s.

The architect analogy then has so far yielded us certain broad headings in the form of these kinds of language awareness, which in turn give us the possible components of language, the rules for their operation and some important parameters. We move on now from the knowing about and how to the skills themselves, the actual ability to perform.

The Four Language Modes

Let me begin by once again defining terms. The *ability* to do or perform consists of four basic skills or *modes,* listening, reading, speaking and writing, each of which has a number of *sub-skills.* Our architect needed both receptive and productive skills and in a kind of circular fashion the one helped the other. In terms of language this is also true. Receiving and comprehending messages are the better for the ability to express or produce well and the latter is improved by a basis of real understanding of meaning. The receptive modes of language are listening and reading: the productive modes speaking and writing. It is these four modes which I shall now go on to discuss, the modes which constitute the ability to perform and which reflect in their performance the degree of language awareness of the linguist.

There is another broad division which must be registered before we go any further and that is the oracy/literacy one. The oracy receptive mode is listening and the literacy one reading: the oracy productive mode is speaking and the literacy one writing. So now we have a grid (Table 1) which yields four useful cells, (1) Oracy/Receptive or Listening, (2) Literacy/Receptive or Reading, (3) Oracy/Productive or Speaking, and (4) Literacy/Productive or Writing. Something further could be added to the grid at this stage. When we receive messages we are said to 'decode' and when we send them to 'encode'. The grid could therefore be constructed as shown in Table 2.

TABLE 1   *The four language modes*

	Oracy	Literacy
Receptive	1 Listening	2 Reading
Productive	3 Speaking	4 Writing

TABLE 2   *'Coding' in the four language modes*

	Oracy	Literacy	
Receptive	1 Listening	2 Reading	*Decoding*
Productive	3 Speaking	4 Writing	*Encoding*

The term 'code' was used above in the notion of code-switching, a skill of communication. Before we go any further, I must point out that we have here two different notions of code, both of which will be reflected to some extent as we proceed. I have used them only because they do appear in the literature and are fairly common parlance. This second use which I have put in Table 2 suggests a code rather like the Morse Code which some of us remember from Guiding or Scouting days. It is a system of symbols attached to a particular set of meanings. Once the knowledge of these has become automatic the user of the code can cope very efficiently with the messages, both sending or encoding and receiving or decoding. He can be said to have cracked the code. Meaning is produced or understood in the light of the code which is known to both sender and receiver.

There was a time, about thirty or forty years ago, when the Morse Code kind of concept in relation to language was very much to the fore, in line with the then current ideas about learning. Language was seen in terms of Code and Message. But times have changed and so has terminology. The association with a very mechanistic kind of learning and arid teaching procedures leading to language-like behaviour rather than language, has turned the teaching profession away somewhat from the concept of code and message, or at least from the terminology. The idea does linger on however, particularly with reference to reading and spelling, and one hears things like 'cracking the spelling code'. My own feeling is that 'code' used in this way is still a useful idea provided it can be made to refer also to the communicative as well as the linguistic side of the language equation so that one could speak about 'cracking the *social* code' of a particular group. Whatever the truth of the matter, it is important for teachers to remember that a psycholinguistic awareness of *all* the language systems including those of use, is an issue to be concerned with when considering teaching options.

The other use of the word 'code', which was popular in the 1970s when Bernstein (1975) highlighted class differences in language styles and spoke of elaborated and restricted codes, has become a term of modern linguistics. It can be used to describe a variety or style of language use within *one* language, such as a regional or social dialect; it is also sometimes used in a wider way to refer to the whole language. So when we say 'code-switching' we mean moving either from one dialect or from one language to another. It is in this sense that we can say that every language user, monolingual as well as bilingual, is constantly code-switching as the social situation seems to demand.

The difference between the two uses of the word 'code' may be a little hard to grasp. I see it as a matter of width of concept. The first suggests a set of components from which messages are generated and understood; the second suggests the total style of message with all possible parameters included. Again, what is important in the classroom is that children are encouraged to understand and to cope with the exciting diversity which exists in every language. Let us return now to the four language modes.

Though they are closely inter-related and share a great many factors, not the least of which is the sum of language awareness as described above, there are, nevertheless, aspects which make each an individual skill with its own sub-skills. For instance, whether the linguist is listening, reading, speaking or writing, he is helped in his performance by his knowledge of the possible linguistic components and the ways they are systematised and by his awareness of the needs of the situation and the rules for choice of components, structure and style. At the same time, whichever mode he is using will involve different physical organs for one thing and perhaps a few other things. Let us consider them now. All four modes will be discussed in light of the physical/practical skills, the skills of comprehension/composition and those of style connected with purpose. The reader should bear in mind as we go along all the things which have been said concerning the knowing about and how, and should refer to the checklists in Part 5 for samples of specific items.

Listening

This is represented by Cell 1 of the grid. It has to do with oracy and with comprehension, so it has much in common on the one hand with speaking and on the other with reading. It has to do basically with discrimination of sound and being able to attach meaning. The physical matter of attention is important so that the ear is able to do its job of perception. What, for example, is to be perceived? There are the discrete sounds of the language in all their varieties, modified as they are used in different linguistic environments. (See Appendix 1.) For instance the word 'to' sounds like 'ti' much of the time. This matter of sound is linked to stress and intonation and to the total rhythm of the utterance. The linguist has to be able to grasp meaning from changes in stress and the rise and fall of the voice, particularly important in English. Contrast for instance is very often marked in this way, as in 'This is *my* book and that is *yours*'.

Next, the linguist has to be able to follow the sequence of an utterance and to comprehend its construction. This can sometimes be hard when the ideas are not expressed very clearly with the hesitation phenomena of the oral pronouncement. He has to bring all his oral awareness into play in order to *predict* what is coming or what should be there. His knowledge of the sound system, the syntax and the cohesive devices, should all help; but perhaps more than anything his understanding of the topic under discussion and the shared meanings in the social situation, very often expressed in subtle gestures and facial expressions as much as by linguistic features, will be clues to the message being encoded. In other words, the linguist has to be able to make informed guesses for his listening to be effective and he will be able to do this the more skilfully for being aware in the ways we have discussed. The opposite is of course also true. A lack of such awareness leads to misreading of the signs and *wild* guessing — what Goodman (see Appendix 2), in connection with reading, has described as miscue.

So to the skills of style connected with purpose. The linguist should be able to listen for gist and to listen for detail. That is to say, there are times when only the general overall meaning of what is being said is important. There are other times when it is vital to have every possible detail clear. These are two different styles of listening. In this connection the factor of redundancy in language could be mentioned. This means the giving of a message in more than one way so that the listener will be *sure* to receive it. Most languages have redundancy built in but some have more than others. The degree of it in English is quite high. Take the sentence 'There are four books on the table'. The message of plurality has been signalled three times — by 'are', 'four' and the 's' on 'book'. A language like Turkish would say something like 'There is four book on the table', when the message of plurality is given only once by 'four'.

What is being suggested is that when he is listening the linguist has to be particularly attentive to this phenomenon, more so perhaps in its communicative guise, as speakers probably in any language tend to repeat themselves or say the same thing in different ways, augmented by the paralinguistic features of gesture and facial expression. The linguist has to be able to sort out what is new from what is being repeated. What must be stressed is that listening is an *active* not a passive operation. There is a physical factor and a cognitive one, the matter of perception and decoding and then of conception. The concepts are stored and accommodated for future use so that they really belong to the listener. He should be able to recall them later. Much of what has been said here is true also of reading, particularly the importance of prediction and informed guessing. Let us move on to Cell 2.

Reading
The physical/practical skills this time have to do with the eye. It is important for efficient reading that the linguist uses economical eye-movements and does not progress jerkily across the page. He has also to be able to move in the right direction, in English from left to right. Whilst the listener has to be able to discriminate sound, the reader has to do so with shape and to understand that these graphics are representative of sound. In place of stress and intonation etc. the linguist who is reading has punctuation to help him, amongst other subtle devices. These aids may not be very adequate but he needs to know the conventions. He has to be able to recognise words quickly using his knowledge of patterns in spelling, word modification for meaning such as past tense, and lexis. He also has to be able to attack new words by means of intelligent deductions from the context and by the use of his phonic skills — blending, etc. (See Ball in Appendix 2.) Above all he must be able to relate the words he is reading to the situations

to which they belong. In other words he must extract the meaning from the text.

Perhaps a short anecdote will help to make clear at least what reading is not! Many years ago when I was in Uganda I had the privilege of being able to start a little school for children who were long-stay patients in the hospital near the university where I worked. The children had no English and I had no Luganda but I yearned to tell them a story. I bought a Luganda primer and noted that the words were written in Romanic script as is English so I *could* make the right noises! I noted also punctuation marks which were familiar to me. Armed with this rather scanty knowledge and what information about the context I could glean from the poor illustrations, I proceeded to 'read' in a loud voice while my pupils were engaged in drawing and colouring. One by one they stopped in their tracks and began to take some interest in my 'reading'. Soon they were all round me, obviously following and eventually laughing. It must have been a very funny story but *I* had no idea what it was about!

The question is — *was* I reading? What *is* reading? It seems that there are four kinds of knowledge being put into operation here if the linguist is 'really' to read. A few have been mentioned already. The first is the graphophonemic relationship, the knowledge of printed symbols and how they relate to speech sounds. Second is the knowledge of syntax or word order. Can he recognise for instance that 'I yesterday came' would be unacceptable in English? Third, there is the semantic knowledge. The linguist has to be able to use the meaning he has acquired from a range of experiences to make sense of this particular message. And lastly, the reader has to use what might be called his bibliographic knowledge, his awareness of books and of the whole concept of print, also the kind of language to be found there which differs quite considerably sometimes from the spoken language. For children the language of story is very important. Given these four kinds of knowledge then, the reader is enabled to predict, which, as we have seen, is a skill vital to fluency.

It is interesting to go back now to my Uganda experience. What was it that I lacked? I had knowledge of the mechanics in the abstract, a universal understanding of grapho-phonemics, syntax, the ways of books, etc. and the manner of decoding. I also had a fair degree of life experience. What I did not have was a knowledge of the particular ways in which these things worked in Luganda. I did not have that particular code. A reader has to have cracked the code to be able to interpret the messages. The sad sequel to my story is that the children assumed I had done so and were amazed and bewildered when I could not respond to their questions and comments. They did not realise that what I had been doing was 'barking at print'. I had not been reading at all.

But of course, reading is much more than cracking a code. The really efficient reader can in a sense hold a conversation with the text. There is a kind of continuum of skill from the simple extracting of a reference through making inferences to making the text part of one's own cognitive and affective schemata (see Chapter 8). The reader, or linguist, generally has to know how to mean. So there are similarities here to the receptive skills of listening. There are the physical and practical aspects and the business of following a sequence. There is also the important meaning factor and the accommodation of the new to what is known. Another thing in common is purpose. As with listening there are different kinds of reading. Sometimes we read in a very casual way as perhaps we would in a dentist's waiting-room if we picked up one of the magazines. At other times we read with more care, paying attention to detail. These two styles are sometimes referred to as skimming and scanning respectively. The second is a vital skill for the student. Indeed the whole concept of reading takes on a new dimension when study skills are considered. There is the reading of all kinds of matter including graphs and other non-verbal materials. Teachers need to consider this issue even in the primary school (see Avann, 1985). What demands will be made upon the pupils and how well can their reading ability cope?

There is one way in which reading differs from listening which is interesting and perhaps also significant for the teacher, and that is the permanence of the reading text compared with the ephemeral nature of the spoken utterance. What is written can be kept and read over and over again. In the matter of extracting meaning, which is what these receptive modes are all about, the linguist has to be able to use different kinds of sign-posts. While listening he has the asset of the face-to-face encounter and meaning which is shared at the moment. While reading he has words which do not go away and certain conventions of the writing business to aid his understanding. These things offset the problems. Let us turn now to the modes of production, beginning this time with the literacy one of writing as it follows on so nicely from this discussion.

Writing

I suppose in a nutshell one could say that the skilled writer has to be able to offer all the things which we have just noted that the reader needs. He has to encapsulate meaning and express it in what/how he writes. Physically and practically he has to manage the eye–hand co-ordination of wielding pencil or pen or typewriter. He has to be able to handle the patterns of spelling etc. and the rules of punctuation and sign-posting. These are what the Kent County Language Policy document (see Appendix 1) calls the 'secretarial skills'. In a sense, each of the four modes has its secretarial skills. Then comes the skill of construction or composition. The writer has to be very conscious of his readership. This has a profound effect upon the kind of writing he will do. Sadly in schools students are often expected to write in the abstract. This produces writing-like behaviour but not true writing. The writer has to be conscious also of the fact that his means of paralinguistic support for meaning are limited and therefore the meaning must lie very much in the words and structures used and in the style of their composing. Skilled writers know the idiom. Some even know when to go impressively against the conventions. In the Widdowson sense they have capacity as well as competence. They are the architects of language who reach the heights. Most of us are content to attain the competence stage and happy when our students do.

Like the reader, the writer has to be concerned with the purpose of his writing. Is he writing something trivial for readers to skim over lightly or is his matter more weighty? Is he reporting something factual or indulging in fantasy? Is he writing to a personal friend or the manager of a firm, or is he writing to express his opinions or feelings — perhaps to a newspaper? The style of his writing will differ accordingly. This sensitivity to style is something to be gained by a wide range of experience of the writings and story-tellings of others so that it becomes almost second nature to code-switch.

The words 'cohesion', 'balance' and 'sign-posting' have been used once or twice already. They are applicable to the whole of language but perhaps especially to writing. Because the writer has to take time and particular care with his production, which is more permanent than the things he utters in speech, he must be able to plan, perhaps to make drafts leading to a fair copy. This will involve sorting out his ideas and a kind of trial and error strategy of putting them together. He must be able to do the work of a word-processor which, of course, is what it is because this is what writers do! So he has to be concerned with the what and the how. Having got his ideas straight he must find the most competent and perhaps the most impressive way of putting them, bearing in mind the why, when and where. His discourse must have linguistic and semantic balance and the reader must be able to find his way about easily or he will lose interest and not extract the meaning.

There are devices for this kind of discourse work. For instance, it is useful for the writer to know about words like 'so', 'but', 'then', or at a more advanced level, 'furthermore', 'in this connection' and so on. The writer has to have the skill of being able to relate one thing to another — 'the man' with 'he', a statement about something with 'this', as in 'it was in this way' etc.

This is what is meant here by sign-posting. It helps the text to be all of a piece and so helps the reader towards meaning. The writer has time to select amongst the items in the builder's yard and to make good use also of his stock of sayings, the kind of prefabricated language as Opal Dunn (1983) calls it, words built already into larger units because someone found this useful. The lore of any language is full of these. We use them in speech often to the point of cliché. We must learn to select. So, again we have been concerned with practicalities, building and style. They will appear once more as we go on now to discuss the last of our modes, that of speaking.

Speaking

Because all the modes are inter-related much has already been said which applies also to speaking. Relating to the 'secretarial skills' we have this time the ability to use the speech organs, the physical business of putting tongue, teeth, palates and breathing equipment to proper use so that the right noises for the language concerned are emitted. There has to be appropriate use of stress and intonation, this time to *give* additional meaning, along with body movement and facial expression. The speech must be accurate and fluent enough to be coherent to the listener, which means that the speaker must make use of his inventory of items on both the linguistic and the communicative sides of language and the conventions for their use. His sensitivity to the needs of the actual situation and his sense of role, his own and those of others, and his ability to code-switch are very important here too. This all builds up to a competence. Equivalent to the capacity of the high-flyer in writing the speaker also can go further if he wants to. He can go to town on the sheer elocution of the business but also on the selection of items and their composition. Lawyers, actors and ministers (church and state) often do this to impress. Again, most of us are content with lowlier skills and teachers should be happy if their pupils reach a stage of speaking which is competent.

The two-way business of language is particularly apparent here. The speaker has to be skilled in conversation. Very few people stand up in public and give a speech unopposed. Every normal person has to handle the give and take of everyday conversation, taking turns, knowing how to wait and when, and how to come in. He needs to know the conventions for attracting attention and devices for holding it. The good conversationalist is both listener and speaker and has to give at least the impression of being interested in what others are saying. He must also have the skill of flexibility, changing his style or even his content as he reacts to the speech and moods of others. This is the strategic awareness in action. Often there is little time to think. Speech has the hazard of being able to cause offence without intent. It also has the asset of spontaneity.

So the speaker composes and the listener comprehends, and the styles of both depend to a large extent on the common purpose. The communicative skills are exceedingly important but so also are the linguistic and psycholinguistic skills. As with all language I believe that true fluency can only be so if accuracy is there as well and the linguist is therefore freed from worries about the medium so that he can concentrate on the message.

The reader should refer back to what was said about purpose in connection with the writer. The same kinds of factors are at work here. Is the speaking informal, amongst friends or even at a meeting of colleagues? Or is it formal as in debate or oratory? Are the interlocutors engaged in working out an argument or making plans or is one relating some story or incident? What and where is the meaning of the situation? How intense is it? How concerned are the speakers? Someone caught in a fire is hardly likely to say politely, 'Can somebody please help me?'. He is more likely to shout with some tension in his voice the single word 'Help!'. Again the strategy of quick code-switching is apparent. In this connection particularly it is interesting to contemplate the problems/assets of the bilingual. He has to code-switch not only from one language to another but, as everyone has to do, from one style of speech to another within one language. All of this calls for considerable skill, supported by a rich depth of language awareness.

Summary

It does appear that language proficiency is a highly complex entity and not at all easy to capture for study. What has been said about the issues of language has of necessity been fairly brief and the writer's personal view. Teachers should avail themselves of some of the reading matter suggested in the Appendices for further and other ideas about what makes the competent linguist. It is hoped, however, that the broad issues highlighted in Part 1 and the more detailed handling here will be a sufficient basis for a methodology of story to build on. We still have to consider one or two issues of learning and teaching implications which I thought should be discussed separately even though language and its learning cannot be kept apart in practice. So we turn in the next chapter from the proficiency of the mature linguist to a consideration of how he becomes so, and more particularly, the special concerns of the foreign and second language learner.

Note to Chapter 4

1. I am using this term in the sense of 'language user' and not to mean the linguist of linguistics.

5 Learning and Teaching

The Early Years

Language, thought and experience

I would not presume in the space of a short chapter to try and describe how language is acquired/learnt. There is a vast literature about this and suggestions for reading are given. My aim here is simply to focus on one or two aspects highlighted by the architect analogy which, along with the issues of language just discussed, should offer ideas for teaching options and influence the selection of the story vehicle, its loading and use.

We noticed that in the early years the architect-to-be was imbibing the messages of the buildings around him, messages from his immediate environment and culture. He also played with his bricks and made his own buildings in imitation of the real thing. So the baby, the budding linguist, responds to the human voice and does so from birth, some say before birth. The sounds and their messages are absorbed together and they belong to the culture of the immediate family and environment. It is said that in his babbling the baby is capable of making all the sounds ever made by man, but that in a very short time he settles for those he hears around him and soon begins to imitate, even the nuances of tone. In a very remarkable way these random noises become systematised for the child. In other words he acquires the rules, both linguistic and communicative, as he gradually becomes socialised within his particular community. He very quickly learns what to say to whom, how, why, when and where.

The manner and rate of this development are still subjects for debate, in spite of centuries of scholarship on the matter, but it is generally accepted that by about six months old the child expects some kind of response to his overtures and that the first words and rules are acquired between eight and ten months. By a year old the child can understand a great deal, much more than he can say. His vocabulary begins to grow very fast as well as his ability to converse. By the age of five most children in most cultures have acquired the basic particulars of their own language and can classify and form concepts. They therefore start school as efficient linguists, competent in both the usage and the use of language. Language and thought have been developing together within the fairly narrow experience of the family circle. Ideally, school should further this development by extending the experience both in kind and degree during which old learning will be consolidated and new learning acquired. But before I elaborate on the task of the school let us think a little more about the development of concepts.

Concept getting and using

There are concepts of the physical and of the social world and, very importantly, the child's concept of self. Part of all this is the child's awareness of language. The inextricable mix of language, thought and experience must always be kept in mind. I have found five words helpful in the study of how concepts seem to develop. They all end in '-tion' and so I call them my five '-tions'. The first is *Identification,* the matter of labelling. The child begins by naming the objects, people and events he is focusing on. Second is *Qualification,* ways of describing the attributes of what has been identified, concerning for example size, shape, colour, number, location in place and time, purpose, mood, etc. Then we have *Relation.* The things identified and qualified can now be compared and samenesses and differences noted. This leads very well into the fourth '-tion', *Classification,* the ability to sort and put into sets or categories. Finally comes *Manipulation,* using the concepts gained in order to hypothesise, expressing cause and effect and possibility, using the imagination to fantasise etc. So the first four '-tions' have to do with concept getting or development and the last with their use.

It is interesting too to consider the kind of language associated with these '-tions'. For identifying there is, for instance, the question form with 'what/who' etc. and the appropriate responses and statements: 'it is — these are — etc.'. For qualifying, 'what' attached to 'colour', 'size', etc. is needed and the word 'which' is used. Relating language would include 'the same as' and 'different from', 'bigger than' and 'the biggest' and the language of classifying, 'sets', 'groups', 'go together', etc. The language of manipulation brings 'if' and 'because' with *their* appropriate structures. As the child's understanding grows and his '-tions' develop so the facilitating language develops apace. It might be useful for EFL/ESL teachers to consider the '-tions' and their language exponents. They are relevant in the learning of another language too and make useful pegs upon which to hang teaching points and materials.

Formulae and rules

Another important thing to say about the child's developing *language,* is that he becomes aware quite early of the chunks of language which always seem to be the same, the formulae or prefabricated language. He can learn these as wholes in the manner of the *Gestalt.* The opening phrase of a story, 'once upon a time' or 'long long ago' would be examples of such language. This is to be compared with his acquisition of the rules and patterns of the language which enable the child to combine and re-combine and be creative as he produces his own particular sentences. Again, this is a useful thought for language teachers. How might we make use of this learning factor in the development of another language? Remember that the learner both analyses and builds, deduces and induces. Sometimes his thinking is global and sometimes atomistic. This is a useful phenomenon for teachers to bear in mind.

School Learning

Confirmation of the old: Accommodation of the new

Our fledgling architect, when he went to college, found that his teacher helped him to confirm the things about building he had acquired on his own. His discoveries were consolidated and built upon by tuition so that his awareness and ability were extended. So the child linguist, beginning his schooling in the language of his own community, has a similar experience. The BICS continue in ways familiar to him and the CALP develops as the language of study is needed more and more. Concept and skill acquisition become increasingly concept and skill using. The child moves from a kind of priming the pump stage to one of creative activity. Learning of language has become language of learning.

For all this to proceed smoothly it seems to be important for the teacher to share or at least to understand the child's concepts and values, to know what the child brings with him. Only then can she confirm or otherwise; only then can she build on a sure foundation so that new knowledge is accommodated (in the Piagetian sense) into the child's existing schemata. This is something of what is meant by a child-centred education. It is the right of all children. For those who come from homes where the community language deviates from that used in school, with all that this means in its relation to thought and experience, the chances of their enjoying such an education are not usually very good. (See below for further discussion on the implications for the bilingual child.)

Mechanics and message

I have spoken of the two sides of the language equation. The acquisition/learning equation offers a kind of matching dichotomy. The young architect and the young linguist begin by acquiring, by making their own discoveries. At school they are submitted to the process of learning. But this is not to say that the acquisition side ceases to function. The eclectic view taken in this book suggests that there is need for a school environment where discovery learning or acquisition is allowed to continue without hassle. There is also a need for monitoring and directing in differing degrees, both used appropriately to give balance.

Another matter highlighted and related to the point just made was the importance of making certain things mechanical so that concerns of the medium become gradually less central to the learner and concentration can really be given to the message. The child must be helped to mean. Everything else is to that end. The experience the child brings to school, the experience shared with others *in* school, and that which comes from various sources, particularly story and literature, must all be harnessed to the aim of bringing sense to the child's world. I believe, however, that one means to this end is the mastery of the basic skills which have to become automatic.

The handling of the tools must become second-nature to the handler. The process of *usage* must become *less* important than the product or message, which is not to contradict the other dictum we looked at, that the process of *use* is *more* important than the product or finished composition. It depends on which product you have in mind at the time. In the Widdowson sense of aim/objective, the overall aim is meaning, but it may be that just at that time it would be appropriate to make a discovery into a habit! So the ESL learner has found out from experience that English seems to pluralise by adding an 's'-like sound. He has found one or two cases of this. Can the teacher point to some more, and to places where plural is made in another way? Or the learner has discovered that the English-speaking people seem to take leave of each other (in the north of England) by saying something like, 'Tara love'. Can the teacher point to other places where this happens, or some version of it, and to the fact that the formal leave-taking might be different from the informal? Can she offer structured experience within which the learner can practise for himself — on the one hand situations where more than one object has to be talked about, and on the other, situations of leave-taking in stories and role-play, gradually increasing the variety? In sum, the child has to be shown *how* to use *what* he knows about language, its skills and its potential, across an increasing number of situations involving messages of different kinds, personal, social, strategic, etc.

The two learning sides suggest two teaching sides, a kind of double bill; on the one hand making mechanical, on the other making meaningful. Linguistic awareness and communicative awareness; learning and acquisition; accuracy and fluency; code and message; mechanics and message; dichotomies concerned with language and learning, all with implications for teaching. It was consideration of these issues which suggested to me the wisdom of opting for an eclectic approach, in education generally and in language teaching in particular. This is exemplified in the construct shown in Figure 1 and elaborated upon in the last section of this chapter and again in Chapter 8. I hope it may serve as a useful framework for the story methodology, not only supporting the 'double bill' of mechanics and meaning but also the *progression* of learning. Let us consider this matter a little further.

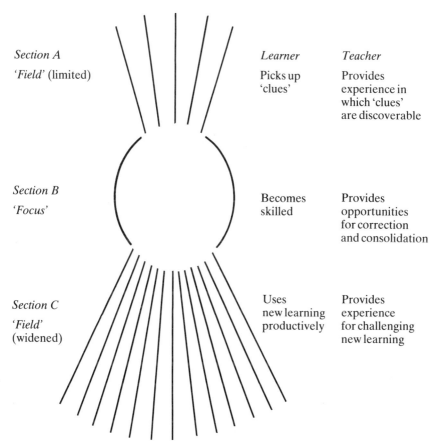

		Learner	Teacher
Section A	*'Field'* (limited)	Picks up 'clues'	Provides experience in which 'clues' are discoverable
Section B	*'Focus'*	Becomes skilled	Provides opportunities for correction and consolidation
Section C	*'Field'* (widened)	Uses new learning productively	Provides experience for challenging new learning

FIGURE 1   *'Field and Focus': A construct for learning and teaching*

Progression

It is believed that learning progresses from that which has been associated with particular experiences to that which has become generalised and productive for the learner over an increasing range and complexity of situations, and that this journey involves a kind of cracking of the code. First the learner needs a limited field in which to browse and absorb, to make discoveries for himself. The next stage is for these discoveries to be made firm, and the final stage is the creative or productive use of the learning. I feel that something of this progression goes on continually in a cyclical fashion and that the learning of language is only one instance of the wider phenomenon of all learning. Be that as it may, in this book concerning the teaching of English and using story as vehicle, it is proposed to bear this three-stage cycle very much in mind, the educational provision helping the learner to control and create.

Implications for the Bilingual Child

Universals and particulars

We must think a little more now about the child who has to face the learning of another language and perhaps learning *in* that language in the primary school. Surely this must be one of the biggest traumas the learner will experience in the whole of his life, with the learning of reading perhaps a close second. I tried to highlight this in the architect analogy. No matter how expert the architect had become in matters of building, to have to operate in an alien culture brought bewilderment and loss of efficiency. He did not know nor had he the time to discover the particular ways in which the new community handled things. This is a fair picture of the child linguist who comes to school and is presented with a regime where his own community language is not used. It is, in particular, a reflection of the situation where the ESL child has to be immediately busy in the matters of his general schooling so that he very often does not have the time (or the support) to sort out his bewilderment. It has special applications too to the threshold situation where the child moves suddenly from an EFL to an ESL kind of teaching.

The problem is the difference in the particulars. The asset is that he *has* an awareness of language and a grasp of things universal through his *own* set of particulars. Does the teacher know what these are? Does she even realise that he has travelled the road before, albeit in a different lane? Somehow the child must be guided to an appropriate code-switch:

somehow what he brings to the situation of the second language must be utilised.

Cashing in on the assets

Here is a special case of the accommodation of the old to the new which Piaget perhaps did *not* stress. What *does* the child bring with him for the teacher to cash in on? If our earlier discussion is valid he has acquired by age five a fair degree of awareness of what language is and does and he is using it to develop his concepts of self, of social relationships and of the physical world about him. What he now needs to know is how English is and does. He requires to go through the five '-tions' again, to discover that the process is the same even though the products may differ, and to discover most of all that he is not so stupid as he thought he was. In fact, if he could but master this second code he would be far better equipped than his monolingual fellows.

The bilingual teacher

Fortunate is the child who has a well-equipped teacher. Ideally, it seems to me, the tutor of the bilingual learner needs herself to be bilingual, preferably in the languages of the learner. This would ensure an understanding of the extent of the difficulties and perhaps some expertise in how to overcome them. The next best thing would be for the teacher to be bilingual in *some* way so that at least the *situation* of bilingualism and the business of code-switching are appreciated. It might not take such a teacher long to discover some of the particular problems of her pupil and to apply her general skill.

But, lest the poor monolingual reading this should despair, let me remind her that we are all in possession of code-switching knowledge and skill to some extent, even within one language. We move from one dialect or style to another depending on the circumstances, much as the bilingual or multilingual does, and our skill in doing it is a measure of our sensitivity to the components of the situation. What I am trying to say is that any teacher, given a proper awareness of the factors involved, should be able to support the bilingual child, but that the best insurance for this support is surely to have a bilingual teacher. There are several implications here for both teacher training and general policy and I shall try to examine them in Part 4. The important issue at stake is the almost certain under-achievement of children in many countries where the learning of language is insufficiently supported in its move towards language for learning, and where the learning of other essential concepts and skills is therefore adversely affected.

English for Special Purposes

Serving the curriculum

It was said that our architect, specialising in one kind of building, needed first of all to have general knowledge of the construction business. There may be a few situations where it would be expedient and effective for the limited ends in view to go straight for the speciality. For instance, a tourist going to a country for two weeks' holiday could well manage with a few useful phrases and words. It would not be necessary for *his* purposes to acquire the linguistic rules, though the communicative ones might be useful. Or again, the foreigner emigrating to a country and starting to work in a factory might for his own safety need to know the words and sentences concerning warning of danger on the machinery. A knowledge of the grammar would be unnecessary.

I could go on posing a hierarchy of situations. Just at what point it would seem necessary to take the wider view it is difficult to say. For the school child whose special purpose is to acquire the language for other learning, a general awareness of the language would seem to be a necessity. It is in this sense that English is being considered here for the child in the ESL situation. The special need is for it to serve the curriculum, to be the tool by which all the other learning is acquired. The implications of language across the curriculum (see discussion on the implications of the Bullock Report in Chapter 10) are vital for all children. Where it is a second language they become particularly significant.

Tool of learning

There is the need for the teaching team to focus on the subject areas and to understand the challenge to the children of the concepts being presented (see Appendix 1). There is the need for an awareness of the facilitating language and for the particular problems this may cause to the ESL child. Has he met such a term before? Does it remind him of some piece of language in his mother tongue which has quite another connotation for him? Are there words or phrases here that have been imbibed by the English mother-tongue speakers over the years and which they are now ready to learn to use in perhaps a slightly different way, to widen their semantic field, when for the ESL speakers there is no field at all and the language comes cold? The learning tool has to be honed occasionally and the teacher has to know how to do it.

But much of the above has seemed to be restricted to the ESL child. Where does the *EFL* learner stand in all this? He too is a bilingual of a kind. He may not need his foreign language to make sense of the curriculum but he may well need it for special purposes in later life. In a sense the teacher in these circumstances has to work even harder making the language learning a meaningful experience for the pupil, as she may not know where exactly and for what reasons the language is going to be important. Extrinsic motivation may be a big factor here and also some knowledge of the *policy* regarding the English language in the country, if there is one! For this pupil English may not be the tool of learning but it could still be a tool for something. At least in the EFL situation in many countries the teachers are bilingual in their pupils' languages, so that is a bonus. But they also need to be educated towards an optimum programme for handling the two languages.

Towards a Methodology

A summary of issues

At the beginning of Part 2 it was stated that the issues raised here would be matched by teaching options in Part 3. We need now to try and summarise these issues, the baggage as it were, for the story vehicle to carry. I hope that the key items selected and featured below will be sufficient *aide memoire* for what has been said. There is nothing sacrosanct about the list and certainly no claim to be definitive.

Language   *Knowledge about* (Kinds of awareness)

Linguistic (Usage); Communicative (Use)

> Psycholinguistic
> Sociolinguistic
> Discourse
> Strategic
> Cognitive/Semantic

Components (Structure, Vocabulary, Purpose/Function) and their Systems. (See Checklists in Appendix 1)

Knowledge how (four basic modes) and *Ability to perform*

> Listening
> Speaking   Oracy/Literacy
> Reading   Receptive/Productive
> Writing
>   and their sub-skills

The *Secretarial and Construction skills* in all four, operating with the various kinds of language awareness

Learning   *Progression* towards productive use
                    Fluency and *Accuracy*
                    Acquisition and *Learning*
                        (Discovery/Habit)
                    Link between *Language, Thought and Experience*
                    Universals/Particulars

Teaching   *Cashing in on the assets* (building on child's understanding)
                    The *Double bill* (making mechanical and making meaning)
                        (The eclectic approach)
                    Provision for *Progression of learning*

We must try to bear in mind also the broader issues raised in Part 1. They are, I hope, reflected in the above list but it might be helpful to look at them again and to cross-reference if necessary. In Chapter 1 consideration of current thinking in English Language Teaching (ELT) gave us the following:

> The *Communicative Approach* with *five salient notions,* thoughts on the *Acquisition/Learning* dichotomy, consideration of the *Cummins Debate* and the link between *Language Proficiency and Education* with the suggestion of a *BICS and CALP* and the implications for *Bilingualism,* suggestion also of a *Common Underlying Proficiency* (CUP) and what this could mean for teaching, the matter of *Graded Objectives* and those of *Language Awareness, Language for Specific Purposes, Learner-Centred Education* and *Return of Grammar.*

Chapter 2, which gives the point of departure and rationale for the book, brought us to:

> The *Nature of Story* as a potential *Vehicle,* not only for *Language Development* (which is our main business here) but also for many other personal and educative gains including the *Affective* development and an understanding of *Universal* and *Intercultural* matters. We saw how story could help to cater for the *Interdependence of Experience and Language,* acting as both *Motivator* and *Cohesive Device* in the curriculum at large. We saw also that it could be useful in a number of situations in both EFL and ESL, *Contextualising the Syllabus, Giving Guidelines of Structure to the Curriculum* and possibly helping the *Move over the Threshold from one Medium to the Other.* In sum, story as *Structured Theme* seemed to offer endless opportunities to the teacher, including, if an eclectic approach were taken, the *Redress of Balance* necessary at times and the *Bridging of several ELT Information Gaps.*

Now, with the further thinking of Part 2 behind us and perhaps a somewhat clearer idea of the classroom issues, we are ready to consider the approach and methodology.

Field and focus

As I indicated earlier, this construct (see Figure 1) has been found useful as a kind of teaching blueprint. It does highlight the accuracy/fluency dichotomy and it suggests a learning progression which is, of course, cyclical. The learner moves from the initial, limited field, where he picks up the clues or makes his discoveries, to sessions of focusing with the teacher so that his acquisitions are confirmed or otherwise. He then proceeds, having cracked the code, to a wider and more challenging field where he uses his learning creatively for his own purposes.

When I first used the construct in *Breakthrough to Fluency* (1976: see Appendix 1) the communicative side of the language equation was not much thought about and the code to be cracked referred to linguistic matters only. It is interesting to me, now convinced that the code applies to both, that the construct still seems to be valid. It can be interpreted as saying that learning progresses in a kind of cyclical way and consists of both acquiring and learning, and that the progression is in matters both linguistic and communicative. In other words, the two run *through* the progression, drawing into them, I believe, all the other kinds of awareness and issues of learning. The approach may help us also to incorporate the various teaching issues summarised. It is the framework for Part 3, the opted-for approach within which story, the opted-for methodology, offers scope for many more options of theme, activity, material and technique. We are ready now to put story to the test. Can it indeed fulfil our expectations?

Part 3
Loading and Using the Vehicle: Options of Theme, Activity, Material and Technique

Introduction

It is the aim of the next three chapters to offer a *strategy* or way of approach. No attempt is made to cover all the possible options matching all the possible issues; rather the intention is to indicate a process. Given a certain understanding of language and learning and given also the particular circumstances of her teaching work, the teacher can proceed in this way or that. It is to a consideration of these options within the methodology of the story vehicle that we now turn. They are options of the theme itself, of activities and materials to support them, and of classroom management and teaching technique. Some ideas are given for the putting together of a story kit in such a way that it could be used as a prototype for others. The notion of prototype is much to the fore throughout both Part 3 and Part 4 where strategies for teachers and for those who train them are examined.

Another salient idea is that of loading the vehicle. In Chapter 6 some consideration is given to ways in which the issues, including that of covering items from syllabus/curriculum, can somehow be incorporated, not only into the story theme itself but also into the related and follow-up activities and materials. It is as though the story vehicle has a trailer, and between the two which form the total kit there is a fairly comprehensive package of learning. So we are concerned with selection, with loading and, of course, using. Chapter 6 deals mainly with selection and loading; Chapter 7 caters for the using aspects. Its title, 'The Story Teller', has been deliberately written in that way as a play on words. What is being suggested is that the teacher, right from her initial selection of the vehicle through its narration and follow-up, is a teller in the sense of the one in the bank. She has to take account of so many things. But of course, attention is also given to the actual narration, both telling and reading, and also to the skills of the wider pedagogy. It is in Chapter 7 too that you find ideas for a bilingual approach to story-telling.

So Chapter 6 deals with the *narrative* and its supporting materials, while Chapter 7 is concerned with the *narration* and the 'noises off' to the drama. The final chapter in Part 3 takes up once again, and in more detail, the important matter of progression — the learning journey. I decided to deal with this after having looked at the kit so that the practical could be informative. As a way of rounding off Part 3 and leading into the teacher training section of Part 4, some suggestions are made for the writing of guidance notes to a story kit. This is for the help of colleagues who might like either to use the kit as it stands or to adapt it in some way, perhaps to indigenise it, another useful idea which should be looked at carefully. These then are the concerns of Part 3.

6   The Story Kit

Section A: The Vehicle

Stories out there

First catch your story. The really exciting thing is that they are all around — out there — just waiting to be caught. Rosen (1985) discusses this 'common possession of humankind — part of the deep structure of the grammar of our world'. He also describes the distinction between 'story', 'narrative' and 'narration', an idea taken from literary criticism. The story is the raw material, the theme of the event. Putting a structure to it, arranging it sequentially, is to produce a narrative, and the art of telling is the narration. It would seem that story carries the potential, narrative is the 'cognitive resource — a meaning-making strategy' and the narration is the *sharing* of it orally or in literature. To some extent these notions are followed here. In this first section we look at the kinds of stories we might catch and why. We also look at the making of narrative and its loading. Section B deals with the related activities and materials, and the business of narration is for Chapter 7.

Story as theme

Something of the nature of story was discussed at the end of Chapter 2. I should like to take up again in particular the point about its being *structured theme* and to develop this notion a little. The idea of using a topic or centre of interest as a key stimulus for learning is nothing new to teachers in the primary school, especially in the lower classes. All kinds of themes are used for this purpose. It might be, for instance, that colour is the current interest. A certain corner of the classroom becomes the focus. This week everything on the table there is blue; next week red and so on. Or it might be that the class has gone out on a visit, say to a farm. For the next week or so the classroom walls will be covered with pictures, drawings and collage showing farm animals and buildings and farmers at work. The changing seasons in some countries make good topics as do festivals and current events. It is also useful to look at the various

institutions in the community — homes, places of worship, shops/markets, etc.,
the more permanent themes in our lives — and then perhaps to run the other
more ephemeral topics through them. In some schools the topic-centred curriculum is the norm and teachers are very familiar with the integrated curriculum and its permeation of the cohesive device or theme.

What is being suggested in this book is that story be used in this way,
and not just as a one-off activity at the end of the day or even at the end of
a week as something to keep the class quiet when everyone is tired! It merits
a much more important place in the learning programme than that. *Let* it
become a key stimulus. *Let* it carry along the learning of all kinds of things,
English language in particular, and let it behave in the same way as other
themes in that it permeates other subject fields, even in the EFL situation,
and that it lasts for longer than one lesson. The time it does last is of course
up to the teacher(s) concerned. It depends on the way the curriculum is
structured and also on the interest and need of the learners. The wise teacher
knows when to switch off. This is not to say that a story could never be
offered in one teaching session and left at that. We have seen that much of
the time this is just what *should* happen, a shared piece of sheer enjoyment
which it would be sacrilege to exploit. But here we are talking about the
story theme which *is* to be used for further learning. It has all the advantages
of theme in general plus the one of offering a structured framework within
which to work. There is a beginning, a middle and an end and other staging-
posts in between if desired, and these act as useful markers to both learners
and teacher, helping memory and suggesting growth-points. In a moment
we will look further at this as we try to turn story into narrative. But first
something must be said about the *selection* of story.

Categories and selection

It is suggested that teachers collect a bank of stories — not in haste, but
over the months of a year and over the years of a teaching career. Times and
needs change. Governments alter syllabuses. The special things a good story
can do are likely to differ from year to year and from class to class while the
general purpose remains the same. It should be possible to have a fairly permanent set of categories which can be used over and over again, while the
actual stories change. In other words, the teacher builds up a useful resource
bank of stories carrying the potential for all the purposes she conceives in her
work (the various kinds of awareness of language for instance) and from this
she selects what she needs for any particular set of circumstances.

What might be the categories of the resource bank? What kinds or
genres of stories are available? What is the range of narratology, to use

another word from literary criticism? The word 'story' suggests fiction but in the context of this book there is also a non-fiction element, the real stories of our everyday world. The dichotomy of *fiction/non-fiction* then would be one way of categorising. If we now take fiction alone there could be several sub-categories to emerge, for example, *traditional folk-tales* and other kinds of story concerned with the lore of a culture, as distinct from the *stories of more modern times* including our own. Across these we might find the *mystery story* as distinct from *plain, factual;* and so on. And if we take non-fiction alone, the *information-giving kind of story,* we might find a division into popular and academic, the latter relating in particular to the stories of the curriculum.

Already we can see that out there is a wide range of choice. There is yet another aspect to consider, and that is the distinction between the stories whose *narratives are given* such as those between the covers of books or dramatised in the theatre or media or even in existence in people's minds, and the *stories yet to be caught* by anyone, the ones really 'out there'. This last category, plucked from the air as it were, is not only the most fruitful very often from the point of view of child-centredness and cashing in on the assets, it is also the one most easily supplied as the resources lie to hand and do not involve financial expense.

The options we take even at this basic level of selecting the categories to work from should be influenced by the issues of language and learning we are concerned with, and the teacher should be able to assess the potential of particular stories against the same issues as she collects them and places them in the categories in her resource bank. These should be continually topped up, some stories being discarded as they become out-of-date or out of favour. Resources have to be found. This involves knowing where to go and whom to ask. It also involves listening and looking, being aware of the things affecting and influencing the learners at the time — asking for *their* news. It might even mean going into the community with a tape-recorder as well as scanning the shelves of libraries and British Council and publishers' lists.

So there must be a strategy for the *selection* of stories. This is the idea of the resource bank and its categories. Next, there has to be some kind of systematised way of collecting them and sorting them out into the categories provided. And finally, it is necessary to make a careful and appropriate selection of any particular story for the current job in hand. As we move on now to consideration of the narrative and its preparation and loading I shall take up this aspect.

The Narrative

Selection and adaptation

Whichever category the story will come from and whatever the special issues affecting the choice, there are certain general criteria which must be borne in mind. The final narrative presented to the children must be motivating. It must stimulate interest and give enjoyment. This suggests that special care should be taken with the level of both concepts and language so that the narrative really is comprehensible input from which the children can anticipate and predict. It also suggests that there should be a strong story-line with very clear staging-posts and possibly repetitions of language and of shape, inviting the listeners to participate. A narrative with these properties is likely to carry the children along and to become a cohesive device for a whole package of learning, a key stimulus to all the rest.

But the selection of the actual story to be treated and used must finally depend on the needs of the moment. Let us try now to imagine a real classroom and to illustrate the strategies of the teacher using a selected story. Let us suppose that this is an EFL situation where an English syllabus is being followed and the unit of the moment demands that the children learn vocabulary of body parts and of colours. It so happens also that in the course of the children's learning, either in English itself or in another subject, the concept of copying/imitating has come up. They have been helped to understand the concept and given the vocabulary in their community language at least. Can some way be found to make it clear in English? Can the idea be transferred? The teacher seeks a story from her resource bank and finds the following (see Story Resources in Appendix 2):

The Hatmaker and the Monkeys

Once upon a time in a distant land there lived a hatmaker. There came a day when he seemed to have quite a number of hats ready to sell so he loaded his barrow with them and set out for the market. It was an extremely hot day and the way was long. The man began to feel very tired. Coming to a shady tree he put down his barrow and sat thankfully on the ground underneath its spreading branches. He was soon fast asleep. Unknown to the hatmaker there were up in the tree some inquisitive monkeys. They were particularly interested in the hats in the barrow. Making sure that the man was still asleep they came stealthily down the tree and took the hats out of the barrow. Each put one on and then they all climbed back to their places in the branches.

After a while the hatmaker awoke. He was almost instantly aware that something was different. His hats had gone. Where could they be? He looked in every direction and at last he looked up into the tree. There were the monkeys sitting smugly with the hats on. The hatmaker was furious. He scowled and shook his fist. Possibly the monkeys also scowled if animals can do such a thing. But they certainly shook their fists. Monkeys are great imitators. They copy or ape the actions of others. This gave the hatmaker an idea. He would get them to copy another action. He took off the hat he was wearing and threw it upon the ground. Then he waited hopefully. His ruse worked. The monkeys did the same. So he was able to retrieve his hats. Feeling rested after his sleep in the shade the hatmaker now replaced his hats in the barrow and continued on his journey to market.

This is the story as it might be given in a book of folk-tales. It illustrates beautifully the concept of imitating. It also offers scope for using the vocabulary of body parts, head, fist, etc., and colours (applied to the hats for example). This work could be extended as hats and heads change to socks and feet, and so on. The teacher is pleased to notice in addition that she could use the story to practise the simple past tense structure and certain vocabulary work relating to sequencing and direction, work already covered but in constant need of revision. So, potentially the story is excellent. The only problem is that the language of the text is too difficult for her learners. There are too many new words and several complicated structures, including reversals (e.g. there came a day) which would be beyond the level of her particular pupils. The story could still be used, the teacher decides, but the narrative would require adaptation. It must be simpler. So how does she set about it?

First of all she makes a précis or outline of the original story and lists the main points, what we are calling the staging-posts. For this story they might be as follows:

Staging-posts of Story

1. Man making hats — enough to sell
2. Puts hats in barrow
3. Sets out to market
4. Hatmaker tired — hot — rests under tree
5. Falls asleep
6. Monkeys in tree look down — very interested in hats
7. Monkeys come down
8. Each takes hat and puts it on — goes back up tree

9. Man wakes up
10. Sees empty barrow
11. Looks all round — finally up — sees monkeys with hats
12. Shakes fist
13. Monkeys copy
14. Hatmaker has idea
15. Throws hat on ground
16. Monkeys copy
17. Man retrieves hats
18. Continues to market.

Secondly, the teacher writes her adaptation at the level at which she thinks her children can cope, using the staging-posts as guide. The following might be the result:

The Hatmaker and the Monkeys (adapted for EFL)

Once upon a time there was a man who made hats. He was a hatmaker. He had enough hats to sell. One day he put the hats into his barrow and went along the road to the market. It was a long way and the hatmaker was tired and hot. He came to a tree and sat down. Soon he fell asleep. There were monkeys up in the tree. The hatmaker did not know this. The monkeys looked down. They saw the hats. Then they came down and took them. Each monkey put a hat on and each monkey went up the tree again.

Then the man woke up. His barrow was empty. There were no hats in it. 'Where are my hats?', he said. He looked left. He looked right. He looked round about. Then he looked up. He saw the monkeys with his hats on. 'Oh, dear!', he said. 'Those naughty monkeys have stolen my hats.' He shook his fist at them. The monkeys shook their fists too. The hatmaker had an idea. He took off his hat and he threw it on the ground. The monkeys took off their hats too and threw them on the ground. They copied the man again. The hatmaker put his hats back in his barrow. Then he went to the market to sell them.

Loading

The narrative is now ready for use in the classroom. The next chapter will pick up from here and continue with the illustration of strategy as it considers options of presentation and accompanying visuals etc. Something more has to be said meantime about the language actually used in this final narrative and about the loading of issues.

The first thing to notice about the language, and indeed about the underlying concepts, is that there is a nice mixture of old and new (for the learners). There are things for them to revise, some very newly acquired perhaps, which need to be focused upon. There are also things totally new which this story is going to introduce them to, and of these some are required by the syllabus and some are not, but are considered useful by the teacher for this particular class and/or for that particular reason. Finally, there may well be still a residue of difficult language from the original text beyond the immediate ability of the learners, but the teacher is not too worried about that. Her aim is to simplify so that the story could be used by *her* class, but it still has to be a real story and that probably means maintaining a little of the original idiom at least. A certain amount of the unknown can be tolerated by the pupils provided they are held by the story, which carries implications for the presentation and 'noises off' as we shall see. So this adapted version is in fact a combination of language needed for the theme and that required by the syllabus, the mixture being carefully balanced by the teacher, and the two just at times overlapping.

The overlapping elements, such as the concept of copying and the simple past form of the verb, could be said to have been already loaded into the story. The given text already contained what was wanted. That is good to find and teachers must be on the lookout for it. But sometimes the teacher has to do a bit of loading for herself. For instance, the original narrative used the word 'each'. This might have suggested to our imaginary teacher here that she could use this staging-post to feed in some vocabulary of sequencing which her class needed to practise. So instead of the sentence, 'Each monkey put a hat on and each monkey went up the tree again', she could say 'The first monkey put a hat on . . . etc. The second . . . (and possibly) the next . . . and the last . . . etc.'. She might also incorporate the word 'all' so that the concepts of 'each and every' were covered along with the words of ordering. But this would depend on how much the children could take. Another example of the teacher loading might be at staging-post 11. The children need to revise direction words and prepositions. The text could be extended to 'He looked down . . . along . . . across, etc.' and finally 'up'. If more were needed, the monkeys could also do some looking around before they finally look down and see the hats in the barrow. So things can be altered just slightly, and the necessary language inserted.

We should note in passing that we have found two uses so far for the staging-posts. One was as an outline for rewriting. The other, illustrated here, is as a series of key points for the teacher to pause on and consider developments. I have spoken before of growth from within rather than, or as well as, end-on learning, by which I mean using one piece of teaching material as it stands and fairly quickly moving on to another, sometimes before the first has been thoroughly explored. So often it seems to me that learning/teaching potential is lost because experience and indeed learner strategies are not exploited sufficiently. Story has been particularly vulnerable in this respect. The good narrative with its clearly marked staging-posts offers place and time for the learner to gather the new around the old and for the teacher to monitor this development. All this is not to say that end-on learning and extending to new material should be held back, only that jumping wildly ahead before adequate use is made of the experience and material to hand is wasteful in both educational and economic terms. On the last point it is worth reminding ourselves that the financial stringency demanded in most countries these days would underline the need for careful husbandry of material resources in any case.

We can go back now to the language of the adapted version once again and consider the new learning which the teacher might like to focus on even if it is not in the syllabus. The work comes at staging-post 14 and is expressed in the sentence 'The man had an idea'. This could well be unknown language to the children and might be thought to be way ahead of what they are doing in the syllabus. On the other hand, what a useful piece of communicative language it is and how very easily it can be demonstrated by augmenting the text with a helpful drama in the presentation. How easy to carry it forward into the follow-up activities. But more of this anon.

It could be that the teacher has so many interesting things to do around her staging-posts that it would be worth writing another version. This is particularly useful if group-work is to be done. (In Appendix 1 three versions of one story are shown. The reader might like to do the same with 'The Hatmaker and the Monkeys'.) What *are* the things which make for greater or lesser complexity? No special linguistic claims are made for these examples and many may disagree with them, but at least they offer a starting-point either for the individual teacher or for teachers working together.

For other situations

The selection and handling of the story so far has been considered in the light of an EFL situation and the use of an English teaching syllabus. Can we see this same story being used in an ESL situation and might there be some differences in the strategy? It will be remembered that in many EFL classrooms there is a need to contextualise the work of the syllabus, to turn language-like behaviour into language. We have tried to demonstrate this a little by the story of 'The Hatmaker and the Monkeys'. Arid practice of prepositions or sequencing vocabulary could be turned into use of real language by means of the story context. It has also been suggested that the wise EFL teacher tries to make use of the concepts understood by the children in the curriculum at large, part of the assets the children come with, to teach the English expression of them. This was illustrated by the central theme of the story, that of imitating. Let us now change the scene of operation to a classroom, say in the United Kingdom, where a few learners find themselves in a minority group amongst the English L1 pupils.

The teacher has come on the story in her resource bank and she has the same original text. Her first criterion for choosing it is that she likes the yarn and feels sure that her class will like it. They had been playing a game of 'Follow-my-leader' and other similar activities where the notion of copying was being explored. This story would enhance the general learning and do so on neutral ground, allowing for a certain degree of objectivity, one of the special assets of folk-tales of the traditional kind. Again the language of the story will need some adaptation, even for her English L1 speakers, so she sets about it. She arrives at the same staging-posts as the EFL teacher does but her rewriting is a little different. Consider the following:

The Hatmaker and the Monkeys (adapted for ESL)

Once upon a time in a land far away there lived a hatmaker. One day he thought that he had enough hats ready to sell so he loaded his barrow with them and set out for the market. It was a very hot day and it was a long journey. The man began to feel very tired. He came to a tree with spreading branches. He was pleased to sit down under it in the shade. Soon he was fast asleep. He did not know that there were monkeys up in the tree. They wanted to learn more about those hats. After the man was sound asleep they crept down the tree and took the hats out of the barrow. Each put one on and then they all climbed back to their places in the branches.

After a while the hatmaker woke up. He soon knew that something was different. His hats had gone. Where could they be? He looked all over the place and at last he looked up into the tree. There were the monkeys sitting with the hats on. They seemed happy. The hatmaker was very angry. He scowled and shook his fist. Perhaps the monkeys scowled too. But they did shake their fists. Monkeys can imitate well. They copy the things people do. The hatmaker had an idea. He would get them to copy him again. He took off his hat and threw it on the ground. Then he waited to see what would happen. His idea worked. The monkeys did the same. So the hatmaker got his hats back. He did not feel tired any more after his sleep in the shade so he put his hats in the barrow again and went on to the market.

The first thing to notice is that this version is much nearer the original than the EFL adaptation. Remember that most of the children in the class are English L1 speakers. Some of them might even manage the original. But the teacher for her *class* narration has opted for a slight adaptation to make the story just that bit more meaningful to the majority. What of the ESL learners? They are continually exposed to English being used communicatively all around them and the chances are that, given that the teacher has adequate teaching aids to illustrate the story, they can benefit from this version to quite an extent, certainly more than EFL learners would do. (The methodology of all this and the handling of special needs in practice is dealt with in Chapter 7.) Let us stay with the narrative for a moment and see what kind of loading the teacher might do for her ESL pupils. She may not have needed her staging-posts to do her rewriting to the same extent as the EFL teacher did, but she would probably gain from using them now as she seeks to find places where the story could help the ESL learners to become more aware of the structure of the language and the nuances of its idiom and vocabulary.

Let us imagine her going down the staging-posts. At the first the children meet the word 'hatmaker'. The agentive '-er' could be new to them or at least might not have registered as a rule. Can something be done here to make it stick? The reader might like to think of ways of loading the story at this point. Could the hatmaker have brothers or sisters or colleagues who make other things or *do* other things? At staging-post 2 the children encounter the word 'barrow', not a very useful word in itself maybe but does it suggest work on other means of transport and *its* vocabulary? Might these be used by the colleagues? The whole concept of 'market' and 'buying/selling' at staging-post 3 opens up many options from both the cognitive and language angles and in addition from the intercultural one. This would be a good staging-post to rest at for some time for all the children where a universal could be explored in many particulars. And so on. The ESL teacher might even use the same loading at staging-posts 6, 7 and 11 as the EFL teacher as she makes her ESL pupils aware of the prepositions and the sequencing language. Language is language is language. The difference between the two situations is one of emphasis and angle. The EFL teacher is faced with certain language and needs to put it in context. The ESL teacher has plenty of context. She needs to focus on the language more. But in effect, the lines are often crossed.

Staging-post 10 serves to highlight the link with the curriculum. The concept of the empty set in mathematics is one which young children often have difficulty with. How useful to let a story make it clear. The barrow was empty. There were no hats in it. There was nothing in it, etc. Some loading of other negatives could usefully be done here. This would be helpful to all the children. But the point to stress is that in the ESL situation where the language being learnt is that of all learning, story can be used to facilitate this process if the teachers are themselves aware of the matters to focus on.

There is obviously a great deal more that could be said about the EFL/ESL balance, including perhaps slight differences of treatment in the varieties of situation as depicted in Chapter 2; for instance a Zambia-like classroom where *all* the pupils are ESL learners would share something of both the EFL and the ESL handling of story, as might that in an international school. But, as has been suggested, the principal differences will arise at the level of classroom management and technique and I hope to bring these out more in Chapter 7. Perhaps enough has now been said about the selection of story and the adaptation of narrative to indicate the vast potential of the vehicle. Different kinds of stories to meet different needs, including the kind I have described as being plucked out of the air, are illustrated in Appendix 1.

In bringing this section to a conclusion it is essential to reiterate *the need for the teacher to be aware of the issues and options,* and for her to have a global view of the work demanded in syllabus/curriculum. This ensures good forward planning. It will be better done if it is a team project. In other words and in the language of 'Field and Focus', the teachers together in a school, or perhaps across a number of schools, should focus on their field before focusing with their pupils. There should then be careful selection of stories appropriate for the work to be covered, and a working together on the narratives. Remember that the general aim is to facilitate the knowing *about* and *how* in language and the integration of skills within interesting themes. Let us now turn to the idea of related activities and materials where this notion can be further developed.

Section B: The Trailer

Pervasion of the key stimulus

It has been suggested that story be the key stimulus for a whole package of learning and that the story theme be made to pervade a number of follow-up ploys of one kind or another. If this is planned well then it is not only the theme of the story which is going forward but also the other learning issues which it was carrying. For instance in the story we have been using, a focus on colour terms and vocabulary for body parts and articles of clothing could be followed through in games where the children have to match an article of clothing to a body part and find and name the colour. Or again, games of various kinds, both quiet and noisy, could be used to follow up the central concept of imitating. If the class had been engaged in these before the teacher found the story, they would now play with greater depth of understanding and the teacher should try to increase the range of activity. The idea is that the children should be swept along on the crest of the story.

Kinds of activities

What options are possible? The answer is — just about everything that goes on in a lively, communicative primary classroom, but for purposes of discussion let us try to categorise a little. There are obviously several ways in which this might be done and it could become a very large task. It is not intended here to attempt a comprehensive description of the primary curriculum but rather, in keeping with the notion of offering a strategy, to take one or two of the important issues we have looked at and to set the activities and their materials against *these*. This procedure has been found useful in teacher-training seminars.

The issues will be of language, learning and teaching. The first is the *Four Modes*. We need to have materials in the story kit relating to activities of listening, speaking, reading and writing; bearing in mind also the importance of the influence each has on the other and the need for work which helps to integrate the skills. Then across all four we should perhaps consider in particular the issue of *structure/vocabulary* and that of *form/function,* some of our activities geared to one side of the dichotomy and some to the other. An important learning issue would be *accuracy/fluency*; and those of teaching, *degree of control, size of group* and *progression,* the latter being expressed in the framework of *Field and Focus*. It is hoped that these issues will offer at least a baseline of sources from which teachers can select the activities and materials for the trailer to the story vehicle. For more detailed selection the total list of issues at the end of Chapter 5 can be utilised. The matters of degree of control and size of group do not in fact appear in that list but are dealt with in more detail when we look at options of classroom management in Chapter 7. I felt that it might be useful to bring them in here as reference points for the selection of activities.

There is also another way of looking at the kinds of activities and materials to select and this relates to what might be called the 'format', by which I mean the physical nature — *Game, song and rhyme, drama/role-play,* etc., not forgetting those activities and materials which relate more to literacy and study skills, including *worksheets* of various kinds. Whilst story and oracy seem to relate closely, we must not forget the development into literacy and the potential of all story-*telling* to become story-*reading,* nor should we forget the contribution of the appropriate story to the learning of the reading skills in the first place.

Options for the trailer

To illustrate the option strategy let us return now to the story of 'The Hatmaker and the Monkeys', and for purposes of conciseness, speak of 'the teacher' and 'the kit', conflating the various issues of EFL/ESL at this level of selection of materials. Let us imagine first of all that the teacher wants to follow up the central concept of imitating. On considering all the issues, she decides to opt for three particular games, two of them adapted and one devised. The first adapted game is a kind of Follow-my-Leader. She had in fact been playing this with her class before she presented her story and it was the idea of copying which had led her to it. Now, with the story fresh in the minds of her pupils and all the enjoyment it brought, she lets them play the game again but this time the leader is the hatmaker and the rest are the monkeys. The actions of shaking fists and throwing hats down will be much to the fore but other actions can follow. The last one to copy is out.

The second adapted game is a version of O'Grady Says. Again, the characters in the story are used — The Hatmaker Says. What is important in both these games is that the story has made the concept clear and presented language to match which can now be practised in these other activities. Something which will have to be understood in this second game is that unless the words 'the hatmaker' are used, the monkeys must *not* copy. So, the instruction 'Do this' would mean nobody moving and anyone who does would be out. If the one who is 'it' says 'The hatmaker says do this', then everybody copies. In some situations it may be necessary to explain these instructions in the community language, but if that is not possible the teacher might be able to demonstrate to the class using a group of the most able pupils who would pick up the idea by direct method more quickly. For her devised game the teacher coins the title, 'What Am I Doing? Copy Me'. Again there is a hatmaker and monkeys. This time there is the fun of guessing the hatmaker's mime before copying. The one to do so becomes the next hatmaker, and so on.

Now, one or two points about these particular games and a few about games in general. These three are part of the focus. They are practising activities. The children are not expected at this stage to be creative. The **activities are** class activities and the children follow the leader who is the teacher, though the games can also be played in groups with child leaders once the activities are understood. The emphasis is on accuracy as certain language, specific vocabulary and a few structures have to be used. So there is a fair degree of control by the teacher. Finally, the games are oral with listening and speaking skills working together.

In the References Andrew Wright *et al.*'s *Games for Language Learning* appears. This is an extremely useful book, brimful of ideas about all kinds of games. It also contains checklists of both structures and types of communication with reference to the games described in the text. Amongst the picture games on page 17 is 'Happy twins'. As its name suggests, this is a game for two players. They work with 16–20 pictures of objects or people which have to be matched into pairs (another reason presumably for the name of the game). They are mixed up and put in a pile. Each player takes a picture and describes it to the other without letting his partner see. When it is agreed that they have a pair they put it on one side. If it is not a pair the pictures go back in the pile. My object in describing *this* game is to show something very different from the three above. This is a fluency activity in that the process of describing is more important than the product of what is described. The teacher may go round helping but she is guiding rather than directing, facilitating the task to be done which is accomplished more quickly if appropriate language is used. The game is also part of the wider field where the learners are making *use* of the language they have learnt rather than practising set structures. The one similarity is that it uses the listening and speaking modes, but Wright offers a variation where, rather than pictures, the children are each given 'a piece of paper on which are written a number of individual words or sentences. All the papers should have some words in common; there will be only two of each kind'. So, the reading mode can be brought in.

That was an option our teacher *could* have used. In relation to 'The Hatmaker and the Monkeys' she would have had sets of pictures of, perhaps, people who make things, body parts or articles of clothing. This would also have served for the follow-up to her vocabulary work on these topics, the same material being used for accuracy activities if necessary. Remember that it is not so much the material itself which is for one or the other but the way in which it is used. This goes also for the stages of field and focus. Another useful set of pictures which our teacher does select in relation to the story is one called 'Tense Sequencing',[1] where there are several *sets* of pictures, three in each, showing an activity about to be done, being done, and then completed. The game is to put them in the right order. This can be done by a child working alone or by two or more working in collaboration. It will require accuracy of language in the product, but if children are working together then the process becomes important too. It will be remembered that the teacher wanted to practise the simple past tense. Here it would be done, again using the story situations and vocabulary, along with the two other forms which presumably the children had also covered (in the EFL situation) and/or been exposed to (in the ESL situation).

So the teacher uses the game format for the follow-up to her story, bearing in mind all the issues and options. She uses the other formats in the same way, song and rhyme, drama/role-play, etc. She has decided for this story not to have activities for reading as such, but she does have some pre-reading worksheets where the children have to match and sort, once more using the story content and language, again making sure of both accuracy and fluency. One pre-reading programme on which such worksheets could be based is shown in Appendix 1. Perhaps the reader would like to use one of the items from it to make a worksheet relating to our story. Perhaps the reader would also like to use the ideas offered for song and drama to develop related activities in those formats. I hope that enough of the strategy has now been offered for teachers to work out their own ideas and to put together trailers to their own stories. Just two more suggestions before rounding off this section, one in the format of song and the other of role-play. The following song has been found useful and enjoyable for young children. It seems very apt for this particular story:

Zozo the Monkey

Zozo the monkey is clapping his hands.
He's clapping his hands, he's clapping his hands.
Zozo the monkey is clapping his hands.
He's clapping his hands today.

Zozo the monkey is nodding his head.
    etc.

Zozo the monkey is stamping his feet.
    etc.

Zozo can be made to do all kinds of things. Relating to the story we could have:

Zozo the monkey is shaking his fist.
    or
Zozo the monkey is wearing his hat.

Another useful song which relates to the story is:

The Hat Song

A red hat, a blue hat, a green hat,
a yellow hat,
A white hat, a black hat,
My hat is on my head.

Now change to shoe and sock, ending with:

My shoe/sock is on my foot.

(See music for both songs in Appendix 1.)

Obviously the possibilities of exploiting further are numerous, use of monkey puppets for instance, drawing and colouring, making paper hats or bringing hats from home. These songs demonstrate practising and accuracy activities. The repetition serves the practice but in fun not boredom. The rhythm of song and rhyme is an excellent aid to the patterning of language in the phonology. So it is wise to have something from this format in most story trailers. In some cultures there is the custom of following the leader in song, producing your own words on the pattern given. It is very often done in the context of the current situation and gathering. Could this kind of tradition be used in school, perhaps, and relating to stories? This would be a more creative activity.

The role-play suggestion is based on another set of material produced by LDA. It is called 'See how you feel', and is a set of pictures showing people in various moods: angry, happy, frightened, etc. The children can play dominoes and snap with the pictures. But my purpose in mentioning this is to illustrate the role-playing format. I have used the pictures as a stimulus to acting and expressing feeling. This can be a group activity where the children collaborate to decide how they are going to act. Then they ask the rest of the class, 'How do we feel?', and proceed to express one of the moods. It has always worked well. Our angry hatmaker would fit in here. Some other LDA material (Photographic Lotto) which also depicts people in different moods is described in the next chapter. More will be said there too about material and method for moving children on to more creative use of language.

Making one's own materials

As with the key stimulus, so too with the follow-up materials in the trailer; it is possible to adopt outright, to adapt or to devise one's own. Any story kit might contain samples of all of these. For some teachers, commercial material is hard to come by for one reason or another, though it might be possible to obtain catalogues such as the LDA produce where the materials are very well illustrated and described. But the adapting of materials already in existence is probably one of the best ways of amassing a set of resources. It is suggested that teachers do a lot of browsing, studying the basic principles of the activities and materials they see and judging their usefulness in light of *their* situations. General issues have been highlighted in this book. The particular come from the syllabus/curriculum in the real classroom.

Ideally the making of materials should be a team task with sharing of both ideas and expertise. How often one hears the wail, 'But I can't draw'! Somebody else can and, if not another teacher, someone in the community or one of the pupils. How much more would be the enthusiasm for the story if the learners had a vested interest in its illustration. A list of suggested raw materials is given in Appendix 1. As can be seen none of these should be too difficult or expensive to acquire for most people.

The notion of indigenisation has been suggested. Let us just think a little about this. For example, a class might be involved with a centre of interest on travel. This could be part of an English syllabus or something in another part of the curriculum field. The teacher finds a story about a journey by bus. It carries many of the general issues she is concerned with. The only difficulty is that it looks different in the illustrations given from any bus that the learners would have seen. It is a double-decker and there are no buses of this kind in the country. Also, the fare is paid on entrance, to the driver, another strange custom. The people queuing (that is not done here either) are wearing thick clothes and look cold. In this country that happens seldom if ever. And so on, through the journey and its scenery. So, is the story worth using at all? It may not be. On the other hand, apart from the matter of learning about other people's life-styles which is important, it may be possible to change the particulars so that they all become immediately recognisable, and the story so that it is structured into a narrative with potential for relevant loading. Again, this kind of exercise would be better shared and would make an interesting ploy for a teacher training seminar. But any teacher could work on it by herself if necessary. There should be numerous stories from a number of cultures with potential for this kind of adaptation in the resource bank. And the same is true of materials for the trailer. Collect possible prototypes under the various categories suggested here so that at any point in time and for any particular story there is likely to be something ready to hand to work on. Some are better than others for certain things. Some stories, for instance, carry mathematics concepts or could easily be made to do so; some illustrate social concepts and ways of behaving or resolving universal problems; others could carry a specific language point like the making of plurals. It is a matter of what *you* need and how story can serve *you,* both in the vehicle and its trailer.

Conclusion

In this discussion of the story kit there is one part which has been omitted so far, and that is the material for the actual presentation of the narrative, for which there are many interesting options. This is dealt with now in Chapter 7 as we consider the narration and class management. It is difficult to separate matter from method and this has only been done so far in order to explain the concept of a kit which is deemed to be useful.

There is something else which should be said about this. The word 'kit' suggests a closed set of things in some kind of container and put there for all time. The story kit *could* be this. As I write I have a memory of several staff-rooms in schools where I have worked where story materials in see-through bags were made to hang up round the walls, each complete and usable by any member of staff as all had shared in the making, and the stories were right for that particular school. This is a useful and recommended state of affairs. On the other hand the kit can also be seen in a wider sense. It could be a much more flexible and changing instrument, so that, for instance, teachers make use of their resource banks more often to pick a suitable story for whatever ploy they have in mind at the time, and then select from their resources of prototype materials for particular follow-up. The same story could be used a number of times with different follow-up; the focusing on certain items could follow different fields.

Whatever method is followed, it is helpful to record the use made of the material so that neither you nor your colleagues have to keep on re-inventing the wheel! Also, some of the activities in the kit are not capable of being captured and put in a bag, such as a class game in the hall or playground. This has to be described. So the kit consists both of activities linked to materials contained, and of suggestions and descriptions relating to those whose equipment cannot be. The story kit is not so much a static set of teaching aids as a dynamic and ever-changing manifestation of a methodology. As such it is possible for any teacher to use it and do her own thing. It is the intention of this book to present the possibilities and not to prescribe. In the same vein let us move on now to options of narration.

Note to Chapter 6

1. For this and many other ideas I am grateful to Learning Development Aids (Duke Street, Wisbech, Cambs., PE13 2AE).

7   The Story Teller

Introduction

The sharing of meaning

So far we have been considering the potential of story and the meaningful strategy of narrative. It is time now to come to the *sharing* of the message, either by telling or by reading it. There are options in the initial presentation, relating both to the attributes of the narrator and to the kinds of materials which can be used, the noises off and remaining part of the story kit. Section A deals with these things, making further use of 'The Hatmaker and the Monkeys' and picking up the strategy at the point where a classroom narrative was prepared. Both the EFL and ESL versions are considered. Another interesting use for the staging-posts is discovered here, linking with the notion of teaching frames and video techniques.

Because the story as theme is being made to pervade other aspects of the curriculum and because the narrator is also a teacher, we are concerned in addition with the skills of classroom management and pedagogy. Our narrator/teacher has to take account of a great many things of which the telling/reading of the story is just the tip of the iceberg. So, in Section B, we consider options of *teaching* strategy. One or two other types of stories are used for illustration of issues and options not yet covered and to show also how things may vary methodologically across the varying learning situations. Some thought is given here to a bilingual approach. Finally, we look briefly at the possibility of teachers sharing their story work with parents and others in the community. It all seems too exciting to contain and full of latent promise for finding new ways to mean. On then to the first steps of the narration.

Section A: Options in the Presentation

Telling the story

The good telling of a story is a combination of several factors. The teacher has to be something of an actress, able to use her whole body but particularly eyes and voice to good effect. In some cultures where an oral tradition is strong, the skills of the story teller are greatly valued. Rosen (1985) describes the experiences of an English visitor to an African school:

> The teacher is telling a story, but not in the way I, an Englishman would tell it. She is dancing it, singing it, acting it. She tells it with her face, her voice, her whole body. The class is completely caught up in the action: toes and shoulders wriggling in sympathy. There is a song involved: the whole class joins in without invitation.

By comparison he also quotes Dell Hymes (1979), worried about the state of story-telling in Western culture:

> There is some reason to believe I think, that the expressivity of tradi-tional narrative styles has often been disapproved of by the upwardly mobile persons and the middle class more generally.

The teacher/story teller cannot afford to be inhibited. Those who come from communities where the oral tradition is vibrant *should* make good use of it in the classroom in the way of the African teacher described above. Those who do not may be fortunate to be able to learn from *pupils* who have these gifts, as do many of the Afro-Caribbean children in British schools. For the telling of stories to young children the teacher must be prepared to become totally involved, loving the story she is telling and passing on this enthusiasm along with the message the story is expressing.

What kinds of skills are available to the teacher? First there are those which lie within herself, for instance a voice capable of a wide range of activ-ity; a face and especially eyes able to move expressively, a body and limbs with which to gesture. Teachers should 'know themselves', to use the Greek dictum in a slightly different sense, so that the widest possible options are open to them for dramatising the widest possible range of stories. Some people seem to be more naturally gifted than others but I believe that certain tricks of the trade can be learnt by everyone. Much of it has to do with the degree of confidence and the ability to lose oneself in the role being played. Another important thing is a sense of audience. Many actors, for example, prefer live theatre to acting on the cinema or television because they feel lost when they try to give their messages to cameras and microphones. The teacher has a *very* live audience! Can she respond to their needs and moods, can she hold them by the turn of her head or the rolling of her eyes? Is she pacing her narration in such a way that the children are hanging on every word and waiting with eager anticipation for the dénouement? These are some of the skills of good story tellers, the best of which virtually make themselves disappear so that the story might take precedence.

How might such skills be used for example with 'The Hatmaker and the Monkeys'? A wonderful opportunity for head movement is the part where the hatmaker wakes up. The narrator (in her role of hatmaker) must look slowly and deliberately in all directions and then make a special, longer pause before looking up, while the listeners wait excitedly with bated breath for the man to see the monkeys. The pause should be long enough for the important informed guessing and predicting to take place, after which the hatmaker's explosion of wrath, coming as the anticipated response, must really meet expectations. If it does there is tremendous satisfaction, a sense almost of having helped to bring this event about. This is the moment when listeners and narrator — learners and teacher — are really sharing meaning. It is pregnant with opportunity.

Another part where body language could be used to great advantage in this story is where the hatmaker realises how he can exploit the monkeys' tendency to copy. In the longer ESL version the sentence 'The hatmaker had an idea' is supported before and after by explanatory language — 'Monkeys can imitate well. They copy the things people do' leading up to the key sentence, and 'he would get them to copy him again', leading away from it. The important point is, as it were, like a little island in a sea of meaning. The children at the level of being able to understand this language should get the message from the words so long as the teacher speaks clearly and uses her voice with all the appropriate tone and emphasis. In the more simplified EFL version the sea of meaning has to be represented by things other than words. And this is not a place where realia (see below) or extra pictures would help. Explanation in the community language would, and might have to be resorted to if it is possible, but it may not be. So what is left? The teacher must somehow combine the limited message in words with that of her body: 'He shook his fist at them' — pause — look at the children — look up — eyes open in amazement — 'The monkeys shook their fists too' — another look at the children — pointing gesture up — slow pacing up and down and stroking of chin — all the gestures of thinking — back to the centre — face the children and then say — 'The hatmaker had an idea' in the pose of the 'bubble' in a children's comic. It is worth a try.

And this is what it is about, experiment with *all* the options. Stories differ in their demands of the narrator. This one does not call for too much work of the voice. Another story where, for instance, different characters are depicted in dialogue would mean the narrator doing vocal gymnastics to make it clear to the listeners which character is speaking. This is quite hard work especially if the sequences are repeated, as they often are — and for good reason — in folk-tales. Woe betide the narrator who gets it wrong! Young children can be very strident in their call for consistency, a point which can be turned to good educational effect relating to the matter once again of prediction.

Reading the story

Much of what has just been said is applicable also to the *reading* of stories, but perhaps just one or two more comments might be made. The most obvious difference is the need for the narrator to have her eyes on the text for much of the time so there is not the same opportunity for eye-contact with the listeners. But there *are* ways round this problem. The reader can for example occasionally stop and look at the children, raise her eyebrows as if questioning or exclaiming about something just read, and then try to suggest, by her gesture or facial expression, eagerness to return to the text to find out what happens next. The odd personal comment is sometimes appropriate also. And by all of this the teacher is giving not only the message of the story but also that of the purpose of books in containing stories, conversation with the text being part of reading behaviour. Whilst listening to stories *told* (in more ways than one) should, in my view, be a vital part of the curriculum throughout a child's school career, the story *read* also has an important part to play whether it comes straight from a book or is written down as an adapted narrative by the teacher. The concept of the written word has to be developed.

The good story reader must make careful use of the punctuation in the text. If she has written the narrative herself then she should be familiar with the signposts. If not, she may have to rehearse a little before reading to the children so that she knows what to expect. The marks of punctuation, limited as they are, serve as guide to things like main statement as distinct from elaboration; statement as distinct from question; spoken words by a character in the story as distinct from the narrator's comments; and so on. This is all important to the overall meaning and must be observed. Some readers render the whole story meaningless by not pausing at the right places and so not giving sense to the chunks of writing, usually because they are not decoding themselves or doing so only partially. They are barking at print. The fluent, competent reader does not read jerkily. She takes in fairly large sections of writing in one movement of the eyes and therefore sees the signpost ahead in good time to benefit from it. Reading aloud well is an acquired art and it is surprising how few people have it. Just listen to the painful stumblings of the secretary reading the minutes at a meeting or the layman reading the lesson in church. The teacher must endeavour to perfect her reading, and this applies equally to those whose community language *is* English. For those who are themselves not English L1 speakers the matter of story narration in English, both telling and reading, is worth working on, especially if they lack confidence in the language generally. It might be true to say in fact that the whole strategy of the story methodology as it is outlined in these chapters, from the selection of the vehicle to its handling in the classroom, could be a useful means of improving the teacher's own English, something for the teacher-trainer also to bear in mind.

One last point should be mentioned before we go on to look at options of accompanying materials, and it relates to the narrative itself. Book language is not the same as oral language although the oral story has much in common with it. Taken together, oral and read stories offer children a whole new genre of language use. The typical story starters are a case in point: 'once upon a time' or 'long, long ago', etc. When would we ever say such a thing except in story? It is interesting to remember also that this kind of starter immediately releases the participants in the story from chronological time and takes them into a world where the exotic is the norm, like the experience of the children going through the wardrobe (see Lewis, 1950). I believe that one of the assets of using *folk-tale* is that it does just this. It suspends personal involvement and allows for a kind of objective keek at the universal which can help equip the listeners for the real world. But there is the special language of it all and the teacher/narrator must make use of it. It is fascinating to see how quickly children both recognise this kind of language and use it for themselves.

However, we must not forget the stories which *do* come from chronological time, and are not concerned with fantasy and make-believe. These are about *us* and the passing scene, and the facts of life as we know them. The language can be very down-to-earth and supportive of the BICS and the CALP. Nevertheless, as soon as story is structured into narrative, the language of story begins to creep in, the genre which says 'Sit back and listen', which thought brings us nicely to the methodology and its materials.

Props for the narration

Story and theatre seem to go well together. It is in this sense that we think of props, short for properties, and including noises off or accompanying effects. There is also another sense. Props are a means of support in a physical way. It seems to be a useful term here. The meaning and essence of the story can be supported in a physical way by materials and activities selected by the teacher and used judiciously in the narration. Is there some way of categorising so that once again selection is made easier? Remember that the main object of the exercise is to help children to mean. There would appear to be a kind of hierarchy of props for this from the use of real objects/ people (realia) through that which represents (pictures, models, role-play, etc.), to use of words alone. Perhaps this idea will help us make a start, related to two others, the use of the senses (including the sense of humour) and the use of the community language when it comes to the words alone. Much depends on the age and stage of the learners as to which of these the teacher goes for, and she may decide to mix them. If her kit has any degree of permanence she will include a selection of all.

To illustrate from 'The Hatmaker and the Monkeys', a barrow of some kind could possibly be brought into the classroom. Hats of various kinds and colours would not usually be a problem, nor would the other articles of clothing which the teacher may have loaded into the story. The children themselves as pushers of the barrow and wearers of the clothes would also be available. All of this is the realia. For representational props a set of pictures might be used which depict the main staging-posts of the story, or possibly figurines for a magnetboard or flannelgraph. In addition, role-playing of hatmaker and monkeys would probably be done at some stage.

Something of the words alone prop was touched on when we were comparing the two narrative versions and how the teacher could compensate for the meaning tied up in the words of the ESL version when she was using the other to EFL learners. These steps show the way we want to go. The young linguist should be able eventually to extract meaning from the text with only the props he himself brings to it, but in his journey towards this end he needs other kinds of props. So in the story the teacher should let those words speak which can, and support with other means those which cannot yet convey meaning to her pupils. For instance, 'There were monkeys up in the tree' may need no help at all, whereas 'The hatmaker had an idea' would probably need a lot. Another useful option is, of course, to have the whole story told in the community language (see this story in Italian in Appendix 1). To a much greater extent it should be possible for the words alone to be relied on for giving meaning when the story is narrated in the familiar community language; which is not to say that no other props should then be used, otherwise children learning in the language of their own community anywhere would miss out on the enjoyment of interesting pictures etc. But it *is* an option and has its purposes.

To generalise, again different stories would call for different props and perhaps the need for appealing to other senses besides the visual and kinaesthetic. A story bringing in foodstuffs, for instance, might involve children tasting and smelling; another where different kinds of noises were an important feature would call for special focus on listening etc., all of which reminds us of the importance of story in catering for all the issues of language and learning followed by appropriate and well-chosen aids in the narration.

But as the visual (pictures in particular) is such a ubiquitous prop, and rightly so, it might be worth spending a little more time on it, teasing out one or two further possibilities. There are of course the pictures in books, and a teacher working with one child or a small group could make use of these as she goes along. But most of the time they are too small to be shared and often not clear, either graphically and/or in terms of a true representation of the story. The exception would be the new variety known as the 'big book', some of which appear in the set of material of the *Oxford Reading Tree* (see Appendix 1). Here the book has been specially designed for sharing and the pictures carefully planned to complement the text. They can in fact tell a story *without* the text. More will be said about big books below. On the point of pictures which complement, whether or not they are in books, it is worth examining carefully the illustrations you put in front of children. Are they *adding to* the meaning given in the words of the narrative, i.e. are they *supplementary* to it, or do they supply meaning which was difficult to convey in words? Are they *complementary?* Or again, do they simply consolidate by expressing in an interesting visual way what the words have said? There is a place for all three types of visual and teachers should know when and how to use each. It pays to study the technique of the good talk/slide-show or television documentary in this connection.

But for the class teacher the best kind of visuals is often those she makes herself. They *can* be in books, sometimes those made by teacher and class together, occasionally with the help of parents, but more often it is better to have them in the form of loose or flip-over pictures, modelled on the commercial wall-chart. They should be bold and uncluttered and they should say exactly what you want them to say. A set of such pictures for each story is an extremely useful prop, along with a suitable place to display them either before the narration as a taster or after as a reminder. In some classrooms this can be a problem. The constraints are many. But even if one picture at a time is shown, taken down at the end of the day and resurrected next day, that is something.

Another format is the figurine. Some stories lend themselves to the use of the magnetboard or flannelgraph, especially where lots of characters are involved. The use of these separate figurines which can be moved about easily by the children is also a very helpful prop to story. The whole operation becomes so much more flexible. (If the figurines are reticulated, the various parts fixed together by bend-back paperclips, they are even more flexible and useful. Also, different garments can be made to cling on to them.) The kind of growth within the story rather than end-on learning which we were considering earlier is much facilitated by having actual materials which can be added at the various growth-points instead of static pictures which cannot be altered or added to. A story such as *The Merchant and His Donkey* (traditional) has various staging-posts where the merchant and his son meet people. The narrator says, 'And they met some more people' and this is repeated several times. How useful if the teacher's loading had concerned attributes of people and their corresponding expression, to make the story take on some varieties at each staging-post. So the man with the long beard appears here and the girl with the spotted dress there, and so on. They can be focused on or not as the teacher wishes but they are there in the experience for acquisition or learning purposes or both.

A further useful idea is to have a set of figurines relating to the community of the school. These can be used over and over again with a few additions here and there, particularly in relation to the kind of stories of *us*, the news of the moment, the stories plucked out of the air. How quickly a narrative can be put together and these figurines brought into use. It is a good idea to have one or two background sheets which can serve in more than one scene. The inside of one building can quickly be transformed to another by the skilful teacher, or a park one day can become a field another, rather in the way of the stage director who moves his rostra around so that totally different effects are created very simply and quickly.

A learning bonus with the use of figurines is the practice of language for position in space which can be undertaken. As a child is re-telling the story and placing the figurines on the magnetboard or flannelgraph, the teacher can rehearse expressions like 'in the middle', or 'next to' or 'up a bit', etc. This in itself is a kind of loading, a story of mathematics being told within the other. No opportunities should be missed by teachers of using the moment so that language is made to serve authentic purposes.

The fortunate teacher who can draw well at the chalkboard has a ready option also and should employ it well. The 'What is this going to be?' kind of game for instance keeps the children guessing and interested, the language of the process being at least as important as that concerning the product. And the drawing can be very simply done, with pin-figures if necessary. Another book by Andrew Wright (1984) is full of good ideas for chalkboard drawing, especially for those who feel very self-conscious about it. There must be many more options open to the teacher in this all-important area of the visual prop. (Further reading is offered in Appendix 2.) However, one other matter should be highlighted now: that of the ever widening possibilities of today's technology. Some of us are more able than others to acquire expensive gadgets, and some of us are more able than others to handle them! I make no attempt to be technical because that is not my field. At the same time I accept the potential of the machine, from the 'steam' age projector to the most up-to-date computer and video, and suggest very earnestly that teachers find out all they can about it, harnessing the new hardware if they can to their story methodology. Again, reading matter is offered.

But even if the new technology is not a present option for many teachers, can any of the ideas it teaches be of help? One that occurs to me is the notion of freezing the frame which is done with video. The operator can stop the moving film and hold part of it, a piece of experience framed as it were and kept in front of the viewers as long as needed for special focusing. It can also be brought back later if required. This idea of learning frames links with that of having a set of loose pictures going with a story, only the operator/teacher has decided in advance where the freezing is to take place. The frames for her are virtually her staging-posts, the main points along the story-line. Here then is another use for them, to guide in the making of pictures or some kind of visual representation of the experience to be frozen. It is as though the teacher were to draw a line round a bit of the story experience and to capture it for focusing on. A set of static pictures is one option; a set of figurines for the magnetboard, as we saw above, is more flexible, especially if the range of ability in a class is very wide. Perhaps it would be advisable to have both, for some stories at least, then there is an option in the telling and its alternative available for the re-telling. Also there would be visual assistance for all levels. The teacher would have teased out all the possibilities of each staging-post and the materials to match would be there in her kit as a set of options to be used appropriately for different groups.

I began this discussion on props for the narration by considering a hierarchy of meaning-making activities as guide, from realia through representational materials to words alone. It is worth recalling now our field and focus framework which also illustrates progression. The narration and its props are virtually the limited field part of the construct. The kinds of activities and materials we were discussing in the last chapter as being in the trailer of the story kit come mostly into the focusing section, and now in concluding this first part of the chapter we must think a little more about what might be put in the kit for the widening field.

For the trailer activities the teacher takes the story into the curriculum at large so that practice of new language skills is possible using known material. The next step is to return to the story, to the staging-posts and their possibilities and to offer some kind of extending work. Again there may be many ways of doing this but here is one very practical idea with linked material for the kit. It involves the sense of humour. Children enjoy the incongruous. So why not have some material which could be designated 'What's Wrong?'? The LDA offer cards which do just this. Various humorous distortions of known experience are put on the cards and the children have to find out and express what is wrong. For work with big groups the cards could become posters or wall-charts. For the story of 'The Hatmaker and the Monkeys' for instance, the monkeys could all become elephants in a picture or the hatmaker could attempt to transport his hats along the road in a boat. What is wrong and why? Could the expression 'instead of' be introduced to facilitate the explanations? The possibilities are endless for taking the children just that bit further on, using what is already understood and enjoyed — and that is important. With care this kind of work may stimulate some children to go even further to exhibit Widdowson's capacity. For example, another activity not related to the incongruous, but which some children may like to try, is making up a story told from the point of view of another character in the original. This could be a group ploy but it would need a fair degree of fluency in the language, and perhaps before the second and especially the foreign language learner could attempt it, something of the kinds of games to be played with the incongruous and the funny visuals in the kit would need to be covered first. The imaginative teacher could, I am sure, think of many more ways of making funny, and indeed of stimulating creative use of language.

It must be remembered that field and focus is cyclical. The extended use of the language to be gained from story can then be put to good account in further focusing activities leading on to further extensions and so on. And there is a limit to what one story can do. What is focused upon in that story could be exploited in another: an interesting new idea would perhaps be better carried further by a different theme. The teacher must have a constant eye to her resource bank, selecting her theme as the needs arise. But it is time now to look more particularly at teaching strategy and the options open in that direction.

Section B: Options in Classroom Management

Ringing the changes

In any teaching situation three aspects especially are apparent. These are the activity being engaged in, the degree of direction or control from the teacher and the size of group taking part.[1] Options are to be found within the various combinations possible. It would be interesting to work out a number of permutations, using a list of different activities, a continuum of degree of control from strong direction through guidance to complete freedom, and one of size of group from whole class through small section to pair and individual. We could make a kind of grid as shown in Figure 2.

Now if we take Activity 3, for instance, and read across, we find that it is one in which the learner has freedom to do his own thing by himself. Or if we take the fifth one we find this to be an activity directed by the teacher for pairs. And so on. There are in fact, with these five activities alone, one hundred and fifty possibilities altogether. It might be fun to work them out, especially against real activities, and to see if any would not be desirable or possible in certain circumstances. How could such a grid be useful to the teacher in her story methodology? Let us try adding two more headings in the blank columns and using real activities, perhaps with a few more. Let us try also to see the grid in terms of the field and focus progression. So we might have the schema shown in Figure 3.

The grid offers the teacher an overall checklist for the kit of any selected story with its options of class management. It attempts to mop up all the issues and options so far discussed. The activities and materials should have been opted for on the basis of language issues with, as we have seen, some heed also to matters of learning and teaching, the content and the method being hard to keep apart. Now in this grid where particular attention is paid to the classroom strategies, the whole thing comes together in a graphic way and acts as a useful reminder of intent. Let us look more carefully at the contents.

There are ten activities. There could be any number the teacher wants to include. Most of these listed here we have already met in the discussion, along with their materials, but one or two are new to enable further points to be made. They are grouped according to the progression of field and focus, the initial field the original narration and key stimulus, the return to the actual story at the end being the widened field and encouragement for creative use of the language learnt. And in between, in no particular order, are a number of activities which take the story theme and the learning it carried into the wider curriculum, focusing on and practising what has been

Activity	Control				Size			
	D	G	F		C	Gr	P	I
1	✓				✓			
2		✓				✓		
3			✓					✓
4		✓			✓			
5	✓						✓	

Where   D stands for Directed   and   C stands for Class
        G stands for Guided   Gr stands for Group
        F stands for Free   P stands for Pair
                                                     I stands for Individual

FIGURE 2   *A grid of possibilities*

Field and Focus	Activity	Material/Prop Description	Control			Emphasis		Size			
			D	G	F	Fl	Ac	C	Gr	P	I
Initial Field	Initial Narration—telling	Set of loose pictures	✓			Key Stimulus		✓			
	Re-telling	Same plus set of figurines		✓		✓			✓		
	Game X	Photographic Lotto—Moods		✓		✓			✓		
Focus	Game Y	Snap-picture cards—Body parts	✓				✓			✓	
	Worksheet	Pre-reading matching		✓			✓				
	Song X	Zozo the Monkey	✓				✓	✓			
	Song Y	Resting under the tree		✓		✓	✓	✓			
	Role-play X	I have an idea		✓		✓	✓		✓		
	Role-play Y	See how you feel			✓	✓	✓		✓		
Widening Field	Story again	What's wrong?		✓		Creative Use			✓		✓

FIGURE 3   *The story methodology/'kit': Varieties of class management*

discovered. The grid now also indicates where the learning emphasis lies — towards fluency or accuracy.

It must be remembered that throughout this progression the two sides of the language equation are present, matters linguistic and matters communicative. This should be covered by the selection of activities. And the two sides of the learning equation also present, in the form of fluency and accuracy, suggest implications for a double bill in the teaching which is taken care of by the variety of options in teaching style.

Before using the grid as a point of departure for more about teaching options, two more things should be said about it. The first is that all the activities listed here come into the representational category in our meaning hierarchy (which can apply to the materials in the trailer also). This is as it happens. Activities using realia or words alone could have been included. But I suppose most children in the 6–10 age-range are capable of understanding representational materials which at the same time are often easier to acquire and use, and most children in the same age-range, learning English as a foreign or second language, will not be ready to benefit from words alone.

The second point refers to the item under Activities designated 'Retelling'. It was touched on very briefly above. It seems to me that before the story is disseminated there should be a little more time spent on it, using both the original materials and one further option at least. These options could be any of the materials we have looked at and probably many more. The point is that the children need to be thoroughly familiar with the theme before it can be used for further learning, and re-telling the story in their own way by the children after perhaps one or more re-tellings by the teacher is one means of ensuring this (Rosen, 1988).[2] I see this period and its materials as being part of the immediate aftermath of the first narration. It also links with the trailer in the sense that it *does* come after. Hence the overlapping line.

Unfinished business

It is proposed now to use the grid and the kinds of options it offers to cover a little bit of extra ground and perhaps to pick up some of the promises made earlier in the text. Let us look first of all at the initial narration and its aftermath. What is shown here is the key stimulus being offered to the whole class by means of telling, supported by a set of loose pictures, and also the use of figurines. The work is directed. One might ask — what other options *are* there? If we follow the grid horizontally we find that every cell offers at least one even in the matter of the progression, if we were to see story as just one activity amongst many. Take the first line. The key stimulus could be presented through a poster or some other thematic means. Then story would *not* be the initial field. However, given that it is, we have the option then of telling or reading. We could use a variety of props to support the narration. Only one is shown in the grid. Perhaps this would be the main one but others could be brought in, such as realia, other representational materials and words alone. The next section is interesting. There *are* options. One could envisage, for instance, children being guided in their listening to a taped story or in their reading of one in a book. The story need not always come direct from the teacher. We have seen also that many stories are told — *not* to be a key stimulus to anything but simply for themselves and left at that, so we must keep *this* option in mind. Finally the story could be given initially to any size of group or to an individual.

If we now take the second line and consider that we *are* using story as a key stimulus, I suppose the first option is not to have an immediate follow-up at all but to let the children's initial discoveries serve, but if we opt *for* it then we could do other things besides re-telling. We could, for example, simply question the children on their understanding either orally or on worksheets or both. And if the questions are in writing there are additional options of how they are to be answered — by ticking one of a multiple choice, by filling in a blank, by writing out the whole sentence, etc. We might use worksheets of a different kind, pictures to be made perhaps by joining up the dots and so on. If we are to use re-telling, the same options are available as were there for the original narration, though we would be likely to select a different one as the main support. Moving on, the re-telling could be very strongly directed in that children would be corrected as they went along, or guided in such a way that if the story went very badly wrong the teacher would tactfully intervene, or free in that no matter what a child said he would be left to get on with it. The teacher's emphasis could be on fluency or accuracy and again the re-telling could be with any size of group or an individual.

Now, lest the reader fears that each line of the grid is to be dealt with in this rather tedious way, let me hasten to reassure her. Once again, I resort to prototype. Teachers should try to work out other options and implications for themselves. So far as the activities and materials are concerned, other ideas have already been given in the text, but teachers may like to add their own, linked to particular stories they are using. Also teachers of children in the upper classes of our age-range especially may want to put more materials concerned with literacy modes into the list. Bear in mind that the prototype here is suggesting a trailer to the vehicle which consists of a number of activities at the same level of difficulty but giving lots of variety and touching many other learning skills and concepts. This is then followed by a return to the story where options have to be found for new and challenging work.

Are there any points to pick up from the set of options just highlighted? Something should be said about the physical environment of story narration. This is quite important whether or not the whole class is involved and whether or not the teacher is doing the narration directly. If possible it is best to have a quiet corner, perhaps part of the book area, set aside for story. If the teacher is telling/reading then the children, whatever size of group, should be clustered around her, possibly on a mat on the floor. The sense of event is important. Story sessions in many libraries make much of this idea, even darkening the room sometimes and using a candle to invoke an atmosphere of mystery. Still with the idea of a sense of event, a story session with a very large group, say several classes together in the hall, could well be done with projection of pictures in a very exciting way, and noises off carefully synchronised. This might even involve parents and other members of the community (see below). On the other hand, the story in the same situation could be *acted* as a community happening. (See short sample in Appendix 1.) This is particularly useful in a multicultural school where story can help to bring about an understanding of diversity, the different communities offering drama from their particular life-styles.

In many countries teachers have large groups to deal with all the time. These ideas, and especially the one of the quiet cosy corner and the lighted candle, will bring a few wry smiles. If it is your lot to have a class of 60 children in a room with fixed desks almost climbing up the chalkboard, then do take comfort from the thought that in the long run it is *how* the story is told that counts and that even if, in addition to these other constraints, teaching props are few, the teacher is her own best teaching aid. Such teachers should look again at the suggestions for options concerning the things which lie within themselves.

In other countries where, for instance, more open plan buildings are used and where in addition teachers' helpers of one kind or another may be available, it is sensible to make the most of all the *physical* options. A certain bay in the large room could be used for children in small groups to enjoy stories together, perhaps using the big books I spoke of earlier. They might also sit round a table which has a junction box so that they can listen to a tape without disturbing the rest of the children. Each listener has his own earphones. It is worth mentioning in passing that the tapes which go with the big books in the *Oxford Reading Tree* contain the narration given by well-known actors and actresses. In at least the early stages of the course, the books have only one sentence of text on each page. All the rest is picture. What a useful technique this is. The children can enjoy the story, beautifully visual in front of them, without distraction of text. At the same time they can listen for the sentence which *is* there and which has been carefully chosen to be a key to the whole section of story that picture represents, the key to a staging-post.

Individual children might go off on their own into these bays, either listening by themselves to tapes or other audio aids, or curling up with a book. One or more could cluster round a parent or other teacher's help and either enjoy a new story together or do some of the follow-up to one which the teacher has told to the class. This might be a good way for a few ESL learners to have the kind of special help they need. But even in more old-fashioned schools, use can be made of corridors. A table just outside the classroom whose door is always open, can be used for the same purpose. Even if the teacher's aide comes only for a short time each week, the teacher should plan her work so that the maximum use can be made of her assistance. A story told to the whole class on Monday with some class and possibly group aftermath on Tuesday, could be followed up by real diversification on Wednesday or Thursday when the helper comes. But she must be in the know. She must not have the story thrust upon her in the staff-room just before she starts work! This should be a planned operation with the teacher, the professional, sharing her kit and her aims in full. It may be that the teacher prefers the helper to be with her in the classroom, helping in a general way. She may plan to narrate the story when the helper is there so that both can go from there. It must never be forgotten that the ways in which this live audience react have a feedback effect on the narrator and on the subsequent work, just as the reactions of a theatre audience can affect an actor. A class with a wide range of ability and needs will require to be very carefully diversified in the work they do following the story. Another option is to tell it at different levels in the first place. Hence the usefulness of our texts prepared for this.

Let us take up this last option and apply it now to a different set of circumstances. It may be an EFL class or one in a country like Zambia where all the children are ESL. What I am talking about is, of course, working in groups which many teachers find hard to do, especially with the large numbers and other constraints such as poor accommodation and lack of equipment. Let it be said here and now. There is no law of the Medes and Persians which says, 'Thou shalt do groupwork — at all times — or even some of the time'! It *can* be a useful option particularly in big classes, given that other conditions are right. If they are, it is helpful for dealing with mixed ability and for making it more possible for children to collaborate and communicate.

Let us imagine then that in this classroom there *is* the possibility of children being grouped to work together. The teacher has done her work on the story she is to use and has a narrative at three levels. She takes each group round her in turn. There could be more than three but some might be at the same level. Then she could combine a couple of groups. However the teacher does it, the story is told at its three levels so that all the children enjoy it and get something from it. What are the rest of the children doing while the teacher is working with a group? I am assuming that this teacher is used to group work, that she has plenty of materials for it, and that she has made sure that all the children are gainfully employed, either within other groups or as a class. This last point offers another option in fact. The class work could continue for the majority of the children while the teacher works with one group, and it could be mathematics or any other subject. For the inexperienced teacher beginning group work this is often the best way to start, gradually having more groups until the whole class is working this way.

Once all the children have heard the story at the level of *their* ability, they need an aftermath. Again there are options. The teacher could work with each group again and possibly have the children re-telling the story with the help of figurines on the magnetboard or flannelgraph. She must try some of the time at least to let this be a guided operation. Remember if the aim is to ascertain understanding, the reins must be paid out a bit. It is very tempting to jump in and correct but this is inhibiting for a child struggling with language. The skilful teacher listens to the inaccuracies and notes what has to be done but not at that particular time. Another small group activity which might be useful with the less able children is for the teacher to take her set of figurines and to work with them in a number of different ways. For example, suppose there are several animals in the story. She could put the figurines behind her back and say something like 'Here is the elephant' — bringing forward the goat! The children would laugh at the mistake and the teacher should then act puzzled. 'What's wrong?', she would say. 'Oh, this is not an elephant. It's a goat'. She could teach the children to say 'Yes it is' and 'No it isn't' in the true pantomime style, a very useful language and cognition ploy.

There are endless things to be done with figurines. They can be compared for differences, put in order, placed in various parts of the room, etc. The whole gamut of the '-tions' can be run through — identification, qualification, relation, classification and then manipulation. In this way the teacher *is* revising the story material and consolidating the vocabulary while at the same time she is beginning to *use* it for helping other learning. Even the 'What's wrong?' kind of activity is a pointer in technique to the later work when she will return to the story after disseminating it.

So the teacher *could* continue her group work into the immediate aftermath and beyond. But, another option some of the time might be to come together as a class again and to let the children work in pairs as they are sitting. Or it might be that she would move the children round a bit so that the more able children were partnered by the less able. A worry in some EFL classrooms is how far it is possible to let children discuss. Their English is poor, teachers say. They cannot use it for communication. In a situation where BICS are dealt with in the language of the community most of the time, perhaps we need to help English BICS. Here is one possibility. The teacher holds up a large picture of something connected with the story. She waits while one child asks the other, 'What's that?' or 'Which animal is that?', and the reply has to be, 'I think it is . . .' or 'I don't know' with, possibly, 'What do *you* think?' added.

This would appear to be a linguistic exercise, aimed at accuracy. The children are trained to say these exact things. It would also be, for most of the children, an exercise in language-like behaviour rather than authentic language because they *know* the answers. The children asking the questions do not need to ask in order to obtain information. So why am I suggesting this in connection with discussion and real communication? What I have described here is the first step. The teacher would then go on to introduce pictures of animals which did not appear in the story. The children may *not* know them. They genuinely *have* to ask and if the partner cannot supply the answer then they have to ask the teacher. In a teacher-directed classroom the children seldom have the opportunity to *ask* questions, only to answer them. We have to try and set up situations where they can ask, as this is an important function of language and it needs to be practised. It is worth noting that in some cultures it is not done for a child to question an adult, at least not in public. Children must therefore be encouraged to question one another.

So here we have demonstrated a pair activity within the class. The teacher is directing from the front while at the same time she is facilitating real communication. If we could now refer back to Figure 3, and consider the game entitled 'Photographic Lotto — Moods', we find the potential for doing similar work but preferably in the small group again. It may be remembered that reference was made to this some time back when we were looking at the kinds of materials which could go into the trailer of the story kit. This activity calls for the children to match the picture being held up with one on the card they have been given. Each child has one of these cards on which are the pictures of a number of people in different moods — angry, bored, frightened, etc. But the people (who are the same on every card) show themselves in different moods on each. The same lady, wearing the same clothes and spectacles, etc. appears in slightly different position with different facial expression and so on, on each card. The aim is to be the first to match all your pictures with those held up. If you have one matching, you get it to cover yours. So the winner is the first to have all his pictures covered.

That is the activity in a nutshell, quite a simple operation. But from the learning and teaching point of view it seems to me to carry many issues and to offer several options. Once again the '-tions' can be tackled, the people in the pictures and their attributes labelled, compared, classified, etc. So the growth of concepts expressed in English can be guided in their development. In fact it is necessary to do this in any case before the game can proceed, in order to set the children's minds for noting samenesses and differences. Then all kinds of useful language work can be done, revising things the children have covered in the syllabus, sequencing language for instance: 'Point to the third picture in the top row' etc. Or the language of attributes: 'Show me the man with . . .' and so on. Let us assume that the teacher has adapted the material to suit *her* needs and, in the context of this book, to suit her story which already catered for these needs. In 'The Hatmaker and the Monkeys' the teacher had loaded her story with further sequencing language. Now in this activity she could continue with this. The hatmaker was angry. She could have loaded a few more moods. If she had not, now she can (see the link with the role-play in Figure 3, 'See how you feel' further down the grid). So there is a tremendous amount that can be done with this material before ever the game is played, and it could be adapted to any story or theme, not necessarily concerned with moods.

Now the game is played. At first the teacher holds up the pictures and says 'Who has this one?'. The child who thinks he has says 'I have it'. The teacher then says 'Let me see', and perhaps, 'Right. Here you are'. The child then says 'Thank you' and places the picture on his card. Or, the teacher could say 'No, that's not right. These are not the same. Look again'. Soon one of the more able children can take over the teacher's role, the teacher standing by to guide. This is all accuracy work but with communicative language! How can we make it more truly a communicative interchange? The teacher can begin to feed in more suggestions to the child leader and also to the group members. For instance, as a child answers, 'I have it', she could whisper to the leader, 'Are you sure?' or she stands behind the child who has just covered one of his pictures and says quietly, 'I have only one to go'.

The group become remarkably adept at picking up these cues from the prompter and the performance goes smoothly on. What exciting possibilities there are here. It is so rewarding for a teacher to be a kind of fly on the wall later when the children are playing this game freely, and to hear the language being used authentically and spontaneously. What in fact has happened? It is the idea once again of the learning frame. The teacher has framed a piece of experience, offered a task, within which the children are allowed to behave and speak more and more flexibly. It is of course hoped that the learning will hold when the frame is removed, but maybe like snooker, the business of real language development has to progress, in some situations at least, by a series of such frames.

This kind of work, however, is best tackled in the small group and the teacher has to be free to concentrate. How marvellous if she has a teacher's aide or a parent who can keep an eye on the rest of the class for her. If not, she must be sure that all the children are usefully employed. Once all the groups have had the story and its aftermath, work of various kinds based on it would be done by the groups working on their own, or done individually. This is where the worksheets come in, another suggested activity on the grid. One pre-reading activity could be a joining up the dots drawing. Another could be colouring and matching hats or ticking the different one in rows of objects/people from the story. If the children are reading and writing, scrambled sentences to put in order might be done, or matching a word or sentence to a picture. Some guided oral composition done either in the whole class or in groups as part of the aftermath would help considerably the individual follow-up. Let us think a little more about this.

The teacher should place her pictures (used for the original narration) in a pile beside her. One after the other should be placed on or near the chalkboard, and one sentence (the key) written above or below. The teacher should then proceed to tell the story of the picture, bringing in the sentence written. Can the children recognise it? Loved and familiar story language is more easily recognised than 'empty' words in a course book. After all the pictures have been dealt with, can the children read the continuous story? Can they now write it, gathering more sentences of their own around each of the keys? With a more able group, space could be left between the pictures for offering connectives. The beginning of paragraphing is seen and the signposts of discourse, the teacher's voice pausing and emphasising — having helped the meaning of it all and guided the construction. Groups could then go away and get on with a collaborative composition, or individuals could write their own. Remember that the growth-points for literacy are to be found in oracy, and the more the children have been stimulated to listen and speak by a story, the more easily the skills of reading and writing can be developed as the story carries the children along.

A few comments about two more of the activities listed on the grid and then we must leave this discussion on options of methodology except for two general matters which will bring this chapter to a close, the business of story done bilingually and that of involving the local community. First the activities. There is a song entitled 'Resting under the tree'. I slipped this in with the story of 'The Hatmaker and the Monkeys' in mind, to illustrate a song aimed more towards fluency. Starting with the known expression from the story, can the children invent, in the manner of those cultures which use this device in their traditional songs, other words to fit the pattern? Can the children help each other by doing things under/over/below, etc. various objects so that these actions have to be sung about? So we have something like the following:

> *Pattern*   He's resting under the tree,
> He's resting under the tree,
> Eh, oh, look at the man,
> He's resting under the tree.

> *Adapted*   She's sitting on top of the box,
> She's sitting on top of the box,
> Eh, oh, look at the girl,
> She's sitting on top of the box.

Some of us getting on a bit will recognise an old-fashioned thing called substitution table here, where the learner has to change the words but keep the pattern. How much more fun it is to do this to music accompanied by interesting actions selected by ourselves. This needs to be a class activity as does most of the song and rhyme work, for obvious reasons.

The other activity I want to highlight is the role-play, 'I have an idea'. Again, our story prompted it. The hatmaker had an idea. We saw how the teacher could help the meaning in her original narration. This activity for the trailer would enhance the learning further, and perhaps it should be done in a group first if possible.

The teacher makes sure that the children are looking at her carefully and listening. She asks the question 'What shall I do?'. She looks about her, perhaps walks round the classroom, stops to think (do we ever let the children see us think?) and then, in the same way that she acted it in the narration, she says, 'I have an idea'. She then proceeds to do the action: to read a book, to write on the chalkboard, to eat her sandwiches, etc. The next step is to get children doing this and using the same language. Next, ring the changes a little. 'What shall I do?' becomes 'What shall I work at?' or 'Where shall I go?'. Again a frame is used to build up options within it. Given a few let the children go. Let them use what they know. Control only to create. The two go side by side. The trouble with many syllabuses is that they do *not* do this. The children are controlled until they do not know *how* to think for themselves and to be creative. They grow up to become teachers and they perpetuate the system.

The other activities listed in the grid have all been touched on somehow in the text. It is hoped that enough has now been demonstrated of the possible options in methodology, also that it would be useful for teachers themselves to use such a grid as a check. The activities, in the nature of the kit we have described, could be of the roll-on/roll-off kind, but the teacher would need to keep an eye on her various categories and be able to read the grid so that she could learn, for instance, that she had not *told* a story for a while or had not done any group work or activities aimed at fluency and so on. It could be both a forecast and a record.

Let us turn now to one of the most controversial options of all, the use of the community language.

The bilingual approach

My own feeling is that *not* to use the language the child comes with is to lose one of the best opportunities of all for cashing in on the assets. In his journey of learning how to mean and how to express this meaning in English, the young bilingual could benefit greatly from the guidance of an empathetic adult, bilingual in the child's languages. And this goes also for English-speaking children whose home dialect is non-standard. To some extent the bidialectal is one variety of the bilingual and can experience something of the same traumas, not forgetting that of social stigma which many bilinguals do not have to suffer. For many good reasons a bilingual approach to education seems to make a lot of sense, as can be accredited in the literature (see Appendix 2), and the interested teacher can read this for herself. The wider approach is a matter of policy at a high level. More is said about it in Part 4. What can be offered to the teacher is the idea of story as a bilingual device if the general policy allows it.

I well remember sitting in on a story session in a British multicultural school. A bilingual teacher's aide was telling the story of Rapunzel (traditional) in Punjabi to a mixed cultural group. She used all the props which had supported the English narration and the entire class was enthralled, British English, children of Caribbean and Asian background, and others. For the Punjabi speakers, of whom there was a large proportion, all the hazy meanings which had reached them through English were now clear. For the monolingual English speakers and those bilingual in other languages the message that meaning can be expressed in a number of ways was no doubt being imbibed, not to mention the other message that this language spoken by their classmates at home had enough validity to be used in school. But what made the occasion particularly memorable for me was the question asked by the little girl in Punjabi when Rapunzel climbed up the lady's hair to reach the window. 'Did it hurt?', she burst out as though she could not stop herself. I cannot remember the response she received but I do remember the satisfied sigh. She could not ask the question in English.

It seems to me that a very large proportion of the world's children are in need of this kind of satisfaction in one way or another. If it is possible in our situation to make story help can we think more about it? The teachers in a multicultural school where perhaps many community languages are spoken may be able to enlist members of those communities to tell stories in school if there is no member of staff who can. In any case I believe this is a good thing to do, whether or not there are many communities involved and whether or not the school personnel could cope. The essence of a school should be that of its community. In schools where perhaps one community language dominates and where in addition the teachers share the language then the logistics of the operation may be easier. However, in all these situations there has to be a conviction of doing the right thing and a commitment to carrying it out. In many countries there is a great wariness of allowing the community language any place at all for either educational or political reasons or both. It is particularly sad when what might be educationally viable and desirable is made impossible for purposes of political expediency.

There have to be clear aims. A sharing of culture is one, intercultural understanding and social tolerance and acceptance, even celebration. Facilitating language learning with all its cognitive and other kinds of awareness is another. To achieve the first the lore of a culture, its stories, songs, dance and the like can be enjoyed by others as they stand. To achieve the second there has to be some kind of translation involving the universals moving from one set of particulars to another. It is interesting how often stories across cultures share components. The same archetypal figures keep appearing, such as the maiden in distress and the wicked stepmother. Jamaica's Anancy, the mischievous spiderman, is present in some form or other in the lore of most cultures. Does this feature of traditional literature suggest that there may be more universals in general than we are aware of?

And we must not forget the wider meaning of story we have been subscribing to in this book. There are today's stories of cultures, the news of the present global village and, in terms of primary school children, these brought into *their* lives and learning. What is the news of the family, neighbourhood, township? What are the school subjects to be learnt? These things need saying, translating and sharing. The BICS of the street and yard; the CALP of the classroom are both involved in this wider story-telling. I believe that story can be gainfully used for the facilitating of code-switching.

It is this last point that I should now like to concentrate on. The possibility of story assisting children to move from one learning medium to another was suggested earlier in the book. It speaks in particular to the situation in some parts of southern Africa where at a certain stage in the primary school children change from learning in their community language to learning in English. As we have seen, this can be a very traumatic experience. The system should be able to give maximum support. I am sorely tempted to linger on this one, thinking through suggestions for a more selective and gradual approach, but it is not my brief here. Also it is not something that classroom teachers can do very much about, whereas *some* support, even though limited at first, may be possible through a bilingual approach to story.

My recommendation to teachers would be to focus very hard on their curriculum (the total curriculum, not just that bit concerned with language) and the challenge it presents to the learners. What are the concepts they are struggling with? What language could facilitate the understanding? What new skills do the children have to learn and how can language help there? This focusing would be specially important for the teachers just before and for those just after the changeover, the first preparing the children to face the new system, the second helping them to settle in it. Teachers concerned should think hard about the implications here. Just one very general suggestion. The lead-up should contain a lot of BICS practice. The time immediately after might be usefully spent doing the same lesson in both languages (at different times), at least for a while, beginning gradually to concentrate more on English CALP.

Teachers should try to find as many suitable stories as possible and to load them with the challenging things. These stories should have dual text (see Appendices). Take, for instance, the notion of time and all its linguistic exponents. Can we find a story where the concepts are made clear and then prepare the narrative in both languages so that the particulars of each code are presented and practised? I am not trying to minimise the problems of translation. There are times when it would be exceedingly difficult to translate a story because of the things which do *not* match across cultures. A totally different way of looking at something needs to be left in its own context. The new concept must be taught in *its* context. This in no way diminishes the usefulness of story at this critical stage of the children's schooling. Let the right stories be found for both purposes.

One very practical matter should be mentioned, and that is that on the whole the same props could be used for both narratives. For those things which *might* differ the flexible figurines really come into their own, one or two being removed and others added. Then of course there is the material for the rest of the kit. The same goes for that, taking up the suggestion above that a lesson could be given in both languages. How interesting it would be to do a photographic lotto session first in the community language and then in English. What kind of BICS in the first would be stimulated in the process? How could instructions in English be made clearer, instructions the children would have to get used to very quickly in their new regime? Differences in the pictures might be necessary if people are involved, or any kind of social concepts. The matter of how far it is necessary to indigenise must be considered. Leila Berg's Nipper series of stories (see References. Berg is a children's writer who is particularly concerned about social issues) was criticised in some quarters because she tried perhaps *too* hard to make her material relevant. Children can take a fair width of the exotic and educationists must learn to sort out their real reasons for objection to materials. The educational and the political tend to become mixed up as is evident in some of the rhetoric in recent years concerning anti-racist thinking in education. I well remember being taken to task by an African writer in Zambia when I mentioned in a talk that the stories we give to children should be relevant to their background and understanding. He seemed to think that I wanted to keep black children down. This is a very sensitive issue in some countries. It must be handled carefully. But there must surely be a way of making materials relevant and meaningful and at the same time outward looking. Education by its very name means a leading out. The trouble comes when values are put upon the differences.[3]

For many people, the whole area of multicultural/- lingual education is fraught with problems of one kind or another, even to seeing the children themselves *as* the problems! To others it is a field of new and exciting challenge, enabling matters of general importance to education to come to the fore. What we have to remember is that it is becoming more and more the norm in the world at large and there are issues which will just not go away. What we also must bear in mind is that teachers do not have to deal with these on their own. The educating of children is a joint project between the community and the school. In concluding this chapter let us think a little more about what this could mean.

Story and the community

There are many varieties of relationship I am sure between a school and its hinterland, from one end of the scale where norms and values are at total variance to a situation at the other end where they are in complete agreement. On the physical dimension also there are differences. At one end of this continuum would be the school with doors open to the community. There might be classes going on for adults alongside those for children, and possibly parents and other adults helping the teachers in their work. There might be leisure-time activities for all the community held in the school and its library and theatre — facilities used by everyone. This is what is called a community school. It is a real part of the community and the community is part of *it*. In other words there is a constant physical mixing of school and community on the school premises. At the other end of the scale, physically speaking, is the school where no parent or member of the community (except perhaps the religious leader) is usually seen. The parents do *their* job and the teachers *theirs* and never the twain shall meet. The school is there for teaching children and closed when that is not happening.

It would be tempting to align these two continua and to see the first of the physical situations described above as having the agreement of values and the second the disagreement, but this might not be so. It is perfectly possible to have much physical proximity along with much disagreement and to have a kind of separateness in which there lies a complete understanding and collusion. Parents may use the facilities of the community school quite happily because they are there. At the same time they may not always agree with the things being taught or the methods being used in the education of their children and may not even have too much voice on the governing body. On the other hand, the parents in the second type of school who never go to it, may be quite sure that the teachers are carrying out their wishes and let them get on with it.

What seems to be important is what was suggested earlier, that the school should really be of the essence of the community. It should be telling the same stories. It is a kind of intuitive fear of losing this which drives small village communities to campaign against the closure of their school, and a similar fear which drives people of immigrant background to set up their own schools. The stories in other schools will be different and in some way bad for the children. Happy are both teachers and parents when each feel supported and the stories match up.

I have described extremes. In most real school situations, whether of the open or closed door variety, there is some degree of alignment of values and some attempt to tell the same stories. I would like now to take two different kinds of schools and very briefly to suggest a way that might be tried in each of sharing in a more imaginative way the business of story in school and community. In a school where parents are often seen and where in addition young people from local secondary schools, students on teaching practice, and teachers' aides of various kinds may be on the premises from time to time, it would be interesting to set up a story project which involved all of these people to some extent. If the school is multicultural it would be useful to try and draw in members of the community who represent these various cultures. The teachers in their professional capacity would stage-manage the operation but they would be guided in their choice of stories and helped in the classroom handling by this vast supportive team. Some kind of planning sessions might be set up beforehand where the teachers could share their aims and methods. Translations for bilingual work could be put in train.

Certain story days or times could be arranged. Different members of the team would take different stories and follow them through, or the more able narrators would do the telling/reading and others of the team the follow-up work. Different parts of the school could be set up for the different stories as props of varying kind would be needed. A certain degree of perma-nence to the story kits might suggest that children move round the various helpers and enjoy all the stories in turn. I suppose the ultimate point of all this is the story-based curriculum. Of course it could be done without the help of the community at large but how exciting to draw in a large group of committed people, including those training to be teachers and younger people who may go on to this. Many secondary pupils make excellent teachers of younger ones. It would be nice too to have the stories going on in the homes later and the aunts and uncles and grandparents all part of the project. (See Chapter 9 for a little more on this.)

With the second type of school the same kind of effect could be attained to some extent by moving in the other direction. Instead of the community coming in to work in the school it may be possible for the school to go out and work in the community. In the black townships of South Africa, for instance, many educational self-help projects have been set up in churches and com-munity halls, especially when unrest closes the schools. The children see the adults in their lives working amicably together telling the same stories. And how this is needed, especially in South Africa. How very badly the children need the traumatic stories of their present situation told and interpreted. How very badly the world needs to hear them. A recent and treasured acquisition of my own is a little collection in English of stories told by the evicted children of Crossroads. For these and many others in the world the narrating of their stories is a therapy. These are not normally the kind of stories one would want to exploit for language teaching, though some may be. If for no other reason, teachers and community must work together to effect this kind of catharsis. Whether it is done on the school premises or in alternative education is immaterial.

Teachers, parents and others could work at the materials, helped by the children. If a story *were* to be further used, teachers could show parents how they do this and how some stories are useful for helping the children's wider education and teaching them to read and write. Just as in the school, a hall could be divided into different story areas and themes of all kinds could be pursued at the same time. Time and space prevent more on this absorbing topic. It has been my privilege to experience the wonderful way in which such things work and the endless resources and ideas which are brought to bear on it. It needs recording. It has underlined for me, if that were needed, the value of story as an educational methodology.

Notes to Chapter 7

1. For this idea I am indebted to my colleague and friend, Janet Higgins, formerly of Hilderstone College, Broadstairs, Kent.
2. In an excellent book by Betty Rosen (1988) which I discovered and added to my references just as this book was going to press, the matter of re-telling is an important issue: see in particular pp. 167–171. The writer reckons that it is in the very personalised versions of the re-telling that the story really becomes valuable. This is a point which deserves fuller treatment than perhaps I have given it in the present book. I recall one instance from my own experience where the story of the Old Woman in the Bottle (see Appendix 1, Stories, Sample 6) was being retold by a group of African children. The fairy became a magician and the castle a bungalow as the children interpreted the story in terms of their own understanding.
3. It is interesting that the use of the same policy can result in the accusation of racism in one country and be seen as a factor in the fight *against* it in another. In Zambia the idea of using African culture and language in education was seen by many as a racist holding down. In the United Kingdom, *not* to permit the inclusion of *immigrant* cultures and languages in the school curriculum had the same effect. The important component of the situation seems to be the political ecology.

8 The Learning Journey

Going Where?

In this last chapter of Part 3 we stand back once again from the classroom teaching for a time and try to pick up in more detail some of the implications for the methodology of the ways in which language learning seems to progress. At various points during our discussion of practice, especially in the context of what has been called here 'Field and Focus', there has been a sense of going somewhere. Let us try now to draw together the things which have been said or implied about the nature of the journey.

I suggest that it might be described as the road towards meaning in which the child's developing language is the medium, and by language here I mean the child's total lingualism. The acquisition of a second, third, etc. language should contribute to the full meaning of life and should offer additional means of expression. In a sense the journey has no terminus except in the mortal sense. A human being continues throughout his lifetime learning how to mean and learning how to make language work for him. The learning about and the learning how of the young linguist are but the early steps of a long journey. In a sense also this journey is not so much a straight road as a series of concentric circles getting wider all the time as initial percepts grow into concepts.

For a short part of this journey most human beings have the assistance of a teacher in addition to all the others out there whose indirect tuition can be influential. As we have seen, the teacher has several roles from instructor through guide and facilitator to what might be termed 'benevolent observer', but whichever role she is playing, she must be conscious of helping the learner along, of travelling part of his journey with him and even of choosing the vehicle. It is the message of this book that story makes a useful means of transport and the preceding chapters have tried to show how this can be so. What remains to be done is just to focus a little more on the way in which the teacher can further the progression, bearing in mind the *components* of the learning. For this we will pick up again the idea of the teacher offering a double bill, making mechanical and making meaningful, and the notion that the second is facilitated by the first. Once more, using the strategy of prototype, the teaching of one aspect is made to serve. I have selected the reading mode.

The Double Bill in Action

It is interesting that as I write, a debate is raging in the London area about real books versus reading schemes. The dispute is between those who see meaning as being obscured by the step-by-step learning of skills, who would agree with Papert (1981) when he says, albeit in a different context, 'The powerful ideas — the intellectual aesthetic — is lost in the perpetual learning of pre-requisites', and those who see some kind of planned programme of pre-requisites as an essential part of the meaning-making process. Surely this is not a question of either/or; not a matter of perpetual learning of anything; but a balanced programme of 'control and create' where the business of making skills mechanical releases the learner to make use of his learning in fluent and creative fashion.

It is my view that there has to be a programme of some kind and that, apart from the educational asset of a good one, there is also the psychological and motivating asset of going somewhere, which both learners and teachers need, not to mention parents. For me the development of reading, like that of language in general, is more likely to advance advantageously on the broad front of eclecticism, and I believe this to be true even at the very early stage of pre-reading in the young child. So, what I am saying in sum is that the reading programme should be a judicious mix of mechanics and message, the teacher's double bill.

As a young remedial teacher in Scotland in the 1950s, I used in the teaching of reading some commercial material called *The Pathway Plan* (Ruxton, 1938). It was a colour-coded programme which covered the phonics of English in a very systematised way, working along two paths of picture matching — one concerning single words and the other full sentences. The material itself must be long out of print. My purpose in mentioning it is that both its title and its way of working seem to make useful suggestions which could be applied to the reading learning journey and its means of support in present-day thinking. On one axis there is a pathway from pre-reading through initial reading and what Clay (1972) calls emergent reading to early and developing and then mature reading. On the other there are two paths, Mechanics and Message. The grid is as shown in Figure 4.

	Mechanics	Message
Pre-reading		
Initial/Emergent Reading		
Early/Developing Reading		
Mature Reading		

FIGURE 4 *'The Pathway Plan'*

Before we become absorbed with what to put in the cells let us focus on what the grid is saying. There is a progression on the vertical axis from pre-reading to mature reading and this in both mechanics and message. There is also, in my view, a kind of two-way progression horizontally. The mechanics help the message which in turn gives more ammunition for the mechanics to work on so that it can better help the developing messages etc. It is all of this developing together which amounts to meaning. In the same way, speaking of language generally, I put form and function under the total umbrella of communication. It must also be said that the names of the stages in the left-hand column are arbitrary and could easily be added to or subtracted from or changed altogether. Teachers might like to put there the particular stages as shown in their syllabuses or even the class names in the school. But remember that we are considering the progression to mature reading and that will come after the learner has left the primary school (see also the point below about changing this molecule into a detailed teaching programme). Finally, in attempting to fill in the various cells, recourse is had to what was said in Part 2 about reading, as I tried to describe what the learner required. Let us remind ourselves now of what these things were in a general sense.

Relating to all four modes I summed them up as secretarial and construction skills, operating with the various kinds of language awareness. In terms of reading, the secretarial skills had to do with eye-movement and discrimination of shape, and with grapho-phonemic understanding, for instance. The construction skills had to do with the ability to interpret the syntax and punctuation and the wider discourse. With all four modes we looked at purpose and with all four modes we saw meaning as the end product. Reading, along with listening, required the learner to be able to predict, and it seemed that four kinds of knowledge were particularly helpful to this end. These were the grapho-phonemic, syntactic, semantic and bibliographic. Can we now begin to place examples of these things against our grid? Again what is selected here is fairly arbitrary and prototypical. The main aim is to indicate process (see Figure 5).

Consider now this example of possible content in the light of what was said above. Consider it also in the particular context of our EFL/ESL learners. The grid concerns reading *per se*. The child coming to read in another language may or may not be able to read in his own. What point of the learning journey has he reached? And might there be some differences to be borne in mind? For instance, on the Message side there would be the obvious cultural differences, though as we have seen, there do seem to be more universals than meet the eye and if our diet of story is rich enough from the start this should present very little problem. What of the Mechanics side? It is likely that the only real difference lies at the Initial/Emergent stage.

	Mechanics	Message
Pre-reading	Eye-movement and discrimination of shape	Story, rhyme, song — topics of all kinds — building a repertoire — development of oral language Concepts of print
Initial/Emergent Reading	'Inventory' of symbols Rules of use — blending etc. Recognition of words and larger units	Widening of the semantic field Picture books and 'real' books Vocabulary development in ever more themes including the needs of curriculum
Early/Developing Reading	Decoding of simple stories Link with first stages in writing Ability to 'refer' and on to 'infer'	Using and exploiting reading — especially to find out things
Mature Reading	Ability to relate the text to personal experience — to 'hold a conversation with the text'	Using reading for an increasing number of purposes including enjoyment

FIGURE 5   *'The Pathway Plan' with examples*

Every language has its own inventory of symbols or alphabet and every language has its own way of dealing with it. Every language has its own particular lexis, rules of syntax and so on. These things need to be acquired/learnt, discovered/taught.

When you think about it, for most people in days gone by (and for many still) this section *was* the teaching of reading, full stop. You started by teaching the child the alphabet and then set him on fairly quickly to his primer, getting him to read aloud, getting all the children to read aloud round the class. Whole pages were memorised and chanted. The same textbook was read over and over again. This is another topic where I should dearly love to linger but dare not as there is so much that could be covered. Suffice it to say, teachers must be aware of the difference between recitation and reading and endeavour to make the latter real, with meaning behind it. This is what the whole grid is intended to show. The business of working with the inventory, indeed the various inventories of a language, is only part of the total picture.

It is, nevertheless, an important part and it would pay the teachers of young children to study ways of helping the learner along and to have some kind of planned pathway for this within the larger one. What are the discoveries the child is likely to make from his growing acquaintance with print? What vocabulary has he met in his recent topic work and story? How can all this be harnessed to the learning of skills so that progress is made in reading? Across cultures and languages the connection between the two sides of the double bill is the same as are the ways in which the one feeds into the other. At the same time, because there *are* differences in the codes, the particulars of the skills programme can differ not only in content but also in handling.

For example, in a language like Bemba or Bahasa Malaysia, in each of which there is a close fit between what is spoken and what is written, the phonic approach is easy and probably sensible. Intuitively the teachers of reading in these languages have been using this approach for years. My recommendation to them is to keep it that way but to balance it gradually with the 'look and say' technique of words, phrases, sentences taken from story etc. Progress is likely to accelerate if both means of attack are used. What these teachers should *not* do in my opinion is to drop altogether, or even to bring in at the wrong time, what has come naturally and easily and has taught thousands of children to decode meaningfully from print because certain modern gurus persuade them they are wrong.

A decoding programme in English, on the other hand, should probably start with the recognition of words and larger units and eventually when enough experience of the grapho-phonemics has been acquired (and the teacher has to decide very carefully when that is, guided by the child him-self), then a phased plan of phonic work can begin. This is because the fit between spoken and written English is not nearly so close or obvious. There *is* a system, more so than many people realise, but it takes a little more effort to acquire.

So, the decoding programme within the larger reading pathway has to be wisely handled. If a child is coming to reading in English and is already lit-erate in his community language, it is important that the teacher knows about (preferably knows) the particular skills he is bringing with him and how far this development has gone. She is then in a better position to guide him into the new set of particulars. To a child coming from his reading in Bemba to reading in English, a word like 'enough' might cause some prob-lems! Having said this, and to go back to an earlier point, I do not consider that this difficulty justifies doing away with phonic methods in the early stages of such as the Bemba programmes. If these methods suit the culture and language and the child gains confidence by them, then out of this basic security he will soon be able to tackle difference.

Before we leave the reading grid, it might be interesting to highlight another kind of mini-progression within the total pathway. This has to do with comprehension of the text, the journey going from simple reference through inference to making the experience one's own. In other words, the learner reader begins by comprehending the surface facts. Later, as his experience of life and language increases, he is able to understand what lies behind the facts, what the writer is implying. In the end he is able to relate to the text in a truly empathetic manner, bringing to it the full force of con-siderable experience and the language to match.

But this journey may be cut short or never really embarked on at all, I believe, if the teacher does not help. Guided comprehension may be a new idea to some. It is equally as important as guided composition and indeed may be even more so. Not so many people are going to do much writing in life. But they will read, and they should be able to read not only the lines of print themselves but between the lines and beyond them. How can the teacher help? A planned system of questions might be one way. Yet another grid illustrates the point (Figure 6).

I am indebted to Peta Constable, British Council English Language Teaching Office in Zambia, for drawing my attention to this. The idea was used by Betty Tasker, United States Information Service, on a visit to Zam-bia, but the framework came originally from Nicholas Hawkes, course wri-ter, and the local content from Peta Constable herself.

Question Types	Yes/No	Either/Or	Wh-
Factual	Did they have lamps?	Was is a night market or a day market?	Where were the traders?
Inferential	Could they see?	Was it light or dark?	How could they see?
Personal	Do you ever go to a night market?	Do you like night markets or day markets?	Which sort of market do you think is more popular? Why?

FIGURE 6   *Question structure, with examples*

The class in an African country have been reading a story about a night market. The teacher questions them on their comprehension. To help the linguistic side of their language she carefully mixes the question structure; to help thought she questions in such a way that a gradual deepening of the relationship with the text is developed. It may well be that only a few of the children can go beyond the factual. The grid is not to illustrate an actual lesson but the potential for lesson planning. And this brings us back to the total pathway plan. This too is simply to demonstrate possibility. The reading mode was used. Any of the other three could have been, just as any story could have illustrated the guided comprehension. Teachers might like to try making grids for themselves. But it is important to understand that they then have to be converted into step-by-step teaching programmes, the steps as narrow or as deep as required. This is really the work of the syllabus designers and makers of materials, but classroom teachers should be knowledgeable about it especially as some of them will eventually be involved in curriculum planning.

What I am suggesting is that out of an awareness of the learning journey and all its mini-journeys (the reader should refer back to other progressions we have studied in the course of the book), exemplified here by these grids, should come the detailed planning, stage by stage, of the classroom activities and materials. It is as though the grid were a kind of molecule to be expanded. It is of course important to get the contents of the molecule right in the first place and the planners have to think deeply about it. But it is felt here that if this were done well for all four of the language modes, each of which should be reflecting the nature of language, with the double bill of the teacher matching the methodology options to the issues, then the classroom would become a place of true communication.

Back to the Story Vehicle

Relating to the journey

It can be seen now perhaps a little more clearly how story can play its part on this learning journey. The skills and sub-skills of the various language modes set against the message coming from the other side of the bill show the vehicle in action. The message *is* story in the wide use of that word, the story of life. It carries all the rest along and helps the total learning by its motivation and its cohesion. The teacher must make use of it and must exploit its potential. With such a complex journey to travel the learner needs a flexible vehicle.

A summing-up of the teacher's task

We have come a long way from the consideration of the issues to be carried, through the various stages of the story methodology and its options. It is time to try and sum up the task of the teacher storyteller and this is done now as simply as possible. The summary is followed by some brief notes for the writing of guidelines which could be placed with a story kit for those who might like to use the work of others as prototype. The notes on the guidelines conclude Part 3 and lead us on to the teacher training implications of Part 4.

The task of the teacher story teller

1. Build up a resource bank of potential stories across a number of genres and a number of cultures.
2. Bearing in mind the learning journey, all the issues, and the double bill, build up a repertoire of ideas and a collection of prototype materials as props for the narration and as equipment for the follow-up.
3. For any particular purpose, select an appropriate story and turn it into narrative for the classroom, loading it with the special issues required. If necessary do the narrative at more than one level.
4. At the same time select judiciously from the follow-up resources for the immediate aftermath and the rest of the trailer.
5. Return to the story, presenting work to challenge and extend the original learning.
6. If this particular story works well, consider keeping the materials selected together in a fairly permanent kit, making notes to remind yourself and others of why this or that was opted for.
7. Keep revising your resource banks, bringing them up-to-date.

Notes for the writing of guidelines for a story kit

1. Have an overall summary of the kit — items listed — with an introductory paragraph or so describing the rationale of the story methodology (this could be the same for all your kits with perhaps just a short particular piece added for each story).
2. For each item in the kit there should be a brief note explaining the purpose. This should cross-reference with the overall list.
3. Show clearly the age(s) and stage(s) of the learners the kit is intended for.
4. State which parts of the syllabus/curriculum areas are loaded into the story.

5. List any useful references, e.g. another story which might pick up the learning from this one.
6. Note further ideas which could be developed. Remember that stories differ in their potential and some are better than others for carrying certain things.
7. Be brief and to the point.

But this will all be more possible if the school is used to the story methodology. You may have to educate your colleagues first!

Part 4
Some Implications

Introduction

The book has been concerned with three big questions. In the context of teaching English to young children we have asked 'What *is* language?', 'How is it acquired?' and 'What might be an appropriate means of providing for its development, particularly in situations where English is a foreign or second language?'. Parts 1 and 2 tried to answer the first and second questions whilst pointing in a general way to the potential of story as a way of providing, and Part 3, by spelling out the methodology, responded to the third. Here in Part 4 we are concerned with the provision of the providers, the business of those who support the teachers. Upon these supporters, the people who educate the teachers and offer resources, those who write syllabuses, design materials and plan curricula, and those who make educational policy, depends so much of the success of the whole operation. It requires that we add another section to the Field and Focus construct. What has this offered so far?

There is initial experience which should be not only stimulating but usefully didactic and heuristic so that learning clues may be discovered. There is follow-up time for consolidation and practice, and there is a widening of the initial field with opportunities given for the learner to make *use* of his learning in new and creative ways, whereupon the whole cycle begins again. This is the operation in which the learner and teacher are engaged. It could be the framework for language development in general, indeed for learning in general. It has been used here in particular with the story methodology in mind. Within it the steps of the teacher's role and task have been examined. As I move on now to discuss some of the possible implications of these for those who should be supporting her, the canvas is widened considerably and a much bigger framework is needed. In doing this for story I aim to highlight the role of teacher support in general.

125

Chapter 9 concerns the teacher educator, some attention being given to both initial and in-service training and to the various situations which exist within EFL and ESL. Section A looks at what the story methodology seems to suggest in the way of the teacher's needs and considers what might have to be done on courses. Section B offers further suggestions to trainers for ways of doing it and includes the important contribution to be made by those who work in libraries and other centres of resource. Chapter 10 deals with the implications for curriculum developers and policy-makers, at the end of which the wider Field and Focus is presented. It is all rather like the House that Jack Built. This is the way that A should support B, C and D who support E who provides for F, or something like that — perhaps not quite so hierarchical in certain areas. However simplistic, the idea may serve as a useful point of departure for further thinking and discussion and act as a kind of summary of the book.

9 Teacher Education

Section A: What the Story Methodology Suggests

A way of working

In a useful article by Rod Ellis (1986), a distinction is made between awareness-raising and experiential practices. Ellis offers a taxonomy which (a) develops the trainees' understanding of the principles underlying the teaching and (b) involves them in actual classroom work. It is a common sense approach which, sadly, is not always followed or, if it is, may be inadequately handled. For instance, some courses seem to concentrate on tips for teachers to the neglect of the rationale. There may be a certain amount of justification for this on short in-service seminars where the teachers are highly motivated to acquiring new techniques, but in the main I believe that every course should endeavour to take the wider view. As Widdowson (1983) says, '. . . being educated means more than being highly skilled'. He goes on: 'I would wish to say that an educated approach is one which develops an understanding of principles in order to extend the range of their application'. Of course, an equally bad state of affairs is when the underlying principles are given in such a highflown and theoretical way that the trainees cannot begin to connect them with what is required in the classroom. And to make matters worse, this often goes along with a lack of supervision and guidance in the practical work itself. The trainee is truly left to grope in the dark.

This chapter has been written, and indeed the book as a whole, from a conviction that teachers in their education need to know the issues and need to be offered a wide range of options. If this is so then the most obvious and primary implication for teacher education is that the trainers themselves need to know the issues and need to have a great many options to offer. It is suggested that the educators of teachers need to keep these two strands, the issues and the options, very much in mind throughout their work, the options of the teacher continually offering further issues for the trainer and in their turn suggesting options for *her*. The matter of understanding leading to action and good practice based on sound knowledge is the essence of any programme of teacher education. Ellis' awareness-raising coupled with experiential practices should be the order of the day.

As a way of working, the story vehicle will be used once again, this time to carry in addition the issues of training. So in examining the implications of the story methodology for teacher education we will discover that in itself it could be an important issue for the trainer. It will serve as a focus. Let us refer back now to the summary of the teacher's task at the end of Chapter 8 and allow it to guide our thinking, along the lines of both making the trainees aware and giving them practical experience. As before some attempt is made to cater for the varied EFL/ESL situations. The seven steps of the task are repeated now for ease of reference.

The task of the teacher story teller

1. Build up a resource bank of potential stories across a number of genres and a number of cultures.
2. Bearing in mind the learning journey, all the issues, and the double bill, build up a repertoire of ideas and a collection of prototype materials as props for the narration and as equipment for the follow-up.
3. For any particular purpose, select an appropriate story and turn it into narrative for the classroom, loading it with the special issues required. If necessary do the narrative at more than one level.
4. At the same time select judiciously from the follow-up resources for the immediate aftermath and the rest of the trailer.
5. Return to the story, presenting work to challenge and extend the original learning.
6. If this particular story works well, consider keeping the materials selected together in a fairly permanent kit, making notes to remind yourself and others of why this or that was opted for.
7. Keep revising your resource banks, bringing them up-to-date.

Needs to be catered for

A general need underlying the seven steps of the task is an understanding of the issues which give rise to the possible options. These are the issues we considered in Part 2 and summarised at the end of Chapter 5. Without an awareness of these things the teacher would have difficulty collecting her story resources in the first place and, in the second, selecting the specific activities and materials for her narrations with the children. Before we look at the seven steps in detail let a broad suggestion for training be made now.

It is elaborated on below. This is to use, as a more or less permanent strategy, a format of working-groups of students who do practical work together. For the short in-service course it is ideal. For longer and for college courses concerned with initial training, it is possible.

The idea is that theory and practice move along together. The students are given a practical task, for example to prepare a story kit, right at the start of the course and begin working in their groups with a little preliminary guidance from the tutor(s) who have carefully planned the steps of the operation. The kit(s) being prepared is/are used in micro or real teaching sessions so that the students can learn very quickly if their ideas work in practice. Over the duration of the course the kits are gradually extended and improved upon as the tutors, helped by their own prototype materials, give further ideas and make the students aware of what their kits should be carrying. So, for instance, a student team might have got their kit to the stage of making the trailer. They have devised material for oracy work. Now, after several sessions on the nature and teaching of reading, they are ready to include in this kit materials to help the children's literacy skills.

It will be assumed from now on that this workshop plan *is* being followed. If we then take the steps of the teacher's task it can be seen that the specific needs can be catered for very well in this way. The first task the students would be given is to collect stories. They would need criteria and information about resources. What a wonderful opportunity here for offering multicultural education, as stories from a wide range of traditions are looked at, cross-referencing with the different genres. There must be numerous examples to hand. If the course is being held in a multicultural area the students should be asked to collect from the communities, going off perhaps with a tape-recorder. This in itself is excellent training. How does one make a start? What are the things to do or not to do in approaching the world outside the college or school? A guided course of supportive reading would be useful here, books *about* story and books *of* stories, including those written specifically for children. Who are the good children's writers? What makes them so? What kinds of things attract children at different stages? The students could also be asked to *write* stories for children, particularly for the children they know — in their families or in the schools where they do their teaching practice. They should be helped also to extract stories and news *from* the children and to use these also for their collection. Working in teams the students gain much from one another and they must learn to share their collections. Even on short in-service courses much can be done to augment each teacher's work by the support of others. A shared idea can result in a wide range of practical output. So there is a team collection of resources. But each individual in it is also collecting her own and has the satisfaction of going away at the end of the course with materials immediately usable in a classroom with children.

The preparing of suitable materials for the narration also bears its crop of training opportunities. This is step 2 above. Again, the tutors need to have all the possible options to show, making sure that the students see them in action and understand their purpose. If materials are to be adapted/devised how is this to be done? Can the language tutor work closely with the department of art and craft so that the students are able to have the maximum help for their story project? Or if it is a short course of teachers in service, are there teachers amongst them with the kind of expertise needed who could help colleagues if the story ideas were harnessed to their skills? And we must not forget the notion of indigenisation. How exciting, for example, to set up some group work where a multicultural course of students were asked to indigenise a story. Both process and product should be extremely interesting.

Then there is the trailer and *its* possibilities. Of course, initially at least, a story kit is being prepared somewhat in the abstract. There is not a particular group of children in mind, though perhaps a year-group or specific language stage could be catered for. This suggests that the students would be collecting *possible* materials which *could* be used, given this story and that age-group and so on. In fact this was the idea behind the suggestion of building up a repertoire and collection of materials by teachers. They may not be used some of the time, or maybe not at all, but they are there and could be picked up at any time to suit the circumstances. The students then have to be trained to recognise the nature of the circumstances and how to select from their resources.

Which brings us to point 3 of the task, the making of a classroom narrative for a particular purpose. Here we find a tremendous range of needs to be catered for, and a tremendous range of opportunities for educating. The turning of story into narrative suggests some exciting work on language and its acquisition and on degrees of complexity. One of the most difficult things for a mature user of a language to do is to write simply. This needs awareness and practice. Another difficult thing might be the listing of the staging-posts to begin with, the making of the précis. A hint I have found helpful is to suggest the analogy of sending a telegram. It is necessary to put the message as succinctly as possible to save money. What is the cheapest telegram which could be sent, maintaining the essentials of the message?

Then there is the loading of the narrative. In the ESL situation, as we have seen, there is a particular need for the teachers to know the curriculum as a whole and, within it, to focus on the special needs. Can the tutors on courses guide their students on how to analyse subject fields? Can they help them to make checklists? This is the English for Special Purposes of the school-child. (See sample of mathematics language in Appendix 1.) There is also the need for teachers in ESL classrooms to be able to cover the structures and functions of English in a general way and to make sure that the children *are* picking up the rules, the things which make for accuracy. A checklist of some kind for this, especially where there is no syllabus for English language work, would be a real need catered for (again see sample in Appendix 1). In the EFL situation and in some ESL classes, there is a syllabus which has to be covered. Do the trainees know the syllabus of the area in which they will teach or are teaching now? Have they a global view of the work the children are to go through? If not, can the course tutor help them? All of this is important to the loading of the narratives. On a year course of training it might well take up much of the contact time in the first term.

Now, linking step 4 with step 2 we can really begin to see how important it is for the students to have an awareness of all the underlying issues. Do they understand what is meant by accuracy and fluency? Have they included activities for both in their kit? Have they made sure that there are activities focusing on form and some focusing on function? What functions would this age-group need? Is there something that this particular story could offer to guide a class in its understanding of a particular concept in history along with its language exponents, or to help them handle the preposition in English? The story of *Rosie's Walk* (Hutchins, 1970), for example, is an excellent tale for assisting with the latter. And what follow-up activities could be done? Would group work be useful? This is another whole term's work, linked to demonstration and practice. What exactly *is* group work and how many ways are there of doing it, for what purposes?

The whole business of progression and the learning journey must be tackled here. The students need to understand the Field and Focus and the two sides of the teacher's double bill. Are they preparing materials accordingly? Are they considering the different degrees of emphasis? What of the immediate aftermath to the narration? Have they been given options for this? And the widening field (step 5) is an important challenge to all, tutors and students alike. It would be worth spending some time in discussing, and allowing the groups to discuss, ways of helping children to *use* their learning creatively and to make story support. The idea of 'funny visuals' and other 'what's wrong?' materials usually captures students' imagination and they enjoy including them in their kits, but there must be other ways of leading children forward. The whole notion of 'control and create' should be worked on, some ESL courses needing more of the control and some EFL courses needing more of the create. The tutor with an all-round knowledge and expertise should know where and how to tip the balance.

So we have virtually covered the steps of the teacher's task up to and including step 5. I have deliberately left out the *use* of the kit for the moment as I wish to discuss the matter of teaching later. Let us now consider steps 6 and 7. The matter of putting your kit in a container and having it available for more than one teaching situation was seen as a useful thing to do some of the time. The idea also of being able to share it with colleagues was discussed, together with the need for guidance notes. Clarifying one's rationale for others is an extremely good training exercise (see a little of this in sample 5 of the story section in Appendix 1). It has been my experience in courses all over the world that many teachers, both young and old and experienced or otherwise, find it very hard to stand back and look at what they are doing, to unearth the principles. The nature of training as it stands has much to do with this. Blind acceptance of teaching techniques unrelated to any principles does not make for an enlightened, thoughtful professional. Teacher educators must make sure that their students are put in the position of having to work things out for themselves. This notion of a story kit and its *raison d'être* is perhaps one means. Why did I select *this* story? What is its potential for X, Y or Z? What language, learning and teaching issues am I catering for and how am I making sure that Unit 6, items 3 and 4 of the Standard 3 syllabus *are* being covered? How could I use this story to help a child having difficulty understanding the empty set in mathematics? And so on. These are the kinds of questions tutors need to encourage students to ask themselves. The responses supply the rationale.

The last step of the task is really for the serving teacher more than the student in training. It is a long-term issue. But even over the span of a three-year training course a student team might have collected a fair number of resources and be in need of revising them occasionally. It is worth remembering that both the collecting and the revising will be more easily done if the initial categorising has been carefully organised. Some ideas for this were given in Part 3, along with various other lists and grids. Tutors may find them helpful or capable of being adapted for their students.

Finally, any course of training, even the longest, has its limitations. The message of the story methodology, it is worth repeating, is to show a process or strategy. Given an understanding of this and given pointers to further resources and reading, the trainees should be equipped to go on creating for themselves. Just as the interesting story is a motivating and cohesive force in the work of the school-child, so its methodology can be in the work of the teacher right from the time of her initial training. The teacher must be aware of its potential as a vehicle, particularly for the development of language. The teacher trainer must be conscious of its potential for developing the teacher of language both in the matter of awareness-raising and in practice.

Teaching practice in particular

The previous section has shown *something* of the above two precepts moving along together but it is necessary now to look at teaching practice particularly. I shall concentrate on activities which relate to the use of the story kit and especially what might be gained by the practice of micro-teaching.[1] In many countries, the handling of this is dull and unimaginative. In the time allowed for a session, perhaps three students will be asked to teach a lesson each, going through the stereotypical steps of presentation, practice and extension as prescribed in the syllabus. Far be it from me to suggest that this kind of exercise (usually in an EFL situation) has *no* place in the training of a teacher. If it is what the teachers have to do then they must learn to do it well and it *will* require practice. But what I should like to suggest is the idea of using the micro-teaching time for practice of specific techniques occasionally, and for doing this in various ways. Let me elaborate.

Within the context of the story methodology, and assuming the students are in working-groups, a *team* might be asked to demonstrate a story in some way. One of them would do the initial narration. Another might do the immediate aftermath and a third some kind of follow-up activity. The whole team would be responsible for the planning even though only three students would be involved in the demonstration. This way the motivation would be high and the entire group would have a vested interest. The students should be encouraged also to explain their rationale and to be prepared to answer questions from their fellow students after the demonstration. If all the trainees are doing this kind of work then the questions are likely to be pertinent and helpful to everyone.

Another idea is for one student to take the class (her colleagues) through the whole procedure from narration through follow-up to extended work, but to vary the proceedings by submitting her fellows to direct teaching some of the time and discussion of the whys and wherefores at other times. The students should be trained to be able to say confidently, 'Now you are yourselves. Let me explain what I am trying to do here and see if you agree with me', or 'You are now school pupils and I am going to ask you to play this communicative game in groups', which of course means that they should see their own tutors doing this on a regular basis! There are so many useful things which can be done using this procedure. Referring back to the idea of categorising materials by format, something else which might be tried is to ask different students to concentrate on the making of certain things. One does games, another puppets, another songs and so on. During the micro-teaching sessions they would demonstrate with them, again saying why they had selected this or that and what it was intended to achieve. Students might then copy the work of others so that valuable time could be saved.

The working-groups could be set the task of considering as many options as possible of *presenting* a story, with a micro-teaching session devoted to this topic, the tutor making sure that a wide variety of the options offered, and perhaps others she could add, was experienced. She might then select one of the presentations and set a further task, that of planning some kind of follow-up to it, her instruction being for example either a very general 'Plan the trailer' or a quite specific 'Design two role-plays' (which will practise greeting or persuading or some other function of language which the story has highlighted) or 'Plan a pair activity' (which will ensure practice of the present simple tense). The groups might also be asked to work out how a teacher-narrator could make a specific bit of language clear to the children. How many ways can they think of and what props might they need? How should the narrator act? An important focus would be ways in which the loaded narratives were to make optimum vehicles for their baggage. Could a student demonstrate how the staging-posts have been used to pause and work on the teaching-points and could that student or another demonstrate the use of the same narrative at more than one level?

I suggested that for trainees whose first language is not English, the story methodology could improve their own use of the language. Work done on story-telling and reading skills should show results in the micro-teaching. The drama department could be asked for help. Trainees should learn how to react to an audience and be made aware of the different aspects of role-playing and communication. The bilingual/bidialectal trainee should have the opportunity to use both codes and to demonstrate code-switching, even if not all her fellows understand. The bilingual approach to story, as discussed in Part 3, would make a very interesting and useful focus for training sessions.

An obvious and important further step is to move from the micro-teaching situation to the real classroom. Teacher educators must help the students to go from simulation to reality but they should not abandon the strategy of micro-teaching too soon. If something does not work so well with real children, why is this so? Does the trainee need to go back to the drawing-board? Is the relationship amongst all the parties in the procedure such that difficulties can be discussed openly and helpfully, and the student's confidence maintained? In an ideal world, school staff and college staff work together to support the trainees and there is mutual gain, the school learning something new from the college and the college kept down-to-earth by the needs of real children in a real school! Colleges which engage in the story methodology might well, through their students on teaching practice, help to spread a fruitful gospel.

The above has tended towards the education of teachers initially and to those in the EFL situation. As we move on now into the next section I hope to redress the balance a little towards in-service training and also ESL.

Section B: Further Suggestions for Trainers

To raise awareness

It was suggested earlier in the book that it is possible sometimes to move from options back to issues. This may be a useful thing to do occasionally, especially with experienced teachers on in-service courses. The idea is to use a prototype set of materials, for example a story kit, and to make it speak for itself. The following procedural steps have been found to work well on several courses, mostly of short duration.

Steps of a seminar

1. Brief needs analysis
2. Taster of a number of language and learning issues
3. Taster linked with prototype materials and materials used with course participants
4. Materials left (if possible) on show in workroom
5. Same materials used in demonstration with children
6. Teachers encouraged to discuss lesson and to go a little more deeply into the issues
7. Teachers make their own materials on the pattern of the prototype
8. Teachers asked to write guidelines for colleagues.

I have found that the issues and options we have been looking at in this book can be highlighted for teachers by concentrating their attention on a set of materials. But the materials have to be well selected and interesting to the particular people on that course, so that even the most reluctant participant amongst them might be tempted to look twice at them. A nonchalant 'What's this for?' might well lead to a whole new enlightenment and motivation especially as the expected dull lecture did not come!

The first step, therefore, is to know the needs of the course members in so far as this is possible. Sometimes the group is very heterogeneous and/or sometimes the trainer is imported and has not necessarily been well-briefed as to what is required. It pays to take time, even on a short seminar, to discuss with the teachers their work and concerns. Gradually this kind of chat can lead into the second step where certain issues of language and learning are just touched on. The materials should be ready to hand so that they can be used to illustrate the points made. At a certain stage the trainer says something like 'But it would be easier to show you what I mean if you actually *do* the activity', and she passes out the material. Several things can happen next. The whole business might fall flat. The trainer has to be prepared for this and to develop contingency strategies. Or it could take off to such an extent that there is no stopping the teachers and the trainer feels like some ogre spoiling the play when she tries to bring things to order.

Let us assume that the latter has happened, that there has been excitement and enjoyment and that there is now a group of people trying to calm down and smiling a little with embarrassment that this silly game should have held their attention for so long. The trainer is then in the position to help them to see *why* it has held their attention, and to discuss what they did and said and how these things relate to the issues talked about earlier. If it is possible to leave the materials around for a while then there is the chance that individuals will browse and develop their awareness a little more. The scene is then set for the demonstration with the children. This has to be well-planned in the light of the work up to that point. Anticipation may be running high and much is expected. Again there could be an anti-climax. The trainer takes a risk here as it is likely that she does not know the children and how they might react. But I believe it is still worth doing. She must be prepared for the post mortem and a frank discussion of the demonstration which, if it has gone well, should give credibility to the materials if not the trainer! This is where the course members are encouraged to go more deeply into all the issues and options, the latter highlighted by the effect of the materials and activities on the children.

So, the trainer has sold her product and the teachers may now be very happy to work on a kit for themselves, individually or in groups, and this could bring about some interesting discussion on indigenisation of material. Guidance on practical matters may be needed and raw materials sought but usually these things are no problem as teachers of young children are accustomed to devising teaching aids as part of their everyday work. If possible, the teachers should be encouraged to share so that each takes away from the course her own work plus. To go away from a course with something useful in one's hand as well as one's head is much appreciated. And the writing of notes so that others not on the course can share the work is also to be encouraged. In some countries this multiplier effect might be the only way to reach large numbers.

The school-based course

In-service courses can be held in a number of places. It is not for me to discuss here the merits or otherwise of the centralised or on-site kind of training. Probably each has its place and is useful for different purposes. I have in very recent memory the experience of a centralised course in Malaysia which was held in a college where I was able to go through the steps discussed above and where students in initial training and teachers in service came together for the demonstration with the children. The accommodation was able to take a large number and was arranged as for theatre in the round!

The great joy (for me at least) was the follow-up discussion. When the children had gone the work was discussed with college trainees and teachers together. The teachers and trainees left and the rest of us (trainers) had our own discussion. This was made possible not only by the convenience of the site but by the good will of all concerned. The matter of conditions for training is taken up again in Chapter 10. For now let us consider a course taking place on-site in a multicultural primary school where ESL learners are in classes with those who speak English as their L1.

The aim is to show the staff of this school how the story methodology might serve a number of useful purposes for them. Most of the teachers will use story regularly and will not need to be convinced of its importance in the life of a young child. The need here is to show how a story project can be helpful to the language development, certainly of all the children but particularly of the ESL pupils who may well be fairly fluent in BICS flavoured with the local accent, and possibly dialect, but who may need special help when it comes to the English of study.

Let us assume that the trainer has done her needs analysis and knows the school well. Let us assume also that she has a prototype kit to use in demonstration. And thirdly let us imagine that this school works closely with the community, some of whose members come in regularly to help the teachers. The story project is to be a team concern and the trainer will act as facilitator and catalyst as much as anything. The first step would probably be to discuss the plans with the whole staff together (that is, the teaching staff), to give them an overall view and to invite comment and contributions. The story would also be told/read and the notion of loading discussed. If the trainer knows the school well then the loading of her prototype story will be relevant to the particular needs already. The idea of work at different levels catering for special needs would be thrashed out, and also the whole business of the trailer and the extended work. As in the last example, materials going with the trainer's prototype story would be used to point up the issues to be carried and demonstration work with children could be done, particularly showing how the story can help towards greater accuracy in the English of the ESL learners.

The next step is to sort out the logistics. It is at this stage too that the total team would be considered. How far should the non-teaching staff take part? What would need to be done in the way of *their* training? All kinds of questions would arise from the plenary session(s) initially, leading to action. For instance, returning to the matter of loading, would it be useful for the trainer to have one or two sessions with the staff on the language of the curriculum? Could some agreed format be found for focusing on and analysing the linguistic demands of the various subject fields so that staff could then continue on their own? Does this particular staff need help with the acquiring of a checklist of general English for the ESL pupils? Where are the special difficulties? Might it be helpful to do an analysis of the written work of these children and list the main areas which suggest problems? Are more sessions needed on the wider issues the story is to carry (again, see Appendix 1 for samples of things mentioned)?

It can be seen that the project could go on for several months, first as a planning and training exercise and then as work with the children, when presumably the trainer would still be involved to some extent, assisting and advising where appropriate. The staff may have decided whether or not to work in year groups and to involve the whole school. These would have been options discussed, along with the possibility of bilingual approaches, particularly if the personnel were available for making it possible. The decision-making would be for the school team. The trainer's part is to offer the issues and options and to focus on the particular parts of the project with which the teachers and their helpers need guidance, for instance the checklists and the loading. One other kind of support which might be appreciated is information on sources for stories (see Appendix 2). The trainer should be able to suggest where teachers can find stories across cultures and across genres and, of course, should encourage the kind of stories mentioned in Part 3 as being plucked out of the air, the children's own news. Teachers of infants are usually more familiar with this and how to handle it, but it can and should still be a source of story in the upper classes of primary schools. Finally, the trainer could well be helpful in the training of parents, secondary school-children and others in their support roles. I well remember a school in Birmingham in the United Kingdom where a class for parents and even grandparents was held regularly on how to help a child's language development.

It was taken by the head and her staff but I was invited to help, and what an inspiring experience it was. There was one particular grandfather who became a tremendous teacher. A school teaching team, augmented by a committed group of others could really make story live in the community and accomplish so much educationally as well.

Some final general points

Wherever the training takes place, with whom and at which level, the trainer must be credible. This is why prototype materials which have been well planned and demonstrations which are useful points of departure for discussion are, in my view, essential equipment and strategy. Most of us have suffered at some stage in our training from the hot air balloon who pronounces from on high but who probably has not seen the inside of a school classroom for a number of years. The trainer *must* work closely with teachers and children and *must* be *au fait* with the real needs and problems of day-to-day classroom life. She must also keep herself up-to-date with new ideas and resources so that she can quickly match one to the other. Only in this way can she be credible.

I suggest that the staffs of colleges should work in consort, just as we hope school teams will do. For those concerned with language (and I include all languages here) a coming together on the story methodology might be very beneficial to all. A general building up of resources and the putting together of training kits which should be continually assessed and brought up-to-date would be a useful asset to the college. The kits could be used for in-service as well as initial training if the college does this kind of work. It is suggested also for those not in colleges, advisers, inspectors, teacher centre wardens, visiting specialists and key personnel of whatever kind, that it is essential to spend some time if possible getting to know the scene and working *with* the people in it before launching into a heavy training programme. Sometimes a local adviser or centre warden does know the situation very well and can go straight ahead, but a lot of the time the trainer is not local and much valuable opportunity is lost because the very good ideas given just do not relate. This can happen particularly where a specialist goes to work in another country. It is essential to meet and to use the local key personnel, and these may not always be official!

It can be seen that there is much in common, especially at the level of technique, in the needs of teachers in EFL and ESL. The main difference springs from the fact that for the latter their pupils need English for life and learning, or learning at least. For the former, English is a subject on the curriculum which may or may not be of much immediate use outside the classroom. As the motivation differs so the emphasis alters. The trainer should be clear about this and in a position to advise accordingly. So, for instance, both kinds of teacher can benefit from the idea of the loaded narrative and the various uses of staging-posts. *What* to load and where it comes from may differ in the two situations, at least in emphasis, the EFL teacher being shown how to cover her English language syllabus, with some attention also to the concepts being presented in other subjects, and the ESL teacher being shown how to highlight the language needs of all the curriculum areas with some attention to general English and also to the things which make for accuracy. In terms of the Field and Focus construct (see Figure 1 on p. 57) the EFL teacher needs more help with sections A and C perhaps and the ESL teacher with B, though work on C may be needed for all.

There are many more implications that could be teased out of the material in Part 3, for instance the possibility of projecting the frames of a story and giving the trainees texts of narrative at more than one level to study with each frame. This could be done in a seminar which was focusing on language analysis and complexity. The trainees, using these texts as guide, could then be asked to go away and work on a story of their own in the same way. Another idea would be to ask teachers on in-service training to bring texts of stories they are using and to set the grid of question types/structures (see p. 121) against these texts. Could they devise questions of the same kind and gradation for their *own* stories? The classroom management grid (see p. 97) might also be useful to trainers. I hope in fact that the trainer reading this chapter will also read Part 3 and try to sort out for herself other implications that could be taken up, that is of course if she agrees with the ideas suggested for the story methodology.

Other trainers

A chapter on the education of teachers would not be complete without some focus on the contribution made by the staff of libraries and resource centres of various kinds, and I speak of public libraries as well as those in educational institutions. Whilst the contribution is mainly in the form of a support service it can also be direct training, as for example when a teachers' centre warden or other key person *organises* a course. Countries differ in their support services and the ways in which these are used, and it is not intended here to go into detail about this. Suffice it to say that these services should be well used and their full potential known by both teachers and those who train them, something which is sadly not always the case.

In the light of our story methodology, an obvious way of support would be the offering of sources for story. This could be the contribution of the library in particular. The staff there might even be able to take on that bit of a course if adequate communication is established between the organiser and the library. They could show teachers how to categorise and what categories there are available. They should be able to guide teachers and trainee teachers in the collecting of their story banks. I suggested earlier that teachers might need a guided course of supportive reading for themselves whilst attending courses. This would be particularly important at initial training level. Here is another place where libraries especially could help.

In some countries there are story-telling sessions in libraries for children on a regular basis. How useful if the library staff knew about the story work in the schools and could co-operate with the teachers — at any time, but particularly if in-service training is in progress. There could be mutual gain for teachers, trainers and librarians. But much depends on the network of communication established. If the staff in libraries know what is happening, what the themes of the projects are, they are only too happy to point to helpful books and other resources and/or to acquire more if the budget allows.

Teachers' centres or resource centres exist in one form or another in many countries, sometimes with a permanent warden and possibly other staff based there, sometimes with teachers and/or others working there on a part-time basis, opening up at certain times only. However the organisation is managed, here is another supportive agency which the teacher should use. Apart from attending possible courses based there, teachers should browse in the library and amongst the other teaching resources, and trainers from colleges and other in-service departments should make close links with centre staff, even to asking for display space for prototype materials. In some places the key personnel who run in-service courses at the centres, and generally help the inspectorate in the supervision of schools, are based at the centres and are very influential, true key figures in the region and perhaps more than any other trainers contribute to the multiplier effect. Seminars on story methodology and the making of materials could have excellent results if supported and organised by them. In other countries these master teachers are perhaps to be found in the schools themselves, people given responsibility and a little more salary for helping to train their fellows. For any imported trainer it would be wise to make early contact with such people and to work with them.

I conclude this chapter on implications of the story methodology for teacher education by emphasising yet again the practical value of a working-group format both in initial and in-service training and in EFL and ESL situations. This means that as soon as possible the participants are active and making *use* of the theoretical input, which is modified by the results of the practice which in turn is improved by informed input and so on cyclically. Input really becomes intake very quickly. For me this is a strategy proven many times. It is hard work but essential and rewarding. We move on now to considerations of what may be implied for the rest of the teachers' support team.

Note to Chapter 9

1. I am particularly indebted for many of these ideas to John Stoddart (see Stoddart, 1981), British Council English Language Officer, with whom I worked in Malaysia.

10 Curriculum Development and Policy

Section A: Makers of Curriculum

The syllabus

An acceptance of our story methodology suggests that it somehow be made to underlie the prescribed work to be done. In this section of the chapter the focus is on the blueprint for action, however that may be conceived, and whether or not there is a syllabus of items to be ticked off. How can the curriculum be supportive? Let us begin by looking more narrowly at the possible implications for an English language syllabus. This document, which often assumes great importance in the eyes of teachers, could I believe be used to give story legitimacy. How might this be done? Syllabuses differ in their format. They also differ in their baseline. Concerning format, some offer suggestions for method as well as matter. This can be shown alongside the matter or separately with cross-reference. In addition there may be suggestions for resources and materials designed for the teacher's use in the classroom. Further than this there may be a prescribed course either adopted or devised locally. In other words the so-called syllabus can in fact be a whole package of materials.

Whatever the format, as we saw earlier, there is some degree of authority about the syllabus which teachers recognise. They can feel constrained by it, often quite unjustifiably, because they have not understood the in-built choices and the growth-points for initiative. There may be a list of items to be covered but the options of method can be fairly wide-ranging. In some countries too there is a choice of courses though the range may not be very wide. It is determined usually by financial rather than educational stringency. Again, whatever the format, there is with most syllabuses the notion of progression. A typical practice is to move forward unit by unit from the lowest class to the highest, each class or year-group expected to cover a certain number of items from the list. It is, of course, this apparently required *class* progression which militates against catering for individual difference and special needs, though I feel that sometimes it makes a good excuse for not doing the dreaded group work! Most syllabuses would allow for this. A more difficult hurdle would probably be the examination at the end of the course, if there is one, but that will not be dealt with here. The concern of the moment is the format of the syllabus, a certain amount of prescribed work to be covered over a certain period of time, and what might be suggested to those responsible for its construction regarding the story methodology.

Another factor to be taken into consideration is what I have called the baseline of the syllabus. This relates to the view of language taken by the writers and which aspect is used for basing everything else on. For example, a syllabus could be structurally arranged with the various units progressing according to the way the writers see the gradation of difficulty in the form of the language. In such a syllabus it is likely, for instance, that more simple verb forms would appear before the usage of the modal 'should' and 'could'. The syllabus may at the same time suggest situations in which these structures should be practised and functions within the various situations. In other words, the two sides of the language equation would be catered for but the structure would be the baseline.

On the other hand, the writers might start with functions or situations, basing the one on the other and also bringing in the structures. So, for example, in a situation-based syllabus there might be an item of a children's playground. The language of the topic (situation and topic can be the same but not always — there is a difference, for instance, between a situational topic and one such as colour) would be suggested, both vocabulary and structure, the former bringing in perhaps a few words and phrases which would not normally be taught so early in a course, because they were relevant to the topic. Or again, the baseline could be functions such as describing and requesting, with structural exponents offered and situations for contextualising them.

The business of syllabus design is a big topic which is not for this book to elaborate upon. The only reason for daring to tread on this somewhat rocky ground is to highlight possible ways in which syllabus writers could, if they were convinced of the usefulness of story, make the way smooth for the teacher. It seems to me that both format and baseline could be made to help. Let us start with the latter. If the syllabus were topic-based, some if not all the topics could be stories. How might this work? A number of suitable stories would be offered as prototypes with the use of some kind of categorisation such as has been suggested in Part 3. The writers, knowing as they should the work being covered in other parts of the curriculum, knowing also the stories of their place and time, should be in a good position to select. They may even go on to make full prototype kits if their syllabus is the kind to include materials.

Would all this inhibit the teachers from thinking for themselves? This is a question which faces most syllabus writers at some stage. Their dilemma is to find a compromise between prescribing too strongly and stopping all initiative, with the danger also of talking down, and offering too vague and free a guideline for it to be any kind of prop whatever. A further difficulty in some countries is that the teaching force ranges from the highly educated and/or well-trained to the very poorly educated and/or badly trained or not trained at all. For the latter the syllabus is truly a lifeline; for the former and others in between the extremes it could and probably should be used as a guide and reference point reminding about what has to be covered but offering much scope for doing one's own thing in the methods. I think if I were a syllabus writer faced with catering for the full range of teacher need I would go for a format of a strong central spine accompanied by lateral elaborations. The teachers who need a lot of help would follow and hold on to the spine in all its steps, using all the elaborations also; those who did not could perhaps use the spine only and not all of its steps. So, in terms of story, here is a format which allows for prototypes to be both spelt out and offered in embryo. (See the idea of story outlines in Morgan & Rinvolucri, 1984.) It should be stated very clearly somewhere what the aim is and teachers should be encouraged to understand 'prototype' and to use it. If such a syllabus *were* in operation this would be a great opportunity for those running in-service courses who could help the teachers to make full use of it. But the syllabus itself could suggest other possible stories in the categories, and ways of collecting and devising.

It will be realised that, as with the teacher-trainers, the success of this approach depends very much on the awareness on the part of the syllabus writers of the issues and options. It seems to me that they need to get together with the trainers and also with the teachers themselves, both experienced and recent comers, to thrash out what these issues and options are. I suggested that work from the classroom could affect the thinking of the planners just as that of the planners could influence the work of the teachers. Let well-tried and much-loved stories, especially those which may have been organised into useful kits, find their way from school classrooms and teachers' courses to the lofty halls of curriculum design and become the prototypes for the prototypes.

Curriculum as a whole

In some situations there is no English syllabus as such. What follows describes in particular one in which ESL pupils are learning their second language along with children who speak it as a first. In such a situation the English curriculum blueprint, if there is one at all, is likely to be a very different kind of document from the one we have just been discussing. It could be more of a booklet for reflection, something which offers a broad description of the various components of an English programme with L1 pupils in mind, perhaps giving some indication of what skills should be acquired by certain ages and stages, but not suggesting work unit by unit or even term by term. In no way could this be a lifeline and not even probably much of a guideline. It is more of an awareness-raising instrument from which the teacher is expected to move into informed action, which she usually can and does. Many teachers include story as an important option in their programme and no doubt put their language awareness to good use as they do so. Even if there are no ESL pupils in the class it is a good thing to do, and to make story carry all the issues of the L1 learner in the development of *his* language. But if there *are* children having to use their second language as the tool of all their learning then it is even more helpful. Story, as we saw in the last chapter, can serve a very wide range of needs.

And one important need of all the children, but especially the ESL pupils, is for the language of the total curriculum to be understood and handled with facility. It was suggested that teachers may need a checklist of some kind for the general English to be covered by the ESL children. Be that as it may, checklists of the language relating to *subject* area would be helpful generally and curriculum developers could give some help in this even if there is no national curriculum, offering prototype lists or at least a prototype way of working. What has this to do with story?

First, I believe that the writers of *any* kind of curriculum documents should consider the place of story in the classroom. This is true especially for language work, but it is also applicable to other subjects, in the sense that they too have their stories, and narrative can encapsulate and make clear their messages. As teachers, by means of the kind of booklet described above, are made aware of the concepts, notions, to be covered in the various subject fields, this idea of making narrative of them should be given. And second, if along with this the language or a strategy for dealing with it were also given, then teachers would be equipped to load their stories in more ways than one. It would be useful if curriculum developers could take one or two stories and develop them to show (a) how a mixed ability class could be served and (b) how the total curriculum could be catered for. My feeling is that this story approach to curriculum should continue into the secondary school where story becomes something called literature. The subject teachers need to become literate in support materials. Once more if such guidance were given in the curriculum, here is the material for teachers' courses ready to be developed.

Where there is no national curriculum and where the format of the blueprint is fairly loose, there is room for innovation. The powers that be should take note of this, especially if the innovation has been tried and practised in schools. The best kind of curriculum design is usually that which has been successful in a real situation. Story as vehicle, not only for language development, the central concern of this book, but as vehicle for many other things educational and personal, could be tried and written about for others to share. Quite a lot has been and suggestions for further reading appear in Appendix 2. (See in particular the 1983 publication by ILEA, in the section 'Story Resources'.)

Some key words

Reference has been made several times to the need for teachers to study the language of the various areas of the curriculum. I should like to concentrate now on this and to offer some ideas which may lead to a strategy for doing it. 'Language (which meant English) across the curriculum' was a kind of catch-phrase coined from the famous Bullock Report, published in the United Kingdom in 1975. This was a government inquiry into the state of reading in the schools. As it progressed it became more and more concerned with language as a whole and ended by entitling its report *A Language for Life*. The report stressed the importance of language as a learning tool, suggesting another catch-phrase: 'every teacher is a language teacher', which led to a third: 'every school should have a language policy'. It might be worth considering these three notions a little further. Regarding the first, 'language across the curriculum', I shall use the preposition as a key word.

For me, 'across' needs a few other prepositions to support it. There is the language 'of' the curriculum, the school-child's English for Specific Purposes. This could be looked at subject by subject or in clusters of related subjects. Matters of vocabulary, structure, function and style are all likely to be affected, the sum total of what is sometimes referred to as a language register. But there is also a language 'for' the curriculum, the general language of study, English for Academic Purposes. It relates to books and the jargon of scholars. The instruction to 'see below' for instance, which is often met with in a textbook, has nothing to do with position on a page. The reader should not necessarily look at the foot of the page for the reference. It could appear at the *top* of a page. What this book language is really saying is, 'Expect this reference to appear *somewhere* in the following text'. The deep structure of the instruction is not apparent in the surface structure and only a knowledge of academic convention will make this clear.

There is an off-shoot of English for Academic Purposes which might be described as 'Teacherese'. For example, the infant teacher dismissing her class may say 'Can you just make me a nice little line at the door?' — and I am not sure that the question-mark should be there at all because again this surface structure is not what it seems. In form it is a question but stylistically it is a euphemistic way of giving the command 'Make a line at the door'. In this case the second language learner might respond to the question structure and not the style and be slated for his impertinence! Kathleen Perera's paper (1981) is worth reading, concerning children's difficulties in interpreting the language of teachers and study; she is referring also to children learning in their L1. She quotes the famous example from *Cider with Rosie* (see Lee, 1971) when the young hero comes home in tears from his first day at school. Asked by his sister what is wrong he complains bitterly that the teacher had told him to 'wait there for the present'. He *had* waited but no present had been forthcoming! Every teacher has her own list of misunderstandings and howlers. We can be amused by them. At the same time we have to think seriously about them, especially in a situation of ESL. The sources of difficulty can be at the level of the word, the sentence or the total discourse. In many textbooks there is unnecessary jargon, the writer imagining that he has to embed technical vocabulary in a kind of prose to match. The result is a readability level far above the ability of the pupil and a reduction in prediction which slows the learning. The teacher should be aware of such pitfalls for the child, remembering that language for academic purposes is an essential part of study skills, the essence of CALP.

The language 'of' and 'for' the curriculum has to do with its *demands*. It is possible to look in the other direction and to speculate on how the curriculum can *serve* language. Language 'by means of' the curriculum is an interesting and perhaps understudied and underrated aspect. This *really* brings us to the second Bullock implication, 'every teacher is a language teacher'. More than any other of the keys it suggests a team approach amongst the staff of a school. It also implies that teachers, whatever the subject being taught, should have a large measure of language awareness. There are important implications here too for the training of teachers, especially of those who are likely to be teaching ESL.

What exactly is meant? Quite simply, it is the using of the different subject areas as language contexts, as comprehensible input in Krashen's terms, but making the various registers *apparent* to the learners, making them aware for instance of the need for a different style of writing when reporting facts in science from that of writing imaginatively, making them aware of the particular vocabulary and structures being used in mathematics as distinct from those in history, and so on, all of which should be giving the message that language can change according to the circumstances, in this case the purpose for which it is used, and that it is necessary to acquire a repertoire or range of codes.

But the phrase 'by means of' subsumes two other prepositions, 'across' and 'through'. The first is the original Bullock word which I am now using more narrowly to mean just that — across — the various subjects at one point in time. The child should be guided by a teaching team to see how certain language features hold good across various situations and how others do not. The universals and particulars of language are brought to the fore. The preposition 'through' suggests development vertically as time progresses, and the important links between past, present and future including the transition from primary to secondary school. How many opportunities are lost for building on what the child comes with because these links do not exist and because teachers do not work as a team.

In order to cater adequately for the implications suggested here, teacher X has to know what teacher Y does about language, which particular aspects are being dealt with in that classroom and the next one. In most primary schools and in the lower classes of some secondary schools there *is* a closer working together (in some countries) and often the same teacher copes with a number of subjects. Even so, the opportunities for language work are not always taken up and the advantages of the comprehensible input from the curriculum are lost. A school needs a clear language policy if its teachers are really to work as a team in these matters, and indeed in the ways implied by these key prepositions. This brings us to the third Bullock notion, 'every school must have a language policy'. In some countries policy-making of this nature is not done so much at school level. A consideration of the implications for policy-makers in general appears in the next section. (But see, in Appendix 1, a small sample of a *school* policy which has been documented; see also the sample of a local authority one.) To conclude this one let us return to story and the developers of curriculum, bearing in mind the above thoughts on English as the tool of learning and the field or curriculum as an aid to its development. How can story help?

It follows then that the designers of curriculum and its materials should somehow build this important aspect into the main body of its work. I spoke earlier of a topic-based syllabus in which some or all of the topics could be stories. Why not a topic-based curriculum where story is the baseline here too? Almost certainly it would call for an integration of subject areas. Almost certainly it would need a different way of designing and organising resources. Almost certainly teachers would need to work together. In many countries, even in the primary school, the teachers of English are not the ones who teach any of the other subjects and they may even be extra to establishment with no base in the school. In situations of this kind it does seem that conditions should be changed so that the English teachers are able to become a true part of the teaching team. Several things are involved here, some of them political, but the curriculum designers could play a useful role by arranging teaching programmes in such a way that integration of teaching would become necessary. Story could help enormously. And what an interesting task it would be, selecting the story themes against this wide canvas, primary personnel working with the secondary mathematicians, historians, artists, etc. to discover the concepts and skills the pupils were to be challenged with, working out the developing steps for the primary pupils and the kinds of activities and materials to support the learning, and finally planning the language to facilitate which should be developed through and across the curriculum.

All this of course presupposes that the field is interesting and *worth* conveying through story, more the business of the curriculum planners and not so much of this book. However, even in the short term story can still be useful and can help teachers do better what they *have* to do now whilst the ideal curriculum, in which story could be even more effective, is continually being aimed for. It could in the meantime augment or flavour the insipid curriculum by supplying certain lacks. The imaginative teacher could use it to plug gaps in the syllabus. She could use it to take the children beyond the narrow and nationalistic for instance, by broadening the range of cultural experience, giving a dimension to the learning which, I believe, should permeate the total curriculum. Above all she can use story to give the children the joy of exploration in the land of fantasy.

There are obviously many questions to be asked and answered about the practicalities and the changes needed in the system for a story-based curriculum to work in any particular situation, but one of the main conditions to be created is one in which dialogue and real communication is possible amongst all the players in the drama, the teachers and the community they serve, the teacher-trainers and suppliers of resources, the makers of curricula and syllabuses and of course those who form the policies and keep the purse. It is to these last that we turn in the final pages of the book.

Section B: Makers of Policy

Language in the curriculum

I use the preposition 'in' to indicate the place given to language within the curriculum and the learning process by those who make policies. It seems to me that the issues highlighted in the last section by all the other preposition keys are relevant also to the making of decisions about *conditions* for learning and teaching, and about the money to be made available. The place of language in learning needs to be understood by policy-makers so that their decisions are tempered by thoughts not only of financial but of other kinds of costs. I have been constantly brought up against situations where what seems educationally desirable is sacrificed to the expediency of political ends. It is sobering to think, for instance, of the cost to the global village of citizens and leaders made less than they could be by the inadequacy in their education of development in the communicative skills. The policy-makers *must* be aware of the importance of this whole area.

This is true about language in general. It applies to the development of the L1, the language of the community, and it applies to the learning of a second, third, etc. language, foreign or otherwise. The child's total lingualism is what the policy-maker has to be concerned with. Given the particular situation — the country, area, school — provision for its fostering must be carefully considered. In this book the particular concern has been ESL and EFL but as we go on now to think about the possible issues for the decision-makers within *these* situations, this wider picture must be kept in mind.

English as a Second Language

In the United Kingdom for instance (and perhaps other countries too) with immigrant communities and ESL pupils in the schools, it might pay the policy-makers to do a rethink of Bullock — *A Language for Life* — in light of Swann — *Education for All*. In other words, if what Bullock is saying about the place and development of language is valid, can it now be considered in the context of the multicultural education depicted by Swann? What difference does the multicultural dimension make to the treatment of language in the schools? I believe the answer to this question to be an important two-pronged policy matter. The first prong concerns — yet again — cashing in on the assets, using the richness of diversity for everyone, the second the special needs of bilingual children. It is interesting that Bullock confined its thinking to the second prong, dealing with the needs of ethnic minority children in one chapter (20). And then it was the *problems* which were emphasised, problems of assimilating to the norms of English. In no way were the *assets* of having another language highlighted either for the child's own learning or for the good of society. Swann at least has widened the thinking to an acceptance of both prongs, laying great emphasis on the first.

It is sad that in spite of this promising change of thinking, present (1988) policies, in the United Kingdom at least, seem not to be supportive. The GERBIL (Great Education Reform Bill) is gnawing away at all the exciting work done for instance by Rosen and his colleagues (e.g. Rosen & Burgess, 1980) in London on language diversity. Also the research carried out with such rigour and at some expense by the Linguistic Minorities Project at the London University Institute of Education into this whole area and its implications for policy, has just got lost somewhere in the cupboards of bureaucracy. This work of the early 1980s had begun to show what was important about diversity and what *could* be done in schools to use and foster it. I believe that it should be resuscitated and given financial backing, and this before the dust settles on the Kingman Report!

Concerning the second prong, the needs of bilingual children, there are some (including the writer) who feel that Swann did not go far enough. Bearing in mind all the reasons, educational, cultural, political, why minority languages should be given place in the curriculum, decisions have to be made about how *big* a place. Should there be full development or only maintenance, or should there simply be some bilingual help towards the learning of English? Swann supported the latter in the infant school, recommended that maintenance and development should be left to the communities themselves throughout the rest of the primary stage, encouraging liaison with the state sector, and suggested that the minority languages then be brought back as options in the secondary school.

It seems to me that this is not a very adequate programme for a bilingual child. With the best will in the world it is hard to create the right kind of liaison between state schools and classes set up by the communities, and, without the maintenance of the language throughout the primary school years, hard also for children to pick it up again at the secondary stage. Worse than this, in my view, the programme makes no allowance for the use of the L1 in the learning process. Of course there are practical problems but I believe that some of these could be got round, given political will. Unfortunately it appears that this last is more lacking than ever at the present time. Provision for the bilingual child should be made within the state school system in such a manner that he is able to use both/all his languages for learning and life. Bullock, in my view, needs to change its title from *A Language for Life* to *Languages for Life*. (It is interesting that reports arising from 'After Bullock' conferences in Wales, were entitled 'Two Languages for Life'.) This new title seems to fit better with the *modus loquendi* of today's *modus vivendi* in Britain and many other countries, and it applies not only to the bilingual *using* his languages but to the monolingual *becoming aware* and to the dialects within English itself. Again, sadly, present politics in the United Kingdom seem not to accept things non-standard.

Another sad thing is that in Britain where, until recently at least, policy to some extent *could* be made at school level, the schools which were reluctant multiculturalists are now happy to let the old order stand, taking the cue from the top. For there is no doubt that if support in the form of staffing and other resources is offered from there, people will act. Policies, backed up by visible means or pushed home by the lack of it, can be influential. I am reminded of an occasion some years ago when in the course of my duties as a local adviser, I visited a secondary school with a fairly large proportion of children of Italian background on roll. I was pleased to find that Italian *was* one of the languages offered but puzzled as to why so few of the Italian-speaking children seemed to be studying it. I was told that this was because not many of them ever reached the required proficiency in French, the school's first foreign language, and they were therefore not allowed to take another language! It was clear that the school saw these children as slow learners and not as a group with particular assets of their own. When I pointed out that the school might gain a few more examination successes if it permitted Italian speakers to take Italian language some changes were made! But to win the school to a true policy of fair treatment for its minorities, others besides Italians, it was necessary to offer help with staffing, materials and strategies, all involving finance from local government backed by central.

This bringing in of the minority languages in no way reduces the important place of English or takes from the opportunities for its development; quite the reverse I think. Nor does the enjoyment of the varieties detract from the place of standard English. It does seem to me that in the United Kingdom at least more rather than less money should be made available for resources, both human and material, to support the two prongs of the multicultural dimension and to ensure that it really permeates the total curriculum. In the context of this book I should like to see, for instance, huge injections of funds to libraries and to the trainers of story tellers in the Chapter 7 sense, promoting the multicultural approach and the lingualism that goes with it.

English as a Foreign Language

It is important in the first place that the reasons for the inclusion of English in the curriculum are clear, and in the second that all parties to the activity know what these are. One can meet a situation sometimes where the government makes assertions about English being a vital *second* language in the country, but the medium of instruction is something else and the methods of *teaching* English are more in keeping with English as a *foreign* language. The terminology is probably not important so long as the strategy is really clear and the appropriate kinds of motivation are set going in the schools. In many countries there is a great need for more communication about the rationale. The teachers need to know why they are teaching English. How is it to serve that particular pupil and/or that particular country? If English is used intranationally how does this affect the kind of English being taught and to whom? Should it be for everyone? Is there a new, indigenous English developing which is accepted within the country and should perhaps be the norm rather than British, American or Australian English? If English is used only by a few in selected areas of the life of the country is this a cause or a result of the teaching policy and does it need sorting out? Will the answer affect the kind(s) of English to be taught? A clear policy communicated throughout the network, which of course includes the pupils and their parents, would enhance motivation and purposeful action. Then of course, having got this straight, the policy-makers have to make sure that syllabuses for both training colleges and schools are aligned, that those who design curricula and courses and other materials are in the know, that in fact all ways possible are found for bridging every information gap. As is illustrated below there are many places where personnel never speak to one another both at departmental and school levels, and as for teachers communicating across schools, that does seem to be an impossibility in some areas for all kinds of reasons. I plead for more dialogue.

Policy-makers in EFL situations usually have to be concerned with a syllabus. They also have to make decisions about when to start the foreign language. What, given the nature of language and the ways in which it is acquired, and given in addition the needs of the country, would be the most appropriate time to start it and the most appropriate ways of providing for it? Perhaps there is another influential body of people who could help the policy-makers with their decision-making, and that is the scholars. I have been amazed to find sometimes that instead of the kind of mutual respect between university staff and those in Education ministries one would hope to find for the greater understanding of all, there is sometimes no dialogue whatsoever and even open hostility as each guards their province. This is a great pity and wasteful of resources. Bilingual scholars who have studied the areas of difficulty very carefully for the children of the country learning English, would be in a good position to guide the writers of courses and syllabuses, and perhaps to restrain the impulsive and short-sighted policy of adopting an approach or a course because it is in line with the latest bandwagon. They might be able to show, for example, how use of the indigenous culture and language did not necessarily mean going back to the bad old days, and that the learning of English might profitably be delayed and/or phased in more gently. If this notion received the stamp of respectability from the prestigious ranks of scholarship and became acceptable as a policy, some exciting things might be done such as the development of story approached bilingually; such as training colleges being encouraged to have their students research and write narratives for this approach; such as curriculum designers and syllabus-writers using the stories of the country in their materials.

In this book I have been advocating an eclectic approach which allows for the occasional redressing of the balance and for teachers to be concerned with the insurance policy of covering all the options, even in the EFL classroom. The policy-makers through the syllabus-designers and teacher-trainers must virtually act as insurance brokers, having an agreed policy about the nature of language and its acquisition which allows for both BICS and CALP, and we have seen how useful the story methodology can be for this purpose. They must also be prepared for changing circumstances and the possible need for greater financial investment, even if it has to come from the World Bank. For instance, as more and more people become proficient in English, and a new English belonging to that country develops, might there be a need for changes in what is accepted and taught and therefore for new curricula and resources?

The swings and roundabouts of policy change need financial backing and teacher support, and teachers need a flexible methodology within which they can put change into operation. It seems to me that story can be a meeting-place of a number of important things. It offers a vehicle for awareness at all levels, including the political. A decision to support literature and all kinds of resources for storymaking and narrating is a wise one for any government. Story has particular motivating properties for foreign language learning, carrying the learner along on a tide of interest and relevance and offering comprehensible input, and at the level of methodology as I have tried to advocate here, the system of categories and options does seem to allow for that all-important manoeuvrability. Teachers can add to or subtract from their categories, can opt for this story or that, as the political messages alter.

Another concern of the policy-makers is the *deployment* of resources. I feel that this could be better managed in some cases. The main cities and conurbations may be well-served but the rural areas are very lacking in any kind of support. This is of course an old story everywhere. The lure of the big city draws people, especially the young and enthusiastic, and to him that hath shall be given etc. A system of resource centres strategically placed with the key personnel responsible for in-service training in the areas which the centres support, is one way of helping this problem. The possibility of a multiplier effect was mentioned above. Courses run at these centres, producing prototype material, might be very effective in this respect. But in the first place the policy-makers and purse-bearers may have to offer special incentives, including monetary ones, to tempt key personnel there. The conditions must be right.

A particular problem of the *cities* in some countries is that schools are so big and life so hectic that teachers never have time to discuss work together. For instance there may be so many children in a particular catchment area that two schools have to use the same site, one in the morning and one in the afternoon. The timetables have to be very carefully drawn up so that everything dovetails and there is a kind of breathless rushing about from pillar to post. This is not easy for anyone and people get very tired. For the teacher of English who is often peripatetic it can be a nightmare. She has no base and has to carry all her materials with her. The amount of energy and time used on the sheer logistics of the operation is bound to detract from the teaching. The lack of base means no display space and worse, no sense of belonging. The only colleague with whom she could really share her worries is the teacher of English in the other school which works on the site but they hardly ever meet for one goes as the other arrives.

In such a situation it does seem to me that the policy-makers should try to alter conditions so that optimum use can be made of human resources, that is if the teaching of English is really important to them. The English teacher(s) need a school base and display space. They also need to be an integral part of the school and not some kind of carbuncle on the main body. They need to be able to talk to other teachers and to work *with* them. What topics are the children dealing with in other subjects? How far have they progressed in the development of their L1? Are they literate in any language? How can anyone try to teach a foreign language without *some* knowledge of this kind? Everything that has been said about cashing in on the assets is relevant here. With the right kind of co-operation, sharing of thoughts and teaching activities and materials — sharing of stories — how much *could* be done to promote the child's learning, and not only of English.

Still on this theme, it has been my experience to find in the same school lively and truly communicative classrooms with exciting work going on in the

L1 or community language which, on the ringing of a bell, became dull and lifeless places with children chanting empty English structures, the only message getting through to them that English is a trial to be borne for forty minutes every so often. What is it that makes a classroom lively? The teachers working in the L1 know about this and they need to share this understanding with the English teachers, to share training. Of course there are things specific to the teaching of English as there are to the teaching of any language or subject, but there are approaches, methods and techniques general to the classroom of young children which should be observed whatever the lesson.

The English teachers, as we saw earlier, often lack confidence. Their own English is perhaps not fluent. They need to be well trained, but not only in the specifics of teaching English. They require to be thoroughly immersed in the whole primary ethos, sharing initial training with other teachers, preferably gaining experience as class teachers in primary schools or at least as teachers of one or more other subjects there, and sharing any in-service training which updates the initial experience. In this way they could learn to put their indigenous skills into action in their English teaching too. I well remember being impressed watching a teacher in an African country dancing his way through a lesson on division in mathematics. The children danced with him, their eyes sparkling with enjoyment and understanding. Why not in the English lesson, I thought ? I remember also another occasion, conducting a seminar for the teachers of English in one place while just across the compound teachers of all the other subjects in primary schools were having *their* seminar — and we never did meet. There *should* be meeting and shared training, at least some of the time. It would be interesting and helpful too for expatriate trainers to attend such training. They would gain so much of the flavour of the schools and their procedures and be in a much better position to offer help if it were needed.

Other situational varieties and considerations

In dealing with ESL above I referred somewhat narrowly to one kind of situation. I hope that some of what has been suggested will be helpful to those responsible for ESL policies in other situations, for example where all the pupils in the schools are second language learners. Certainly all that has been said about the place of language, and in particular English, in the general learning process is important there too. A special factor is for policy-makers to ensure that the English teaching syllabus really serves the learning needs, with teachers of all subjects working together.

As reading is such an important mode for study, policy-makers have to make very careful decisions about its initial teaching. The fact that the medium of instruction in the schools is English, does not necessarily mean that young children should acquire their initial reading skills in that language. There is some research (see the paper commissioned by the English Curriculum Committee of Zambia's Ministry of Higher Education, 1984) to show that reading in a second language can be enhanced if the learner is first made literate in his L1. This certainly makes sense to me. When one considers the factors involved in the reading mode, the issues we looked at in Part 2 and again in Chapter 8, particularly the predictive skill, it becomes plain that real reading can come only from a fluency of language generally, in the case of the young child at least. This is a vast subject which it is difficult to hit and run from, but in looking at the implications of our story methodology for policy-makers I feel that there is something very important here. They may need to think again about reading policies and to use a kind of bridging strategy from the L1 to English with story used bilingually an important factor (this may also be relevant to some minority group children in countries like Britain).

Perhaps another matter of policy in this particular kind of ESL situation is the one referred to above under EFL (many of the things said there are also applicable here), and that is the need for teachers of English to be less special and more part of the school. As the medium of instruction *is* English this should be easier, and shared training sessions could consider the English of the curriculum in ways we have looked at earlier. But the policy-makers need to make this possible and by their provision give the clear message that English *is* integral to the curriculum as a whole.

If we turn now to the situation referred to as threshold, where EFL *becomes* ESL, we find again that many of the things said above for both ESL and EFL hold good. The additional factor here is the trauma of the move for both learner and teacher. Conditions should be created, I believe, whereby the teachers of the year-group who have just changed should be allowed to work closely with those in the year just below and those in the year just above, these two groups in particular. Across this range there *must* be a sharing of topics — again of story — and everything possible done to smooth the passage. Ideally, in my view, the process should be less abrupt with experiments tried in a more gradual changeover, perhaps some subjects before others. But a full discussion of this is beyond the brief of this book. In some ways this threshold situation is the one which needs most careful thinking about and most support for the teachers immediately concerned, who have to be well prepared and trained to cope with it. I repeat my advocacy of story as a powerful aid and vehicle for the transition but the teachers must be allowed to work together and to use bilingual approaches.

	Teacher-trainer	Librarian and other resource person	Syllabus/curriculum/materials designer	Policy-maker
A.	Gives guidance on 'clues' and on selection of experience.	Informs about and supplies appropriate books and other resources.	Makes experience-based ('story') learning seem important. Suggests topics. Offers prototype materials.	Makes a clear statement linking experience and language in learning. Supplies the conditions to translate this into practice.
B.	Gives guidance on techniques.	Supports other trainers and teachers generally on specific work of story follow-up, especially in making of materials.	Shows clearly in guidelines items of work to be covered and practised within story methodology. Caters for different kinds of help needed.	Creates opportunities for teachers to 'focus' together and to make materials. Provides conditions whereby teachers can 'focus' with children in small groups if necessary.
C.	Gives guidance on extension of previous experience, selection of new experience and on techniques of challenge.	As at A. Also offers display space for prototype materials. Adds ideas both gleaned from other parts of the area and 'born' in the place.	Shows how topics can develop cyclically. Accepts the challenge of innovation and is prepared to use ideas originating from the classteachers.	Is prepared to invest more money on the development of experiment and new ideas.

FIGURE 7 *'Field and Focus' revisited and completed: Support services*

Finally, a word for those in policy-making positions in international schools and other kinds of language schools where English may or may not be the only medium of instruction and where the motivations for learning it may range widely. Concerning English as a learning tool and its place in the curriculum, concerning the specific language needs, many of the same things apply and will not be repeated. In this situation the question might be asked in addition, especially in the schools which are international in clientele, as to how far story is allowed to carry the international message. There are such wonderful opportunities in many of these schools for a true intercultural meeting at a deep level. Are the universals and particulars being studied and handled in the curriculum to the mutual benefit of all? Some of the schools are community schools and very much supported by highly motivated parents. Do other people's stories matter to them? Can the conditions of learning be such that there is real communication and enlightenment across the network of the community? Does a little more money need to be spent on resources which would help? All of these and many other questions need to be asked and answered and they all touch on story in the wide sense of that word. Let us now bring this one to a conclusion by returning to the construct of Field and Focus and filling in the last section relating to the services which support the teacher (see Figure 7). Perhaps enough has now been said to allow the figure to speak for itself.

Postscript to the construct

As so much depends on the last column of this last section, the one concerned with the 'what *will* happen' of the Papert quotation used earlier (p. 30), it is relevant to make one last overall statement. The policy-maker must make sure that conditions are appropriate for allowing the learning journey to proceed and be accomplished. This book hopes that he will speed the story vehicle on its way.

Epilogue

This book has been about the teaching of English to young children. The three big language questions in relation to English have been asked and, I hope, answered to some extent at least, in the context of another — why story? The message has been that story seems to serve all three, the nature of language, its learning and the condition of its teaching. It is a vehicle which carries the pupil along by its momentum on the journey of learning. We have seen for instance how it is a preparatory ground for enjoyable and meaningful reading especially in the early years, a diet of exciting narrative helping to develop the predictive skill so important to comprehension. But we have seen also that if handled skilfully story will help all four modes, promoting more efficient listening, more fluent speaking and the ability to read and write easily and competently. As a methodology for the furthering of language awareness and skills it has undoubted potential.

So for the children, also for the teachers. As a strategy of training the vehicle can serve again, and the method of prototype kits has been put forward as a way of doing it, even to the suggestion of topic (story)-based syllabuses and/or curricula. All the world loves a story, adults and children alike. We have seen how wise use of it in school and community can serve several purposes beyond and around the development of language, and it is essential to stress that whatever the learning situation story is not an educational frill but an important and integral part of the curriculum, an important and integral part of life.

Perhaps this emphasis is a fitting note on which to end the book. Is it not a fact that people everywhere are seeking guidance and security, and that the flux in some countries of cultures and languages in contact makes for constant change and a need for interpreters of the story? This is not to mention the violence and misery amongst which many of the world's children are presently being reared. Apart altogether from the narrower educational issues which story can carry, we have to consider these broader matters. We owe it to our children to give them the sense of continuity and hope that story can bring, the language strategies being the means by which they can explore it for themselves. We must try to open a door to the land of books and worlds beyond their own. We must endeavour to give them the means of coping with their present experience, whatever that may be, from Northern Ireland to the black townships of South Africa, and help them climb beyond it to new heights of learning and living.

Part 5
Resources

Appendix 1: Sample Materials

This Appendix contains:

1. *Checklists*

2. *Stories*

Sample 1: *Daniel and the Coconut Cakes* (Monolingual, ESL, from a book)

Sample 2: *Shared Story Writing* (Bilingual, ESL, 'plucked from the air')

Sample 3: *Sonal Splash* and others including an Italian version of The Hatmaker and the Monkeys. (Bilingual, ESL, book, traditional and 'plucked from the air')

Sample 4: *The Mischief Maker* (Monolingual, EFL, traditional, to be used for narrative-making)

Sample 5: *Our Village Bus* (Monolingual, Threshold, book, sample of guidelines)

Sample 6: *The Old Woman in the Bottle* (Text at three levels)

Sample 7: *The Storybox Project*

3. *Other materials*

Sample 1: Music for: *Zozo the Monkey* (see p. 81) and *The Hat Song* (see p. 82)

Sample 2: *A Community Happening*

Sample 3: Materials which could be useful in the workshops

Sample 4: Language Policy from (a) an education authority, (b) a school.

Sample 5: Introduction to the *Oxford Reading Tree.*

1. Checklists

Sample 1

To illustrate that ESL teachers may find an EFL course useful as a guide. (Taken from: *Now for English* by Keith Johnson (Nelson, 1983), Teacher's Book 1, p. 1, contents of first ten Units.)

Contents

Unit	Main Teaching Points (Structures)	Topics (Lexical areas and functions)
Introductory lesson	What's your name? My name's John	names (asking for names and saying who you are) colours countries of the world
1 Good morning everyone	I'm Anne I'm not Peter Who's this? It's Sam	the characters in the book introducing yourself
2 Who's this?	This is Mr Porter This is my father he's/she's numbers 1–10	family relations (talking about the family) children's ages
3 Oh Sally!	What's this? It's a — (positive, negative, interrogative, short answer)	objects commonly found in the street or house
4 What a mess!	Whose is this book? Whose book is this? It's Sam's It's his/her book Is that/it your book?	common classroom objects talking about who owns things
5 Kate's farm	What colour is it? It's red It's a red horse this/that	farm animals
6 Games to play	revision and progress Test 1	
7 Gee up, Sam	I'm a — You're a — (positive, negative, interrogative, short answer) a/an	exciting jobs (talking about jobs)

8 Circus time	He's a — She's a — (positive, negative, interrogative, short answer)	the circus
9 Stop, Bella, stop	Imperative (positive, negative)	simple actions giving orders
10 Shirts and skirts	What are these? They're — These are — Plural nouns No article + plural Noun/a + singular noun	articles of clothing

Sample 2

To illustrate the language of a subject area and how this subject can be used for *teaching* language. (Taken from: *Language Through Maths: A Scheme for Teaching Language Through the Mathematics Activities of the Infants' Classroom*, p. 12; prepared by Catherine Johnson and Jessica Wiltshire, with the help of Beverley Dunbar and Yvonne Clark. Any comments or questions may be addressed to: Jessica Wiltshire, Consultant for ESL/Multicultural Education, Central Metropolitan Region, Professional Services Centre, 65 Albert Road, Strathfield, NSW 2135, Australia.)

Counting: Number Lines

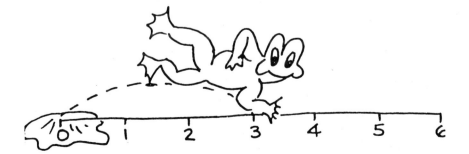

In using number lines children are generally required to follow instructions and give simple, often one word answers. If an explanation is required, the language used will probably be that of counting.

> *Questions and Instructions*
> Where is 5?
> Where is the 5th place?
> What is in the 4th place?
> What comes before 5?
> What comes after 5?
> What comes between 7 and 9?
> Put this flower in/at the 5th place
> Walk 3 places
> Walk *along* the number line
> Go *as far as* the 5th place
> Walk *to* the 5th place

(Select one way of giving an instruction and use it until it is thoroughly understood.)

Some Teaching and Practising Activities

The frog game: Given a number line with a frog drawn at its beginning, the child draws in the number of jumps his frog might take to reach the end of the line.

Stepping stones: The child uses a chart with pictures of stepping stones across a river, and counters or plastic figures to 'cross the river' in two, three, four, etc. steps.

Playground markings: Can also be used for outdoor activities with number lines.

Sample 3

To illustrate: (a) the steps of a strategy; (b) the framework for the analysis of the language; (c) the checklist itself. (Taken from: *Breakthrough to Fluency* by Edie Garvie (Blackwell, 1976); now out of print.)

I have used most of Chapter 3 because it seems to serve a number of purposes relating to the present book, particularly the strategy it describes for teachers in a team working on the language of their curriculum. These were Bradford (UK) infant teachers, concerned to help their ESL pupils with the language needed for the activities of early reading and mathematics. I hope that the checklist may also help to augment what has been said in the present book about the nature of language.

Steps of the Strategy

1. List the learning objectives, that is, the skills and concepts which underlie the activities the children have to engage in, e.g.

Pre-reading	*Mathematics*
Visual/motor skills	Relationships
a. Matching through all stages	Sorting
b. Discrimination: same/different	Enumeration
c. Eye/hand co-ordination	a. Simple recitation of the 'jingle'
d. Ability to do jigsaws of increasing difficulty	b. One-to-one correspondence
	c. Simple naming of the figure
Left/right orientation	d. Matching the numeral to the group and the group to the numeral
Auditory/speech skills	Conservation
Sequencing	Ordering

2. List the activities and materials being used and try to put them to some extent in order of difficulty.

The following is one example from seven pre-reading programmes arrived at in this way.

Visual/Motor: Discrimination: Same/Different
A. *Posting Box*
B. *Set of 3 objects* — 2 alike, 1 different
  Use of hoops, sorting-boxes, etc. Look for differences of: colour, size, direction (N.B. the differences must be very obvious)
C. *Tupperware ball* and *Shapes on to posts* etc.
D. *Strip Books* — alike and different
E. *Set of 3 pictures* — 2 alike, 1 different
  Look for differences of: colour, size, direction, position, family. Look for something left out and something added
F. *Discrimination sheets:* match cut-out pictures on to strips of pictures, noticing alike and different. Point out which is different from 3 or 4 pictures on a strip. If the child is working on his own, a counter can be placed on the different picture. If enough copies are available, the different picture could be coloured in.
  Shapes:
    Colour the two similar shapes the same
    Make all shapes the same
    No colour: pure shape discrimination
  Strip books for letters:
    2 strips only
    3 strips

Letters on sheets:
Cut out on card and match on to sheet
Find the one that is different.

3. Use each of these items with children and note the language used, either by recording it or writing it down as it is spoken. An observer can do it for you. If time allows, the same item should be dealt with in this way several times with different children involved.

Here is an example using one of the items taken from the above list of activities.

Teacher	*Child* (Item E)
Look at these pictures.	
What's this?	It's a ball.
And what's this?	It's a ball.
Yes, it's a ball too.	
And what's this?	It's a ball too.
What colour is this ball?	Red.
That's right. It's a red ball.	
Say, 'It's a red ball'.	It's a red ball.
Good. What colour is *this* ball?	It's a blue ball.
etc.	

(There could still be a place for this kind of activity, preferably with an individual.)

4. Do an analysis using all the samples of recorded language.

Framework Used

Vocabulary:
Nouns
Verb parts
Adjuncts (covering adjectives and adverbs)
Other structural words

Basic sentence types:
Statements
Questions
Responses
Instructions
Exclamations

Formulae (prefabricated language)

Rules and patterns

Sample of: The Actual Checklist

Nouns: ball, bead, box, brick, button, card, colour, counter, dice, dish, doll, domino, end, game, glass, group, half, hole, jigsaw, lace, ladder, line, lot, marble, money, music, name, number, order, pair, peg, pegboard, piano, etc.

Verbs: add, be, begin, belong, bring, break, build, can, change, clap, come, colour, copy, count, cut, do, draw, empty, feel, fill, find, finish, fit, etc.

The words listed above had the highest frequency of use by the teachers in their pre-reading and mathematics work. They arise from the needs of the particular learning involved and from the activities and materials. But it can be seen that many of them have much more general application, for example the noun 'end' and the verb 'begin'. These two parts of the list are very open-ended, particularly the nouns. Much depends on the activities and materials being used.

Adjuncts

Colour: red, blue, green, yellow, black, white, brown, fawn, grey, pink, orange, purple, light, dark.

Shape: round, circular, square, oblong.

Texture: hard, soft, rough, smooth, sharp, blunt.

Size: big, small, large, little, long, short, tall, wide, narrow, high, low, fat, thin, thick, deep.

Quantity: a. one, two, three, four, five . . . ten

b. once, twice

c. many, some, more, less, most, least, several, few, enough, plenty, much, any, each, all, exactly, no, not, else, full, empty, just, every, another, other, both.

Sequence: a. first, second, third, etc.

b. next, last.

Position — Place: here, there, top, bottom, middle, centre, side, etc.

Position — Time: now, then, before, after, early, late, today, yesterday, etc.

Degree: very, too, nearly, almost, quite, only.

State, manner, mood: well, sick, poorly, ill, hungry, thirsty, cruel, angry, happy, etc.

General evaluation: good, bad, nice, pretty, etc.

The teachers' analyses of the words they used suggested the above grouping. The groups vary in the degree to which they are open-ended, ranging from counting words at one end of the scale to those in the section on state, manner, mood at the other end. The latter are very open-ended and can easily be added to. Once again there are words which are particular to the situation and those which are useful generally.

Other structural words
1. a, an, the.
2. this, that, these, those.
3. I, my, me, mine.
   he, his, him, his.
   she, her, her, hers.
   it, its, it.
   we, our, us, ours.
   you, your, you, yours.
   they, their, them, theirs.
   one (this one).
4. myself, yourself, himself, herself, itself, ourselves, yourselves, themselves.
5. any-body/how/one/thing/time/where.
   every-body/one/thing/where.
   no-body/one/thing/where.
   some-body/how/one/thing/time(s)/where.
6. what, which, who, whose, whom, how, when, where, why.
7. and, but, or, nor, so, then.
8. as, than, till/until, unless, while, after, before, if, because, though/although.
9. about, above, along, among, amongst, at, behind, below, beside, between, by, down, for, from, in, in front of, inside, into, near, next to, of, off, on, outside, over, past, round, to, towards, under, underneath, up, with.

Teachers should be aware of the broad division of words into those which can be described as content words, such as the nouns and verbs and many of the adjuncts, and those which are mainly structural. Some of the adjuncts come into the latter category, e.g. 'here' and 'there'. But all of the words listed above under 'other structural words' are of this kind. They are very important and teachers should make sure they do all they can to help the second-language learner to use them appropriately. Content words are much easier to learn.

Basic sentence types
   Statement: Gives information, e.g. It's raining.
   Question: Seeks information, e.g. What are you doing? Is it time to go? Do you like my dress?

Response: Answers a question or acknowledges a remark, e.g. Yes it is/No it isn't; That's right; Have you?
Request/instruction/command: Calls for action in another, e.g. Put the light on; You do it.
Exclamation: Expresses strong feeling, e.g. Oh, dear! Well!

Only a few examples have been given. Teachers should think more about this and try to fill out this section.

Formulae (prefabricated 'chunks' of language): e.g. Once upon a time; Long ago; How do you do.

Again this is a very small sample and the list should be filled out. The formula is to be distinguished from the form which is productive, such as 'I am doing', a pattern which can be elicited and used again.

Rules and patterns

Nouns

a. *Singular/plural:* Three forms of plural with 's', e.g.
   after voiced consonant: dog — dogs (*z* sound)
   after unvoiced consonant: book — books (*s* sound)
   after sibilant: house — houses (*iz* sound)
   Irregular plurals, e.g. teeth, men, children, sheep.
b. *Countable/uncountable,* e.g. pencils, sticks, glasses (countable); water, sand, jam (uncountable).
c. *Possessive,* e.g. the dog's bone (*z* sound), Frank's book (*s* sound), Shiraz's hat (*iz* sound). Note we say 'the leg of the table' and not usually 'the table's leg', but 'Mary's hat' and not usually 'the hat of Mary'.
d. *Agent,* e.g. '-er': one who teaches is a teach*er*, one who speaks is a speak*er*.

Verbs

a. *Time:* Suggested tense forms to cover —
   Present continuous, e.g. She is running
   Simple present, e.g. She runs
   Present perfect, e.g. she has run
   'Going to' future, e.g. She is going to run
   Shall/will future, e.g. She'll run
   Past continuous, e.g. She was running
   Simple past, e.g. She ran.
b. *Continuity:* I am/was speaking (continuous action); I speak/spoke (non-continuous action).

c. *Object:* With an object, e.g. He is eating his lunch; without an object, e.g. He is running.

d. *Regularity:* e.g. count, counts, counting, counted (regular); give, gives, giving, gave, given (irregular).

Special irregulars: be and have.

be	*have*
am/is/are	have/has
being	having
was/were	had
been	had

N.B. There are three forms of the regular past with '-ed' (in sound) which correspond with the three in plural and possessive with 's', e.g.

after vowel sound: show — showed (*d* sound)

after unvoiced consonant: jump — jumped (*t* sound)

after t and d: count — counted (*id* sound)

There are also other irregulars such as 'met' and 'cut'.

e. *Phrasal,* e.g. Sit down; Put on.

f. *Helpers,* e.g.

be, as in 'I am speaking'

have, as in 'I have finished'

do, as in 'I do feel happy'

go, as in 'I am going to sing'

can/could, as in 'I can/could come'

may/might, as in 'I may/might come'

will/would, as in 'I will/would come'

shall/should, as in 'I shall/should come'

must, as in 'I must come'

ought to, as in 'I ought to come'

let, as in 'Let's do that'

dare, as in 'How dare you do that!'

Adjuncts

a. *Comparative and superlative,* e.g. long, longer, longest (regular); good, better, best (irregular); beautiful, more beautiful, most beautiful (most words of two or more syllables).

b. *Forming adverbs with '-ly',* e.g. quick — quickly; slow — slowly.

Sentences

a. *Agreement of parts,* e.g. The boy is here; the boys are here.

b. *Positive/negative,* e.g. It's raining; it's not raining.

c. *Nearness/farness,* e.g. This book here is mine; that book there is yours.

N.B. A simple sentence like 'The boy drank his milk' can be extended by *word:* 'The boy drank his milk quickly'; by *phrase:* 'The boy in the red jumper' etc.; by *clause:* 'The boy . . . before he went out'. Putting all this together we have: 'The boy in the red jumper drank his milk quickly before he went out.'

For help with words, see the list of adjuncts.

For help with phrases, here are a few 'time' examples. Teachers should try to list other kinds, e.g. of place:

at two o'clock	on Sunday
at playtime	this/next/last week
at Christmas	every day/time
in March	all the time

For help with clauses, see the list of 'other structural words', group 8, for clause starters. Some of the question words in group 6 can also be used as clause starters. All of these give suggestions of clause extensions of time, place, reason, etc.

The rest of the checklist which appears in Chapter 3 of *Breakthrough to Fluency* attempts to describe categories of experience in which children acquire language in situations in which the why, when and where affect use. In the 1970s this was a very new field. I hope that the present book has been able to go a little further in that direction, whereas the linguistic side of the equation perhaps needed to be spelt out a little more. The linguistic systems seem to hold good over time and over topics as these Bradford teachers found. The only part of their checklist which was specific to the reading and mathematics fields at this early level of language use was the vocabulary, and also one or two collocations of words which kept appearing. It might be worth listing a few of these, just to make the point:

> *Pre-reading and Mathematics*
> the same as
> are the same
> are alike/different
> both of them
> in the right order
> a pair of
>   etc.

But as we have seen, the special language of subject areas becomes more obvious and complex as the children advance. The strategy used here for analysis is still valid. One last point — these particular teachers, in the course of this work, became very much more aware of the linguistic systems. They had discovered them for themselves!

Sample 4: The Sounds of English

Symbol	Keyword		Symbol	Keyword

Vowels

1.	i:	deed	di:d
2.	i	give	giv
3.	e	bed	bed
4.	æ	black	blæk
5.	ɑ:	laugh	lɑ:f
6.	ɔ	odd	ɔd
7.	ɔ:	bought	bɔ:t
8.	u	good	gud
9.	u:	lose	lu:z
10.	ʌ	love	lʌv
11.	ə:	bird	bə:d
12.	ə	china	'tʃainə

Diphthongs

13.	ei	aid	eid
14.	ou	goes	gouz
15.	ai	five	faiv
16.	au	loud	laud
17.	ɔi	voice	vɔis
18.	iə	dear	diə
19.	ɛə	dare	dɛə
20.	ɔə	door	dɔə
21.	uə	tour	tuə

Semivowels

1.	j	yes	jes
2.	w	wet	wet

Consonants

1.	p	pass	pɑ:s		12.	f	face	feis
2.	b	bus	bʌs		13.	v	vote	vout
3.	t	tie	tai		14.	θ	thick	θik
4.	d	do	du:		15.	ð	this	ðis
5.	k	car	kɑ:		16.	s	see	si:
6.	g	go	gou		17.	z	zoo	zu:
7.	m	miss	mis		18.	ʃ	shoe	ʃu:
8.	n	now	nau		19.	ʒ	pleasure	'pleʒə
9.	ŋ	sing	siŋ		20.	tʃ	chin	tʃin
10.	l	let	let		21.	dʒ	just	dʒʌst
		tell	tel		22.	h	heart	hɑ:t
11.	r	rest	rest					

The phonetic symbols are not important but they do help us to remember that we actually use in speech many more sounds than our alphabet would indicate.

Sample 5

Language functions of young children (see also in Tough, 1976, in Appendix 2).

Halliday (1969) describes the following functions of language mastered by young children:

1. *Instrumental:* to get things done — 'I want'.
2. *Regulatory:* to control others — 'do as I tell you'.
3. *Interactional:* to interact socially — 'me and you'.
4. *Personal:* to present one's identity — 'here I come'.
5. *Heuristic:* to learn — 'tell me why'.
6. *Imaginative:* to create environment — 'let's pretend'.
7. *Referential or representational:* to inform — 'tell me about'.

It might be interesting to consider these in terms of the EFL/ESL learner and perhaps to list possible language exponents which could be offered.

2. Stories

Sample 1

Daniel and the Coconut Cakes by Inger and Lasse Sandberg (monolingual, ESL, from a book) developed across the curriculum by Eve Burch of Cecil Road Infant School, Gravesend, Kent, UK.

This story comes from a book series, *Kate and Daniel* books (A & C Black). The story is simply told and the children enjoy it and can relate easily to the characters. Extension work is exemplified in the flowchart and work-sheets. (There is also a bag of games.) The teacher took the children to a real baker's shop to see how *they* made cakes and then they made their own in the classroom.

There is a useful moral! The story is particularly good for the language of maths.

Another useful story developed in this way has been recommended by Jean White, Head Teacher of St. John's V.P. (c) Infants' School, Ordnance Street, Chatham, Kent. This is *Geraldine's Blanket,* by Holly Keller (A Hippo Book). Geraldine is a pink pig who will not give up her special comfort blanket. She goes to great pains to keep it. The children very quickly empathise with Geraldine and predict how she will behave.

Now follows the flowchart for *Daniel and the Coconut Cakes* and a few examples of the activities suggested.

Eve Burch (Cecil Road Infants)

Suggestions for · · · · · · · · · · · · · · · ·

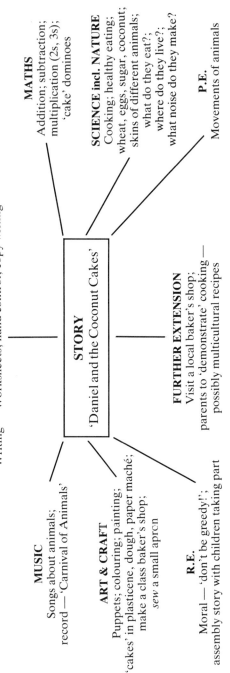

STORY

— developed through the curriculum

LANGUAGE

Listening — Story; initial sounds; animal song & rhymes; 'I Spy'; riddles

Speaking — Re-tell story; animal songs; act story; rhymes; 'information gap' games; describe & guess games

Reading — Sound, word & sentence matching; worksheets

Writing — Worksheets; hand control; copy writing

MATHS

Addition; subtraction; multiplication (2s, 3s); 'cake' dominoes

SCIENCE incl. NATURE

Cooking; healthy eating; wheat, eggs, sugar, coconut; skins of different animals; what do they eat?; where do they live?; what noise do they make?

P.E.

Movements of animals

STORY

'Daniel and the Coconut Cakes'

FURTHER EXTENSION

Visit a local baker's shop; parents to 'demonstrate' cooking — possibly multicultural recipes

MUSIC

Songs about animals; record — 'Carnival of Animals'

ART & CRAFT

Puppets; colouring; painting; 'cakes' in plasticene, dough, paper maché; make a class baker's shop; *sew* a small apron

R.E.

Moral — 'don't be greedy!'; assembly story with children taking part

Some important *Functions of Language* (as suggested by Joan Tough) included in a cross-curriculum approach, i.e.

Reporting   Asking questions   Reasoning   + Vocabulary & structures as required

Directing   Predicting   Explaining & imagining

Instructions for: NUMBER GAME – 'Daniel's Cakes'

Played in pairs or 2 small groups, with 2 real patty tins, 24 plasticene 'cakes', dice 0–5 or 1–6

Put cakes in centre of table

Either take turns to *fill* the tins or take turns to *empty* the tins

(Children must get exact number on dice to finish game)

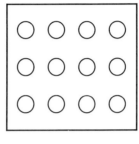

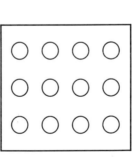

'Maths' language use —
recognise and value; more/less; full/empty; most/least; only

Counting in 2s (in the story)
Counting in 3s (in the game)

Daniel and the

Coconut Cakes.

Daniel

This is Daniel.

Mum

This is Daniel's

Mum.

This is the elephant.

This is the horse.

This is the crocodile.

This is the sheep.

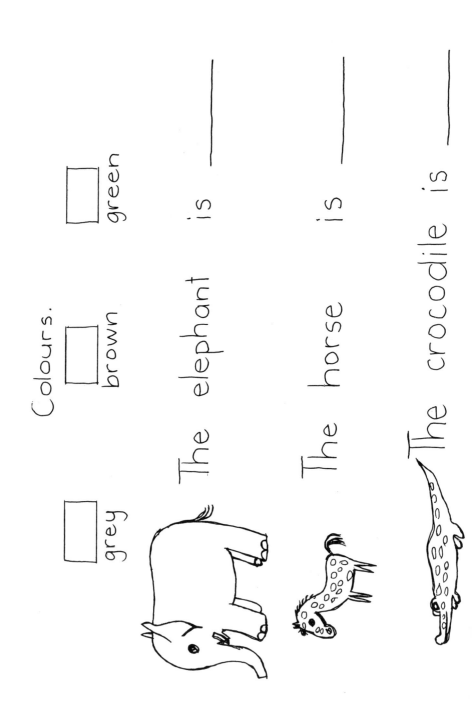

Colours.

grey   brown   green

The elephant is ___

The horse is ___

The crocodile is ___

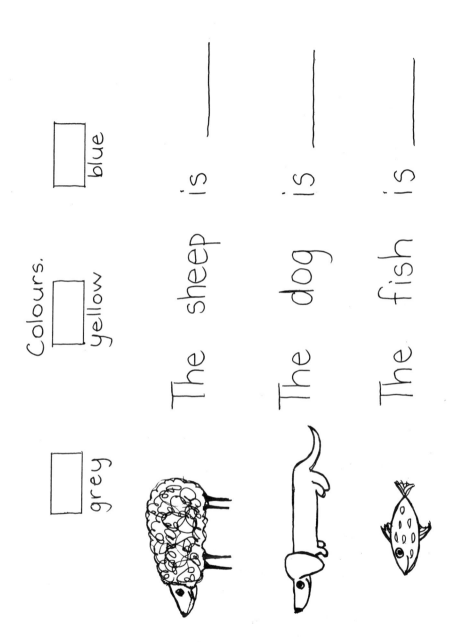

Colours.

☐ grey   ☐ yellow   ☐ blue

The sheep is _____

The dog is _____

The fish is _____

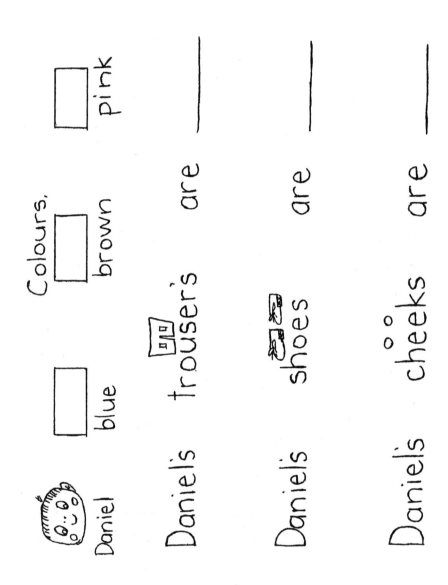

Colours,

Daniel   blue   brown   pink

Daniel's trousers are _____

Daniel's shoes are _____

Daniel's cheeks are _____

How many are there?

What do they eat?

chicken

hay

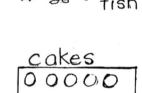

Daniel

people and fish

horse

cakes

dog

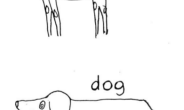

corn

crocodile

bone

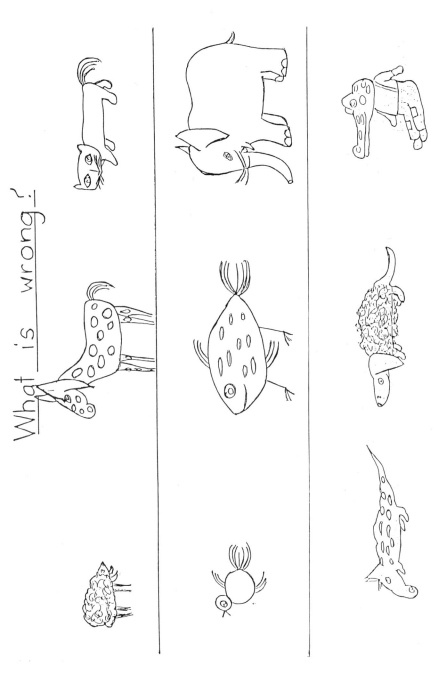

What is wrong?

Sample 2

Shared Story Writing (bilingual, ESL, 'Plucked from the air' — see Part 3)

The following was written by Mrs J. Reed and Mrs S. Kelly of Avery Hill College after a story workshop in Gravesend organised by Lena Vaughan, Convenor of the Bilingual Group at North West Kent Teachers' Centre. Let the teachers speak for themselves.

Using Story as a Vehicle for Language Development:
Shared Story Writing

Aim

To make use of bilingualism as a tool to encourage general language development.

Intended age range

Nursery to lower infants, but could be extended upwards to any age group.

Organisation

Ideally, this would be a small mixed race group of approximately six children working with the class teacher and a bilingual assistant.

Note: This activity and its follow up has been planned with Bangladeshi children in mind, but it could equally well apply to any group.

Starting point

This is to be a story composed by the children themselves from their own experiences, e.g. getting lost, going to a fairground, a beloved pet dying; or from fantasy, or a combination of the two. It is important that the story comes from the children, although in some circumstances the teacher would be able to structure the subject matter to fit in with a particular topic, for example. It is better, though, if the activity is by way of a response to the children's need to express themselves about something they have experienced first hand.

The activity

The story would be composed by the children working collaboratively with the class teacher and bilingual assistant acting as scribes. (This should also apply to older children; the teachers acting as scribe would relieve the children of the 'burden' of writing and allow them to concentrate on the content of the story.)

The bilingual assistant would then write down the story in Bengali as the Bangladeshi children made it up, the class teacher would write down the equivalent in English *underneath* the Bengali script (having listened to a translation from the assistant). This use of dual language has been tried in a situation such as this and does not impair the flow of the story. We feel that to have the Bengali script above the English would show the children the teachers value it.

Once the first draft of the story has been completed the children can then act as editors, changing the story-line if necessary or replacing individual words with more appropriate ones. This is likely to engender considerable discussion! The children can explore the type of language used, particularly if they have chosen to use dialogue. 'Is this really how so-and-so speaks? I don't think she would have said that', etc.

When the final draft has been agreed upon then the story can be divided into pages (chapters with older children) and the children can then illustrate it. The individual pages can then be put together either as a big book, flipover cards, a zig-zag book or in some other way. The text would be in *dual language,* Bengali and English.

Follow-up activities

1. *Curriculum areas*

Using the children's story as a starting point, activities could be devised within the curriculum areas to develop language particular to each area. Taking as an example a story entitled 'Ali gets lost' the following might be encouraged:

Maths — use of prepositions, under the bridge, up the hill, down the road, beside the bus-stop, etc.
— classification, games involving identifying people by their clothing.

History — sequencing, putting the events of the story into chronological order.

Science — taking everyday events such as Ali having his breakfast and looking scientifically at some aspects of this, e.g. cooking and growing. Type of language to develop: observation/ describing, prediction, hypothesising, recording and evaluating.

Drama — role play, conferencing, exploring different endings through mime, tableaux, etc.

RE/Social studies — use of labels, putting together of labels, e.g. red and Shalwar. Colours (through looking at clothes) and cultures, e.g. red and gold, Rastafari.

Art — calligraphy as an art form.

Geography — mapping Ali's journey, addresses, also as labels (see maths numbers as labels).

Music — children composing own percussion and voice pieces; harmonium and tabla.

2. *Types of language*

The children would hopefully become aware of: use of dialogue — this would include everyday and formal, dialect, idioms; story-book language — once upon a time there lived . . . ; syntax — differences between Bengali and English, therefore sentence construction generally.

As a result of producing a story such as 'Ali gets lost' the children might well be prompted to write a multilingual information book along the theme of 'Say no to strangers', for use in the school. Here lies the possibility for the bilingual children to act as teachers using their mother-tongue to help other children in the school.

Sample 3

Sonal Splash and others (bilingual, ESL, book, traditional and plucked from the air)

This story and others are published by Harmony Publishing Ltd, 14 Silverston Way, Stanmore, Middlesex HA7 4HR (directors, A. Abrahams and E. Abrahams). *Sonal Splash* is told in English and Gujarati, *Sameep and the Parrots* in English and Bengali and *Topiwalo the Hatmaker* in English and Gujerati. Each story has an accompanying tape, English on one side and the other language on the other.

Mrs Abrahams writes:

> When children first come to school with little or no English, I build upon their existing language in order to teach English. I always work through their mother-tongue — and it always works! Of course, the richer the mother-tongue, the richer the English. *Sonal Splash* was in fact invented by me with about nine or ten eight-year-old children. We had been playing a game in our playground which was full of puddles at the time and then returned to the classroom for a creative writing lesson — and *Sonal Splash* was born.
>
> *Sameep and the Parrots* was a figment of the imagination. Sameep was one of my very naughty boys in school and I told him I used his name more than any other name and that I would write a book about him! He promised he would be good if I did — so

Sameep and the Parrots was created. As for *Topiwalo* — well, I have always loved the story so I simply adapted it for the children in our school and asked my artist for pictures which would concentrate on the 'listen and identify' skill demanded of little children, listening first in mother-tongue and then in English.

Suddenly the old man woke up. He glanced up into the tree and was very surprised to see the monkeys – and very cross when he discovered that each monkey was wearing one of his hats!

The Hatmaker and the Monkeys: An Italian version

For this translation I am indebted to Mrs Louisa Shippey, formerly of Cambridgeshire Education Authority, UK, who used a bilingual teaching approach in the schools there.

The Hatmaker and the Monkeys (Italian)

C'era una volta un uomo che faceva cappelli. Era un cappellaio. Aveva molti cappelli da vendere. Un giorno mise i cappelli in un carrettino e s'incammino' per la strada del mercato. La strada era lunga ed il cappellaio era stanco ed aveva caldo. Arrivo' ad un albero e si sedette. Presto si addormento'. C'erano delle scimmie sull'albero. Il cappellaio non se n'era accorto. Le scimmie guardarono in giu'. Videro i cappelli. Poi scesero e li presero. Tutte le scimmie si misero un cappello e tutte le scimmie risalirono sull'albero.

Poi l'uomo si sveglio'. Il carrettino era vuoto. Non c'erano piu' cappelli. 'Dove sono i miei cappelli?' disse. Guardo' a sinistra. Guardo' a destra. Guardo' tutto interno. Poi guardo' in su. Vide le scimmie con i suoi cappelli. 'O povero me' disse. 'Quelle scimmie dispettose hanno rubato i miei cappelli'. L'uomo mostro' il pugno alle scimmie. Le scimmie anche mostrarono il pugno. Il cappellaio ebbe un'idea. Si tolse il cappello e lo getto' in terra. Anche le scimmie si tolsero il cappello e lo gettarono in terra. Stavano imitando l'uomo un'altra volta. Il cappellaio mise i cappelli sul carrettino. Poi ando' al mercato a venderli.

Sample 4

The Mischief Maker (monolingual, EFL, traditional)

This traditional Kikuyu story, narrated by Gwida Mariko, is ideal for the making of narratives. Mrs Jenny Du Plessis of Kathorus Teacher Training College in South Africa has used it in her training work, in particular to show students how story can be made to cross the curriculum, especially from threshold level onwards, and to show them also how to manage group work. It appears in *The Best of African Folklore* by Phyllis Savory (Struik, 1988). Mrs du Plessis writes:

> 1. Tell children story. Have pictures/hand puppets of a lion, a jackal and a hare. Children can dramatise story if they so wish.
>
> *Graded workcards for English:*
>
> a. *Top group*
> Answer the following questions.

    1. Which two animals were friends?
    2. What was the hare's name?
    3. Was the hare a friend of the lion and the jackal?
    4. Name one kind of food mentioned in the story.
    5. Name one animal which was killed for food.
  b. *Average group*
     Fill in the missing words.
     1. Lion come quickly and . . . with me.
     2. The lion bared his . . .
     3. The lion and the jackal . . . the hare.
     4. The lion and the jackal were . . . friends.
     5. They called . . . to each other.
     loudly, killed, eat, fangs, devoted
  c. *Weak group*
     Draw a picture for each word and write the correct name under
     each picture.
     lion, jackal, hare, honey, forest.

Amongst the activities suggested for the extension of the story into the curriculum at large is the *sewing* of a picture. Otherwise most of the subjects shown in the ESL flowchart in Sample 1 are also suggested here, with the addition of the vernacular lesson which does bring in the bilingual dimension.

The Mischief Maker (Kikuyu)

For many years a lion and a jackal had been devoted friends. Each had his own private hunting-ground in the forest, and when he had made a kill, he would call loudly for the other to join him. They would then eat and chat happily together and discuss the news of the forest.

But Sunguru the hare was highly jealous of this friendship, because they hadn't invited him to join them. So he planned to make mischief between them. 'I'll put one against the other', he decided, and it was not long before he thought out a plan.

The next time that he saw the two friends set out for their hunting-grounds, Sunguru hid between the two areas and waited. Before long he heard the lion call, 'Friend, friend, come quickly! I have found some honey.'

Imitating the jackal's voice as well as he could, the hare called back, 'Eat by yourself. I'm tired of being friends with you!'

The lion was most upset when he heard what he thought was his friend. He did not understand why the jackal should be so rude. However, he went sadly on his way and said nothing. So all that day and for several days after, the jackal listened in vain for his old friend's voice.

Sunguru stayed in hiding between the two hunting-grounds, and eventually the jackal made a good kill after which *he* called loudly to his friend, 'Lion, lion, come quickly and eat with me! I have killed a bush pig.'

'Then eat it alone! I don't want to be friends with you,' the hare called back in a voice as much like the growl of a lion as his small throat could manage. The jackal could hardly believe his ears. 'How can an old companion treat me like that ?' he muttered sorrowfully to himself. 'One day I'll get my own back.'

Life was now very lonely for the two animals. Each one wandered about on his own until one day the lion could bear it no longer. 'There must have been a mistake!' he said to himself. 'I'm going to call my friend over the next time I have something to share.' So the very next time he found some food, he swallowed his pride and called out, 'Friend jackal, come and share!'

However, Sunguru was still stirring up trouble, so he replied loudly in the jackal's voice, 'Eat alone, *I tell you!* I don't need your friendship!'

This time the lion was very angry. 'Wait until I meet that jackal!' he snarled. 'I will kill him for treating me like that.'

The jackal was equally annoyed when he too found his attempt to heal the friendship was answered with another insult. The two friends drifted farther and farther apart, each furious with the other — until they met accidentally one day in another part of the forest.

The lion bared his fangs and prepared to attack the jackal who promptly backed down an ant-bear hole. From there, he decided he could safely tell the lion what he thought of his rude behaviour.

As they listened to each other's story, it wasn't long before they realised that someone had planned to make mischief between them. 'We must find out who it is,' said the lion. So they decided to go to their own hunting-grounds, where the lion would once more call the jackal to his kill. The jackal would be waiting to catch whoever answered.

It did not take long before they heard the hare answering rudely as before, but the hare found himself caught as the jackal crept up quietly behind him. The lion joined the jackal, and they told Sunguru angrily that they were going to kill him then and there for his treachery (which they did). After that they made a vow to hunt his children and his children's children for ever more. And that explains why the jackal hunts the hare to this very day, and the lion continues to call the jackal to his kill.

Sample 5

Our Village Bus (monolingual, threshold, book)

This story, from the book of the same name by Maria Mabetoa, has been developed as a teaching pack (kit) by Deborah Botha of the Materials Development Group of the READ (Read, Educate and Develop) Educational Trust in Johannesburg. The following comes from the Teacher's Book and I include it especially to illustrate guidelines. The teacher's book goes on to give lots of ideas for the use of the pack.

● **WHAT IS IN THIS STORY PACK?**

● **A Book**

● **Teaching Aids**

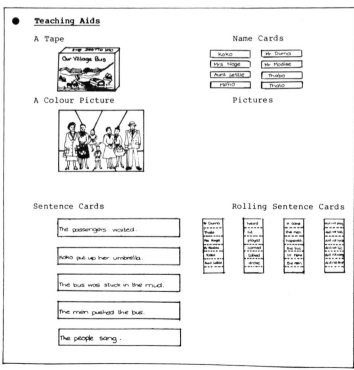

● **WHAT IS IN THIS PACK?**

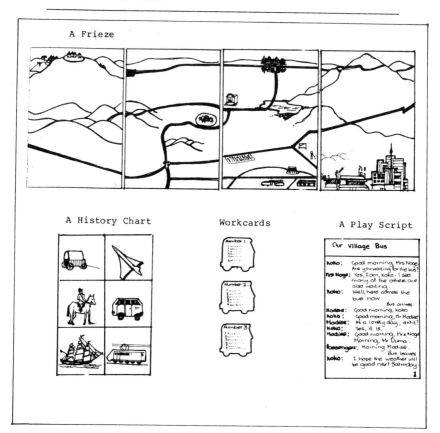

A Frieze

A History Chart   Workcards   A Play Script

● __The Teachers' Book__, which you are looking at now, contains:

Lessons Suggestions for you to use
Worksheets for the children to use.

● **WHAT IS A STORY PACK?**

A Story Pack is a collection of teaching aids based on a **story book.**

What does this Story Pack contain?

It contains a book called <u>Our Village Bus</u>, by Maria Mabetoa, published by Ravan Press. It also contains a cassette tape, pictures and charts, name cards and sentence cards, worksheets and lesson suggestions.

Why did we develop this Story Pack?

For the pupils:

● To help them enjoy books, and to encourage them to read

● To help them improve their English language skills through books

● To encourage them to participate in lessons and to think for themselves.

For the teachers:

● To help you plan your English lessons and Book Education lessons using a specific book as a theme

● To provide materials that will make your teaching easier and more stimulating

● To provide examples of methods that you may not have tried, such as theme teaching, group work, learning through games, and creative questioning

● To show the many uses of books in teaching

● To provide an example so that **you** can contribute to future story-packs

● To encourage you to think critically about the material that you use.

Sample 6

The Old Woman in the Bottle (text at three levels)

This is a traditional story, probably European, originally entitled *The Old Woman who lived in a Vinegar Bottle.* (The story is dealt with in more detail in *Breakthrough to Fluency,* Chapter 6.) It has been divided into twenty-two frames. These could be made into transparencies and used with students, as is suggested in Chapter 9 along with the text at different levels, if it is not possible to give each student a set of the pictures. As was said earlier, there is nothing definitive about the levels. They are simply a guide, and may be useful for workshops on other stories. Note the 'here and now' nature of Level 1 in particular, a kind of discussion of the pictures, accounting for tense changes.

1. Once upon a time there was an old woman.
   She lived in a bottle.
   Look, she is in the bottle.
   This is her chair. This is her table. This is her cat.

2. Once upon a time there was an old woman.
   She lived in a bottle with her cat.
   She had a chair, a table and a light.
   There was a cup and saucer on the table.

3. Once upon a time there was an old woman who lived in a bottle
   with her cat. She had hardly any furniture, only a chair, a table
   and a light. The only dishes she had were a cup and saucer.

1. One day the old woman was crying. She was very sad.
   The cat was crying. He was very sad.
   Look, they are crying.

2. One day the old woman was crying. She was very sad.
   The cat was crying. He was very sad too.
   Look, they are both crying.

3. After a while she became very sad and one day she began to
   cry. The cat was sorry for her and he cried too.

1. Suddenly a fairy came. Look, this is the fairy.
   This is her magic wand.
   'What's the matter?' the fairy asked.
   The old woman said, 'I don't want to live in a bottle.
   I want to live in a little house.'

2. Suddenly a fairy came. Here she is. She has a magic wand.
   'What's the matter? Why are you crying?' the fairy asked.
   The old woman said, 'I don't want to live in a bottle. It's too
   small. I want to live in a little house.'

3. All of a sudden a fairy appeared, with a magic wand in her
   hand. At first the old woman and the cat were frightened.
   Then they knew that the fairy had come to help them. The fairy
   listened while the old woman told her how much she wanted
   to live in a little house. She wanted more space
   and more furniture.

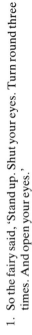

1. So the fairy said, 'Stand up. Shut your eyes. Turn round three
   times. And open your eyes.'

2. So the fairy said, 'Stand up. Shut your eyes. Turn round three
   times. And open your eyes.'

3. The fairy decided to make a magic spell.
   While the cat watched she told the old woman to stand up,
   to shut her eyes, to turn round three times and then to open
   her eyes.

1. So the old woman stood up. She shut her eyes. She turned round three times. And she opened her eyes. The fairy waved her magic wand — and —

2. So the old woman stood up. She shut her eyes. She turned round three times. And she opened her eyes. The fairy danced on the table and waved her magic wand — and —

3. The old woman did all these things and the fairy did a little dance on the table. At the same time she waved her magic wand and said some magic words.

1. — the old woman was in a little house. Look, she is smiling. She is very happy. And the cat is very happy.

2. — the old woman was in a little house. Look, it has a chimney, a roof, two windows and a door. The old woman is smiling. She is very happy. The cat is very happy too. The house is bigger than the bottle.

3. When the old woman opened her eyes the bottle had disappeared and there was a beautiful little house with two windows, a fireplace and a chimney and lots of nice furniture. The old woman was delighted and so was the cat.

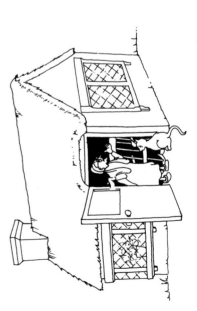

1. Then one day the old woman was crying again. She was very sad again. The cat was crying too. He was very sad. Look, they are crying again.

2. Then one day the old woman was crying again. The cat was crying too. They were both very sad again. Look at them crying.

3. But soon the old woman became sad again and she began to cry once more. Again the cat was sorry for her and he cried too.

1. Suddenly the fairy came again. Here is her magic wand. 'What's the matter now?' the fairy asked.
The old woman said, 'I don't want to live in a little house. I want to live in a big house.'

2. Suddenly the fairy came again. Look, she has her magic wand again. 'What's the matter now? Why are you crying again?' she asked. The old woman said, 'I don't want to live in a little house. It's too small. I want to live in a big house with rooms upstairs.'

3. All at once the fairy appeared again. Once more she asked the old woman what the trouble was and this time she found that the old woman wanted a bigger house, one with more rooms, some of them upstairs.

1. So the fairy said, 'Stand up. Shut your eyes. Turn round three times. And open your eyes.'

2. So the fairy said, 'Stand up. Shut your eyes. Turn round three times. And open your eyes.'

3. Again the fairy decided to make a magic spell. The cat watched very closely while the old woman did what the fairy told her. She had to stand up, to shut her eyes, to turn round three times and then to open her eyes. The fairy hopped about on the table and twisted her magic wand.

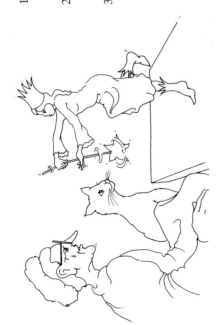

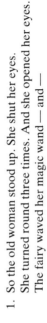

1. So the old woman stood up. She shut her eyes. She turned round three times. And she opened her eyes. The fairy waved her magic wand — and —

2. So the old woman stood up. She shut her eyes. She turned round three times. And she opened her eyes. The fairy hopped on the table and waved her magic wand — and —

3. Then she gave one very big hop and waved her magic wand in the air.

1. — the old woman was in a big house. Look, she is very happy. And the cat is very happy too.

2. — the old woman was in a big house. It was much bigger than her other house. Look, here is a window and here is another window. There are lots of windows. This is upstairs and this is downstairs. And this is the garage. The old woman and the cat are very happy.

3. When the old woman opened her eyes she was surprised and delighted to find that she had her wish. There was a big house with rooms upstairs and downstairs. It had lots of windows and lots of lovely furniture. It even had a garage. There were also two dustbins. Even the cat was delighted.

1. Then one day the old woman was crying again. The cat was looking at her.

2. Then one day the old woman was crying again. She was very sad once more. The cat was looking at her.

3. Then, oh dear, the old woman became sad again. This time the cat did not cry with her. He thought she was silly.

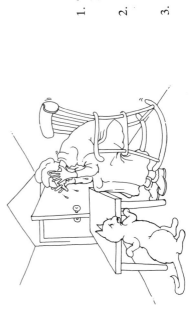

1. Suddenly the fairy came again. Look at her magic wand. 'What's the matter now?' she asked.
The old woman said, 'I don't want to live in a big house. I want to live in a castle.'

2. Suddenly the fairy came again. She was cross. Look at her magic wand. 'Now what's the matter? Why are you crying again?' she asked. The old woman said, 'I don't want to live in a big house. It is not big enough. I want to live in a castle.'

3. Again the fairy appeared but this time she was a little cross. The old woman told her that now she wanted a castle, a very big house indeed. The cat wondered what the fairy would do.

1. So the fairy said, 'Stand up. Shut your eyes. Turn round three times. And open your eyes.'

2. So the fairy said, 'Stand up. Shut your eyes. Turn round three times. And open your eyes.'

3. She was cross but she decided to work her spell once more. She told the old woman to do all the same things as before. The cat was a little bit surprised.

1. So the old woman stood up. She turned round three times. And she opened her eyes. The fairy waved her magic wand — and —

2. So the old woman stood up. She turned round three times. And she opened her eyes. The fairy ran round the top of the table and she waved her magic wand — and —

3. While the old woman had her eyes shut the fairy made a big spell. She ran round the top of the table and she waved her magic wand in the air. She made lots of stars and the cat was a little bit frightened.

1. — the old woman was in a castle. Look, she is very happy again. And the cat is happy too.

2. — the old woman was in a castle. It was much bigger than her house. Look, here is a big tower and here is another big tower. And here is a middle-sized tower. This is a flag. There are many small windows. The old woman and the cat are very happy.

3. This time when the old woman opened her eyes the house had gone and instead there was a huge castle with big towers and little towers. There was a flag on top of the middle tower and there were hundreds of rooms and hundreds of windows. The furniture was very beautiful. It was a wonderful place to live. The old woman was so happy and the cat was happy too though he thought she was silly to want so much.

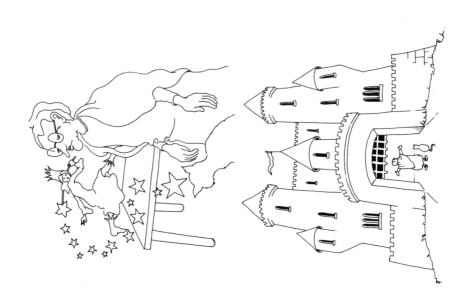

1. Then one day the old woman was crying again. The cat was not looking at her.

2. Then one day the old woman was crying again. Look, she is sitting at the top of a tower. The cat is looking down.

3. One day the old woman and the cat climbed to the top of one of the towers. The woman sat in her chair and she cried and cried. The cat thought she was very silly. He did not look at her.

1. Suddenly the fairy came again. Look at her magic wand.
'What's the matter now?' she asked.
The old woman said, 'I don't want to live in a castle. I want to live in a palace.'

2. Suddenly the fairy came again. She came to the top of the tower. See the cat looking at her. The fairy is very cross. 'Now what's the matter? Why are you crying again?' she asked.
The old woman said, 'I don't want to live in a castle. It is not big enough. I want to live in a palace.'

3. The fairy did come again but this time she was very cross. She wondered why the old woman was crying again when she had so much. The cat was cross too. Then the old woman said that the castle was not big enough. She wanted a palace now.

1. So the fairy said, 'Stand up. Shut your eyes. Turn round three times. And open your eyes.'

2. The old woman waited and the cat waited. Look at them both. Then the fairy said, 'Stand up. Shut your eyes. Turn round three times. And open your eyes.'

3. The cat said to itself, 'This time the old woman has asked for too much. She won't get a palace.' He waited and he watched. But the fairy told the old woman to do the same things as before.

1. So the old woman stood up. She shut her eyes. She turned round three times. And she opened her eyes. The fairy waved her magic wand — but —

2. So the old woman stood up. She shut her eyes. She turned round three times. And she opened her eyes. The fairy danced on top of the wall and waved her magic wand — but —

3. She did all these things while the fairy danced on the wall and the cat shut his eyes, lay on the floor and waited. The fairy waved her magic wand and made lots of stars. There was another magic spell — but —

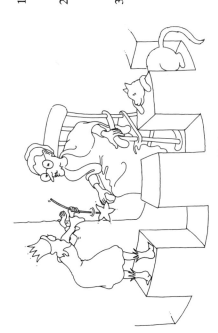

1. — the old woman was not in a palace. She was not in a castle. She was not in a big house. She was not in a little house. She was back in the bottle. Look, she is in her bottle again. The cat is in the bottle again. Here is the chair. Here is the table etc.

2. — the old woman was not in a palace. She was not in a castle. She was not in a big house. She was not in a little house. She was back in her old bottle again. Look at her in the bottle once more. Here is the same chair, the same table and the same light. The cat is there too.

3. — when the old woman opened her eyes this time there was no palace. There was no castle or big house. There wasn't even a little house. There was only the bottle. The old woman was back in her old bottle again, with her cat, her old chair and table and the same light hanging down. Only the cup and saucer were not there. The fairy forgot those.

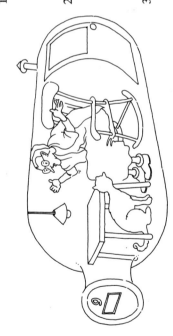

1. The old woman was very sad. Look, she is crying again. But the fairy never came again. The cat is laughing.

2. The old woman wanted too much. She was greedy. Now she is very sad. She is crying again. But the fairy will not come any more. The cat is laughing at her.

3. The cat is laughing because the old woman got what she deserved. She was far too greedy. She kept on wanting more and more and more but in the end she had less than she had when she started.

Sample 7

The Storybox Project

Storybox is a multilingual project sponsored jointly by the Department of Teaching Studies in Bradford and Ilkley Community College and Bradford Education Authority. Its main aims are:

— to celebrate multilingual skills through story-telling;
— to promote the potential of a variety of media for multilingual story-making;
— to develop a network of resources for the production of multilingual story materials;
— to provide a context for research in the multilingual classroom.

The project owns a number of 'prototype' STORYBOXES, the 'Boat', the 'Forest' and the 'Palace', designed and crafted by BA students in the Department of Art and Design, Bradford and Ilkley Community College. Each of our STORYBOXES is a set of play-shapes and hinged boards which are painted and patterned to form environments that represent a universal setting of storylore, epic or fantasy. They are intended to provide the stimulus for bilingual story-making for young children through play, with puppets and toys, in writing, in directed drama, for audio and video recordings. Each STORYBOX can also serve as a model for craft and design project work suited to Middle and Upper Schools or Further Education students.

The PROJECT works each term with a number of schools on the basis of a contract made between the school and the PROJECT. Teachers seconded to the PROJECT work in school with STORYBOX materials, and appropriate resources available through our network. Each school joining the STORYBOX PROJECT undertakes:

— a link with another school, usually of a different age-range, with the agreed goal of promoting bilingual skills;
— production of a set of materials;
— an aspect of evaluation and development of the language curriculum.

[Details taken from the information sheet.]

3. Other Materials

Sample 1

a) Zozo the Mon-key (key of D)

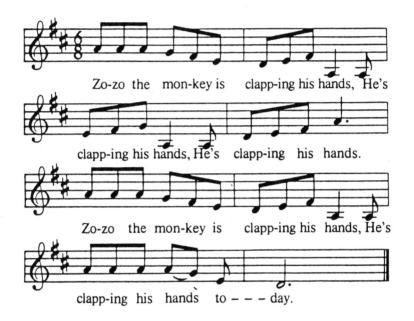

Zo-zo the mon-key is clapp-ing his hands, He's clapp-ing his hands, He's clapp-ing his hands. Zo-zo the mon-key is clapp-ing his hands, He's clapp-ing his hands to – – – day.

b) The Hat Song (The Keel Row)

Sample 2

A Community Happening

Using two teachers as the main performers, with the rest of the community, teachers and children, as the chorus you could enact:

The Lost Shoe

Teacher 1:	*(enters with one shoe off, visibly showing signs of distress)*
	Oh dear! oh dear! I've lost my shoe
Chorus:	Oh dear! oh dear! She's lost her shoe.
Teacher 2:	*(enters, pauses to look at the first teacher and asks the chorus)*
	What's the matter?
Chorus:	She's lost her shoe.
Teacher 2:	*(turns to the first teacher and asks her)*
	What's the matter?
Teacher 1:	I've lost my shoe.
Teacher 2:	*(confidentially to the chorus)*
	Let's try to find it.

All start looking for the shoe which has been carefully placed beforehand and is found by one of the teachers in the chorus (this could be a child eventually).

Teacher from chorus:	I've found it, I've found it.
	Look! I've found it.
Chorus:	Look! She's found it.
Teacher 2 to Teacher 1:	Here you are.
Teacher 1:	Oh, thank you. Look I've got my shoe.
Everyone together:	She's got her shoe. She's got her shoe.

The same scene could be acted over and over using different teachers and eventually children as the main performers. Also the objects lost could be varied, so that new vocabulary is practised as well as sentence structures.

Notice the constant repetition. Done this way it loses some of the aridity of a drill. Notice also the change from 'I've' to 'she's' and vice versa. It is important in teaching a second language to show what can be substituted in the same slot of the sentence. Another thing to notice is the use of 'oh dear' and 'look'. These interjections and exclamations are very common in English and the only way they can really be learned is in a context like this; but not too many at once.

Sample 3

Materials which could be useful in the workshops

manilla card
felt pens
scissors
newspaper
old magazines and catalogues for pictures
large sheets of paper for background
bits and pieces of material for collage and puppets
the means of making overhead projector transparencies
paper clips (especially the kind which bend back to fix parts of a figure
    together)
lots of scrap paper and various kinds of paper such as tissue
card for templates
magnetboard or flannelgraph with magnets or magnetic tape
bluetack and/or other adhesives — sellotape, glue, etc.
drawing pins
sticks for puppets/old gloves/sand-trays to stick them in
tracing paper
empty boxes for carrying and storing
means of display
overhead projector pens and other pens and pencils
sticky labels
coloured sticky paper
envelopes/bags (little cash envelopes are useful for keeping bits and pieces
    of language games, and see-through bags for keeping story kits in — these
    can be hung on the wall of the classroom/staffroom and people can see at
    a glance what is inside).

Sample 4

(a) *Language policy from an education authority (Kent)*

4.3 Planning and organisation

4.3.1. Children will benefit by having available a variety of writing and drawing instruments, different sizes, colours and textures of papers, book making
equipment, and appropriate art materials.

4.3.2. Children will need time for contemplation, the development of ideas,
discussion, questioning as well as time to complete the task.

4.3.3. Beginner writers tend to write as they speak. For some tasks this is not always appropriate. A child's understanding of written convention develops slowly. There may also be cultural or language differences between the child's home and school life. Teachers will need to provide models which will introduce children to written conventions.

4.3.4. When children write, it is often, though not always, appropriate to make a first draft. Drafting allows the child, as writer, to re-order, amend, extend, contract and rewrite his/her composition as much as is necessary so that the content has time to develop, communicates successfully what the writer wishes to say, and is presented accurately and appropriately.

4.3.5. Thus when assisting in the development of children's writing it is necessary to develop the skills of composition through the children's own creative and personal writing, as well as considering ways of facilitating the secretarial skills of handwriting, spelling and punctuation. Furthermore, children will need to develop language with which to talk about writing.

Group discussions will focus upon children's own writing, with the teacher encouraging children to find their own strengths and weaknesses and introducing a language with which they are able to express opinions and ideas.

4.3.6. It is necessary for teachers to decide which technical terms would be useful for the development, as writers and users of language, of the children they teach. When a list of grammatical terms and figures of speech has been decided upon, a common approach to their introduction needs to be agreed by all staff. These terms should be used only to support purposeful learning, and only when the children are at a stage where they can and will use them in their own discussion of language. English exercises text books are unlikely to help in developing children's understanding and knowledge in the use of language.

4.3.7. By giving such close attention to the planning and organisation of written work, particularly drafting and redrafting, the emphasis will be placed on quality rather than quantity.

b. *Language policy from a school*

Marryatville Primary School Language Arts Policy (Australia)

Introduction: This policy has been designed to be both a classroom document, and a school statement within the school's overall policy. We intend to act on the policy immediately and review it annually in order to ensure that what is stated is happening in the classrooms (R–7). As an ongoing statement, we believe that there will be changes due to evaluation and review. In addition, in each of the 4 main categories, there is a 'belief and evaluation' sector that is in accordance with our Overall Policy Statement.

1. We believe that Language Arts is the inter-relationship of reading, writing, listening and speaking. To foster, develop and reinforce skills in this area a wide variety of books, activities, resources both human and material, and topics should be made available as these 4 categories are incorporated in all facets of children's learning.

2. We believe that language is central to learning, understanding and experiencing. Therefore children should be given lots of time for talking, discussing, writing and using drama every day in all curriculum areas.

3. We believe that children develop at different rates; therefore skills should be introduced, taught and reinforced in context, and when the need arises.

Writing

We believe that the following are essential to the children's development as writers:

— a positive attitude towards expressing ideas and emotions
— a positive self-image as a writer
— writing with a sense of purpose and meaning.

Therefore we aim to ensure that the children:
— write with confidence and enjoyment
— feel free to express feelings, opinions and ideas
— have respect for their own writing, as well as showing respect for the writing of others
— become aware of the role and importance of writing in their lives
— be positively influenced by the teacher's interest and enthusiasm for their writing
— feel secure in their attempts at writing, especially in their first years at school
— progress at their own rate and develop a sense of their own learning and writing development
— be encouraged to continue to write through positive and constructive response to their writing, as a result of sharing, displaying and publishing their written work.

We believe that children are to be encouraged to become accountable for their own writing and see personal relevance in all writing tasks.

Therefore we aim to ensure that the children:

— take ownership of their writing through choosing topics, form and publication
— have opportunities to make and justify decisions independently when writing
— proof-read and self-revise their own writing, prior to conferencing
— are allowed as much scope as possible when writing in prescribed subject areas, across the curriculum.

We believe that writing is a developmental process which involves:

> Pre-writing
> Draft-writing
> Proof-reading
> Conferencing
> Publishing
> Responding (by an audience)

'. . . regular experience of the "full" process of writing is important to every child.' (R. D. Walsh, *Every Child Can Write)*

Therefore we aim to ensure that the children:

— have regular opportunities to write and, thereby, become familiar with the Writing Process
— become aware of individual approaches to the writing process by using 'real' writers as models
— develop individuality, independence and control over their own process for writing
— have opportunities to think, talk, read and research before writing
— feel free, within the first draft, to develop their message and style without over-emphasis
— feel confident in discussing their writing in the conferences (either with the teacher or peer groups), so that they develop a sense of value towards their own ideas and feelings.
    > 'At the core of the conference is a teacher asking the child to teach her about the subject. The aim is to foster a burning desire to inform.' (Donald Graves)
— respond to one another's writing, in process, through assisting each other during the various stages
— be aware of the audience when writing final drafts and publishing.

Sample 5

Teacher's Guide 1 for the Oxford Reading Tree

The approach

The *Oxford Reading Tree,* published by Oxford University Press, is a reading scheme for five–seven year olds which uses a 'whole language approach' and a 'story method'. The main reason for adopting this approach and method is the recognition of the importance of story experience for all children and the belief that although young children cannot 'understand' separate letters or isolated words on a page, they can understand and retain a simple story told in natural-sounding language patterns.

When we read we use the information from the context to predict what is to come, confirm it, and carry on. The sequence of learning underlying the approach of the *Oxford Reading Tree* may be expressed as follows:

MEANING → SENTENCES → WORDS/LETTERS

(the sequence underlying most vocabulary-controlled schemes is: letters/ words → sentences → meaning).

Appendix 2: Suggestions for Further Reading

Theory

Bilingualism

BAETENS-BEARDSMORE, H. 1982, *Bilingualism: Basic Principles*. Clevedon, Avon: Multilingual Matters.

BAKHSH, Q. and HARDING, E. 1985, *Teaching the Bilingual Child*. The Gravesend Study: Commission for Racial Equality, UK.

CUMMINS, J. 1979, Linguistic interdependence and the educational development of bilingual children. *Review of Educational Research* 49 (2), 225–51.

—— 1984, *Bilingualism and Special Education: Issues in Assessment and Pedagogy*. Clevedon, Avon: Multilingual Matters Ltd.

HOULTON, D. and WILLEY, R. 1983, *Supporting Children's Bilingualism: Some Policy Issues for Primary Schools and Local Education Authorities*. York: Longman/Schools Council.

SKUTNABB-KANGAS, T. 1984, *Bilingualism or Not: The Education of Minorities*. Clevedon, Avon: Multilingual Matters Ltd.

TROIKE, R. 1978, Research evidence for the effectiveness of bilingual education. *NABE Journal* 3, 13–24.

The communicative approach

BRUMFIT, C. J. and JOHNSON, K. (eds) 1979, *The Communicative Approach to Language Teaching*. Oxford: Oxford University Press.

CANALE, M. 1983, A communicative approach to language proficiency assessment in a minority setting. In C. RIVERA (ed.) *Communicative Competence Approaches to Language Proficiency Assessment: Research and Application*. Clevedon, Avon: Multilingual Matters Ltd.

CAZDEN, C., JOHN, V. and HYMES, D. (eds) 1972, *Functions of Language in the Classroom*. New York: Teachers College Press.

MUNBY, J. 1978, *Communicative Syllabus Design*. Cambridge: Cambridge University Press.

RIVERA, C. (ed.) 1984, *Communicative Competence Approaches to Language Proficiency Assessment: Research and Application*. Clevedon, Avon: Multilingual Matters Ltd.

Language

BARNES, D. R. *et al.* 1971, *Language, the Learner and the School: A Research Report.* Harmondsworth: Penguin (revised edn).

CRUTTENDEN, A. 1979, *Language in Infancy and Childhood.* Manchester: Manchester University Press.

EDWARDS, V. 1983, *Language in Multicultural Classrooms.* London: Batsford.

Every Child's Language 1985, An In-service Pack for Primary Teachers. Multilingual Matters Ltd and Open University.

HALLIDAY, M. A. K. 1973, *Explorations in the Functions of Language.* London: Edward Arnold.

—— 1975, *Learning How to Mean.* London: Edward Arnold.

HOLDEN, S. (ed.) 1987, *English in the Primary School:* British Council Sorrento Papers 1987 (2), ELT Division (Section 14). London: Macmillan.

HUTCHINSON, T. and WATERS, A. 1987, *English for Specific Purposes: A Learning-centred Approach.* Cambridge: Cambridge University Press.

WILLIAMS, R. (ed.) 1981, *Contact: Human Communication and its History.* London: Thames and Hudson.

Learning and teaching of language

BRUMFIT, C. J. 1979, Accuracy and fluency as polarities in foreign language teaching. *Bulletin CILA* 29.

BYRNE, D. 1986, *Teaching Oral English.* London: Longman.

DUNN, O. 1984, *Developing English with Young Learners.* London: Macmillan.

DURKIN, K. 1986, *Language Development in the School Years.* London: Croom Helm.

FREUDENSTEIN, R. (ed.) 1979, *Teaching Foreign Languages to the Very Young.* Oxford: Pergamon.

HEATON, J. B. 1986, *Writing Through Pictures.* London: Longman.

HOLDEN, S. 1980, *Teaching Children.* MEP.

KRASHEN, S. D. 1981, *Second Language Acquisition and Second Language Learning.* Oxford: Pergamon.

STEVICK, E. W. 1982, *Teaching and Learning Languages.* Cambridge: Cambridge University Press.

TOUGH, J. 1976, *Listening to Children Talking.* London: Schools Council/Ward Lock.

VYGOTSKY, L. S. 1962, *Thought and Language.* Cambridge, Mass.: MIT Press.

WELLS, G. 1984, *Language Development in the Pre-School Years.* Cambridge: Cambridge University Press.

WILKINSON, A. 1975, *Language and Education.* Oxford: Oxford University Press.

Learning and teaching: Courses

Active English for Today (1983). London: Longman.

English Today: D. H. HOWE (1987). Oxford: Oxford University Press.

Jigsaw: B. ABBS and A. WORRALL. (1980). London: Mary Glasgow.

Now for English: K. JOHNSON (1983). Hong Kong: Nelson.

Outset (an international primary course): O. DUNN (1987). London: Macmillan.

Pathway: N. HAWKES and D. DALLAS (1985). London: Longman.

Stepping Stones: J. ASHWORTH and J. CLARK (1989). London: Collins.

Linguistic diversity

HOULTON, D. 1984, *All our Languages: A Handbook for the Multilingual Classroom.* London: Edward Arnold.

LABOV, W. 1969, The logic of nonstandard English. In J. ALATIS (ed.), *Monograph Series on Language and Linguistics* (No. 22). Washington, DC: Georgetown University Press.

Linguistic Diversity in the Primary School (LDIP) 1987–89, A three-year development project funded by the European Commission. University of Nottingham, School of Education.

MILLER, J. 1983, *Many Voices: Bilingualism, Culture and Education.* London: Routledge and Kegan Paul.

RALEIGH, M., MILLER, J. and SIMONS, M. 1981, *The Languages Book.* ILEA English Centre, London.

RICHMOND, J. and SAVVA, H. 1983, *Investigating our Language.* London: Edward Arnold.

Reading

ARNOLD, H. 1982, *Listening to Children Reading.* Sevenoaks: Hodder & Stoughton.

BALL, F. 1977, *The Development of Reading Skills.* Oxford: Blackwell.

BENNETT, J. 1979, *Learning to Read with Picture Books.* Stroud: The Thimble Press.

CLAY, M. M. 1982, *Observing Young Readers.* Exeter, New Hampshire: Heinemann Educational Books.

GOODMAN, K. S. 1967, Reading: A psycholinguistic guessing game. *Journal of the Reading Specialist* 4, 126–35.

GOODMAN, K. and GOODMAN, Y. 1979, *Reading in the Bilingual Classroom: Literacy and Biliteracy.* Rosslyn, Virginia: National Clearinghouse for Bilingual Education.

HENDRY, A. 1981, *Teaching Reading: The Key Issues.* London: Heinemann.

SMITH, F. 1978, *Reading.* Cambridge: Cambridge University Press.

—— 1983, Afterthoughts. In F. SMITH, *Essays into Literacy.* Exeter, New Hampshire: Heinemann Educational Books.

WALLACE, C. 1986, *Learning to Read in a Multicultural Society: The Social Context of Second Language Literature.* Oxford: Pergamon Press.

WATERLAND, L. 1985, *Read With Me: An Apprenticeship Approach to Reading.* Stroud: The Thimble Press.

Practice

Classroom props

Drama/Puppets

BURGESS, C. 1985, *Short Plays for Small Groups* (Books 1–4). Hulton.

DUNN, O. 1979, Ideas to be found in Range of Story Workbooks, e.g. *Mr Black Ant and Mrs Red Ant* and *Red Hen's Cake.* London: Macmillan.

—— 1984, Ideas to be found in *Developing English with Young Learners.* London: Macmillan.

Games

HOWE, D. H. 1987, Ideas to be found in: *English Today,* a 6-part activity course for young children. Oxford: Oxford University Press.

LEE, W. R. 1987, *Language Teaching Games and Contests* (new edn). Oxford: Oxford University Press.

Rhymes and songs

DUNN, O. 1979, *Mr Bear's Book of Rhymes.* London: Macmillan.

HOWE, D. H. 1987, *English Today.* Oxford: Oxford University Press.

STOLL, D. and HINTON, M. 1985, *The Otter's First Song Collection.*

General (on all of the above and more)

MANLEY, D. 1986, *Look, No Words!* York: School Curriculum Development Committee, Longman.

Teaching English as a Second Language to Young Learners: An Annotated Bibliography. The British Council Central Information Service.

Visual in particular

BYRNE, D. 1981, *Using the Magnetboard.* London: Allen & Unwin.

WRIGHT, A. 1976, *Visual Materials for the Language Teacher.* London: Longman.

Technology

CHANDLER, D. (ed.) 1983, *Exploring English with Micro-computers.* London: Council for Educational Technology.

HOPE, M. (ed.) 1986, *The Magic of the Micro: A Resource for Children with Learning Difficulties.* London: Council for Educational Technology.

KEITH, G. R. and GLOVER, M. 1986, *Primary Language Learning with Micro-computers.* London: Croom Helm.

LONEGAN, J. 1984, *Video in Language Teaching.* Cambridge: Cambridge University Press.

NORMAN, J. 1987, *Information Skills and Information Technology: Case Studies and Training Materials.* London: Council for Educational Technology.

TOMALIN, B. 1986, *Video, TV and Radio in the English Class.* London: Macmillan.

Story Resources: Useful Addresses

Baker Book Services Ltd: Single and dual language books from all over the world. Manfield Park, Guilford Road, Cranleigh, Surrey GU6 8NU, UK.

The Storybox Project (see Appendix 1, Stories, Sample 7). Bradford and Ilkley Community College, Great Horton Street, Bradford, Yorkshire, UK.

Books to Break Barriers (1986): A review guide to multicultural fiction 4–18. Oxford Development Education Centre, UK.

Books for Keeps. Children's book magazine, School Bookshop Association, 1 Effingham Road, Lee, London SE12 8NZ, UK.

The Books for Keeps Guide to Children's Books for a Multicultural Society 0–7, 8–12 and 12+ (1986/1987) — compiled by Judith Elkin, ed. Pat Triggs. School Books Association/Library Association Youth Libraries, with help of Lloyd's Bank.

Centre for World Development. Regent's College, Inner Circle, Regent's Park, London NW1 4NS (lots of useful literature for story themes).

Education in a Multicultural Society: A selected bibliography compiled by Rachael Evans, up-dated bi-annually. Kiln Cottage, Culham, near Abingdon, Oxon, UK.

Molteno Project (1974–): *Bridge Plus One* and *Bridge Plus Two:* Bridge Book Box and two training films. Contact: Institute for the Study of English in Africa (ISEA), 2 Rhodes Avenue, Grahamstown 6140, South Africa; and ISEA and BP Breakthrough Educational Unit, 408 Braamfontein Centre, 23 Jorissen Street, Braamfontein 2001, South Africa.

Resources for Multicultural Education: An introduction, new edition (1984). Compiled by Gillian Klein. Schools Council Programme 4, Individual Pupils (Longman).

Stories in the Multilingual Classroom: Supporting children's learning of English as a second language (1983). ILEA Learning Materials Service, UK.

We All Live Here: A multicultural booklist for young children (1983). Compiled by Anne Kesterton. National Book League, UK.

World Studies Journal (quarterly). World Studies Teacher Training Centre, University of York, Heslington, York YO1 5DD, UK (for story themes).

References

AVANN, P. (ed.) 1985, *Teaching Information Skills in the Primary School*. London: Arnold.

BERG, L. 1968, *Nipper Series*. London: Methuen.

BERNSTEIN, B. 1975, *Class, Codes and Control: Theoretical Studies Towards a Sociology of Language*. New York: Schocken Books (originally published: *Class, Codes and Control* Vol. 1. London: Routledge and Kegan Paul, 1971).

BOWERS, R. 1987, Grammere that grounde is of alle. *EFL Gazette* (London), July 1987.

BULLOCK REPORT 1975, *A Language for Life:* Report of the Committee of Inquiry appointed by the Secretary of State for Education and Science under the Chairmanship of Sir Alan Bullock, FBA. London: HMSO.

CHOMSKY, N. 1965, *Aspects of the Theory of Syntax*. Cambridge, MA: MIT Press.

CLAY, M. M. 1972, *Reading: The Patterning of Complex Behaviour*. Auckland, NZ: Heinemann.

DODSON, C. J. and PRICE, I. T. W. 1968, *Towards Bilingualism* Vol. 1. Cardiff: University of Wales Press.

DUNN, O. 1983, *Beginning English with Young Children*. London: Macmillan.

ELLIS, R. 1982, Informal and formal approaches to communicative language teaching. *ELT Journal* 36(2) (January), 73–81.

—— 1985, *Understanding Second Language Acquisition*. Oxford: Oxford University Press.

—— 1986, Activities and procedures for teacher training. *ELT Journal* 40(2) (April), 91–99.

GRADED OBJECTIVES 1982, What the Graded Objective Approach is. In *Tongues*. Education Department of South Australia.

HALLIDAY, M. A. K. 1969, Relevant models of language. *Educational Review* 22(1), 26–50.

HAWKINS, E. 1984, *Awareness of Language: An Introductory Guide for Teachers*. Cambridge: Cambridge University Press.

HUTCHINS, P. 1970, *Rosie's Walk*. London: Puffin Books in association with Bodley Head. (Now also in dual text: English/Greek, English/Urdu, English/Turkish.)

HYMES, D. 1979, Language in education: Forward to fundamentals. In O. GARNICA and M. KING, *Language, Children and Society*. London: Pergamon.

KINGMAN REPORT 1988, Report of the Committee of Inquiry into the Teaching of English Language set up by the Secretary of State for Education under the chairmanship of Sir John Kingman.

KRASHEN, S. D. 1982, *Principles and Practice in Second Language Acquisition.* Oxford: Pergamon.

LEE, L. 1971, *Cider with Rosie.* London: Penguin.

LEWIS, C. S. 1950, *The Lion, the Witch and the Wardrobe.* London: Fontana Lions.

MORGAN, J. and RINVOLUCRI, M. 1984, *Once Upon a Time: Using Stories in the Language Classroom.* Cambridge: Cambridge University Press.

PAPERT, S. 1981, *Mindstorms: Children, Computers and Powerful Ideas.* Brighton: The Harvester Press.

PERERA, K. 1981, Some language problems in school learning. In N. MERCER (ed.) *Language in School and Community.* London: Arnold (originally published as *The Language Demands of School Learning* as supplementary reading course No. 232. Oxford University Press, 1979).

PIAGET, J. 1953, *The Origins of Intelligence in the Child.* London: Routledge and Kegan Paul.

—— 1955, *The Child's Construction of Reality.* London: Routledge and Kegan Paul.

ROSEN, B. 1988, *And None of it was Nonsense: The Power of Story-telling in School.* London: Mary Glasgow.

ROSEN, H. 1985, *Stories and Meanings.* Sheffield: National Association for the Teaching of English (49 Broomgrove Road, Sheffield S10 2NA) (new edn 1986).

ROSEN, H. and BURGESS, A. 1980, *Languages and Dialects of London Schoolchildren: An Investigation.* London: Ward Lock Educational.

RUTHERFORD, W. E. 1987, *Second Language Grammar: Learning and Teaching.* London: Longman.

RUXTON, I. M. 1938, *The Pathway Plan.* London: University of London Press.

SAYERS, P., GEORGE, T., GREENWOOD, S. and PETERSON, R. 1979, *Signing Off: A Teacher's Resource Book (English for Adult Immigrants Seeking Work).* National Centre for Industrial Language Training, Southall, Middx, UK.

STEVICK, E. W. 1980, *A Way and Ways.* Rowley, MA: Newbury House.

—— 1986, *Images and Options in the Language Classroom.* Cambridge: Cambridge University Press.

STODDART, J. 1981, *Microteaching: Current Practice in Britain with Special Reference to ESOL.* University of London, Institute of Education, Department of English for Speakers of Other Languages: Working Documents 3.

SWANN REPORT 1985, *Education for All.* Committee of Inquiry into the Education of Children from Ethnic Minority Groups. London: HMSO.

TRINITY COLLEGE 1988, *Syllabus of Grade Examinations in Spoken English for Speakers of Other Languages.* London: Trinity College.

WIDDOWSON, H. G. 1983, *Learning Purpose and Language Use.* Oxford: Oxford University Press.

WRIGHT, A. 1984, *1000 Pictures for Teachers to Copy.* London: Collins.

WRIGHT, A., BETTERIDGE, D. and BUCKBY, M. 1984, *Games for Language Learning.* Cambridge: Cambridge University Press.

ZAMBIAN MINISTRY OF HIGHER EDUCATION 1984, *First Steps in Reading: In English or in a Zambian Language.* A paper commissioned by the English Curriculum Committee and produced by the English Department, Curriculum Development Centre, Lusaka.

Index